Street by Street

BRIGH
WORTHING
HOVE, LEWES, NEWHAVEN
Ferring, Lancing, Peacehaven, Portslade-by-Sea, Rottingdean, Seaford, Shoreham-by-Sea, Sompting, Steyning, Upper Beeding

Ist edition May 2001

© Automobile Association Developments Limited 2001

This product includes map data licensed from Ordnance Survey® with the permission of the Controller of Her Majesty's Stationery Office. © Crown copyright 2000. All rights reserved. Licence No: 399221.

Published by AA Publishing (a trading name of Automobile Association Developments Limited, whose registered office is Norfolk House, Priestley Road, Basingstoke, Hampshire, RG24 9NY. Registered number 1878835).

Mapping produced by the Cartographic Department of The Automobile Association.

A CIP Catalogue record for this book is available from the British Library.

Printed by GRAFIASA S.A., Porto, Portugal

The contents of this atlas are believed to be correct at the time of the latest revision. However, the publishers cannot be held responsible for loss occasioned to any person acting or refraining from action as a result of any material in this atlas, nor for any errors, omissions or changes in such material. The publishers would welcome information to correct any errors or omissions and to keep this atlas up to date. Please write to Publishing, The Automobile Association, Fanum House, Basing View, Basingstoke, Hampshire, RG21 4EA.

Ref: ML018

Key to map pages	ii-iii
Key to map symbols	iv-1
Enlarged scale pages	2-5
Street by Street	6-73
Index – towns & villages	74
Index – streets	75-88
Index – featured places	88-90

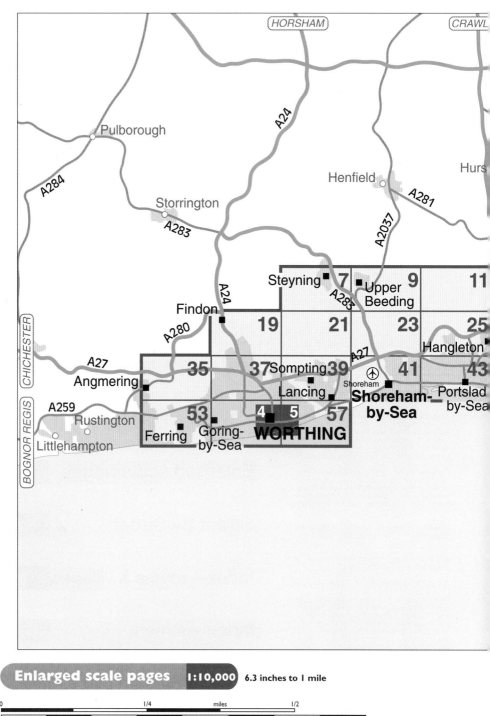

Enlarged scale pages 1:10,000 6.3 inches to 1 mile

miles
0   1/4   1/2

kilometres
0   1/4   1/2   3/4   1

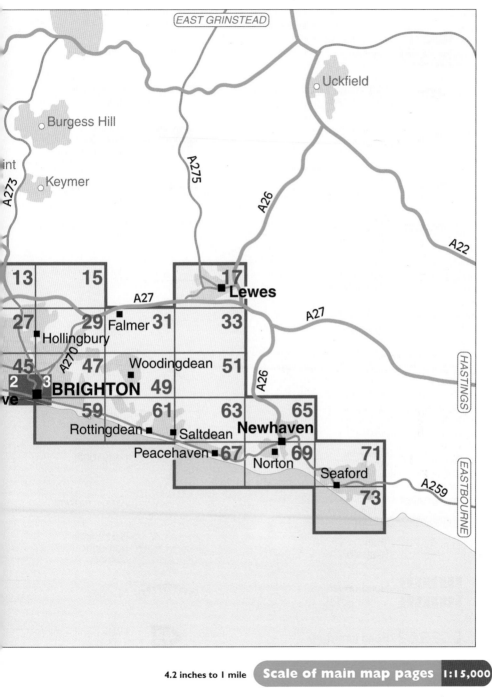

EAST GRINSTEAD

Uckfield

Burgess Hill

A275

int

A273

Keymer

A26

A22

13   15

A27

17

Lewes

27   29 Falmer 31   33

A27

Hollingbury

A270

45   47   Woodingdean   51

A26

2 3 BRIGHTON   49

ve

59   61   63   65

Rottingdean   Saltdean   Newhaven

Peacehaven   67   69   71

Norton   Seaford

73

HASTINGS

EASTBOURNE

A259

4.2 inches to 1 mile   Scale of main map pages   1:15,000

0   1/4   miles   1/2   3/4   1

0   1/4   1/2   kilometres 3/4   1   1 1/4   1 1/2

iv

Junction 9	Motorway & junction	**P+**	Park & Ride
Services	Motorway service area		Bus/Coach station
	Primary road single/dual carriageway		Railway & main railway station
Services	Primary road service area		Railway & minor railway station
	A road single/dual carriageway	⊖	Underground station
	B road single/dual carriageway	⊖	Light Railway & station
	Other road single/dual carriageway	+++++++++	Preserved private railway
	Restricted road	*LC*	Level crossing
	Private road	•—•—•—•	Tramway
← ←	One way street	----------	Ferry route
	Pedestrian street	··················	Airport runway
	Track/ footpath	—·—·—·—	Boundaries- borough/ district
	Road under construction	▼▼▼▼▼▼▼▼	Mounds
	Road tunnel	**93**	Page continuation 1:15,000
P	Parking	**7**	Page continuation to enlarged scale 1:10,000

River/canal, lake, pier

Toilet with disabled facilities

Aqueduct, lock, weir

Petrol station

465
▲
Winter Hill

Peak (with height in metres)

PH Public house

Beach

PO Post Office

Coniferous woodland

Public library

Broadleaved woodland

i Tourist Information Centre

Mixed woodland

Castle

Park

Historic house/ building

Cemetery

Wakehurst Place NT National Trust property

Built-up area

Museum/ art gallery

Featured building

† Church/chapel

City wall

Country park

A&E Accident & Emergency hospital

Theatre/ performing arts

Toilet

Cinema

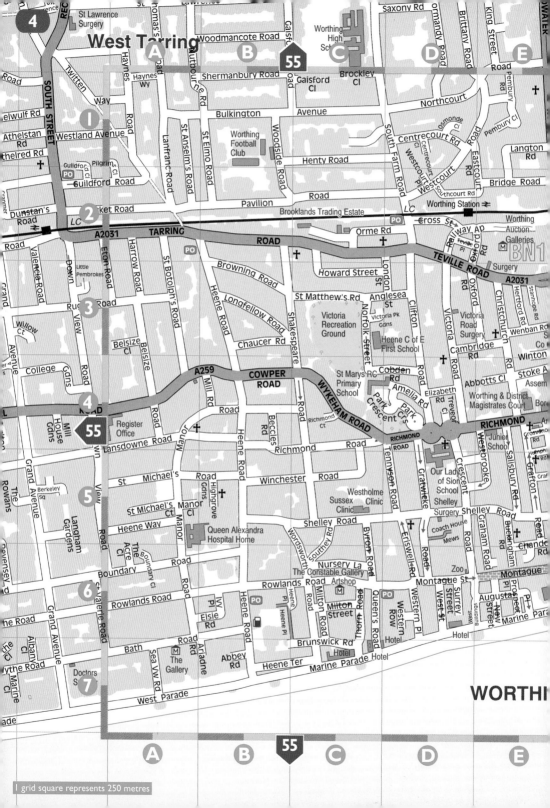

F **G** **H** **J** **K**

Hazelwood

Willo

ROAD

Thackeray Rd

Ham Bridge
Trading Estate

Fairlawn
Wilfred's
Congreve
Marston
Rd
St Andrews
C of E High
School for Boys
Sackville
Road
School
Sackville

ashetts
The
Tivesay
Garrick
Rd
Sackville
Way
Road
Road
Ango
Ruskin
Road
Warner
Rd
Juskin
Road
56
Meredith
Kingsley
Cl
Ham Close
Ham Way

ashfords Lane
Crescent
Sackville
Road
King Edward Avenue
Ashwood Cl
East
Worthing
Station
HAM ROAD
B2223
I
Oakleigh Rd
Mansfiel

ourne Avenue
The Quashetts
King Edward
Close
King Edward Avenue
King Edward Avenue
Chesswood Road
Chesswood
Close
Pages Lane
Oakleigh
Cl

rs Surg
y Arch Road
Dagmar
Rd
Station
Road
Chesswood Road
Chesswood
Middle School
Halsbury
Close
Stuart
Cl
Davison C of E
Secondary School
for Girls
Chester
Av
Chester
Avenue
2
HAM
Rd
Archbal
E
W

lnox Rd
Gordon
Road
Newland
Rd
Newland
Stanley Road
Ltd High St
Ashdown
Park
Road
Tower
Rd
Road
Worthing
& Southlands
Hospitals
N H S Trust
Park
Av
Park Avenue
Halsbury
Close
Thurlow Rd
Halsbury Rd
Alverstone Rd
Sugden
Cranworth Road
Ladyde
Rd
Selborne
Rd
Cottenham
Rd
Eldon Rd
Dawes Av
Dawes
Colebrook
Lyndhurst
CP School
Lyndhurst Road
Chester
Av
Pendine
Avenue
3
Chatham Rd
Church
WK

Sussex
Road
A&E
Worthing Health
Authority
PO
Selden
St
George's
Gannon Road
Windsor
Road
Walk
Hotel
B2223
Navarino Road

NORTH STREET
Town
Hall Annexe
Northbrook
College
Superstore
Providence Ter
Lyndhurst Road
Park Road
Beach
House
Park
Madeira Avenue
Farncombe
Selden
Road
Church
Alexandria
Road
West Sussex Area
Health
Authority
Road
4
56

Union Pl
PO
l Worthing Mus
Police Station
Charlecote
Rd
Ash
Gv
High
Street
Warwick
Elm
Rd
Warwick
Pl
Sandhurst School
Merton
Rd
The Esp
5

Pl
Connaught
Theatre
Chatsworth
Road
Market
St
Ann Street
Sup
Cl
The John
Horniman
School
New Pde
Parade

Liverpool Rd
Chapel Road
Warwick St
Stevne Gdns
York Road
Alfred
Pl
BRIGHTON ROAD
A259
Warwick Rd
Aquarena
Swimming
Pool

Shopping
Centre
Shopping
Centre
South
Street
The Stevne
Hotel
Library
Place
Bedford
Row
Marine
Place
Hotel
Parade
Beach
6

street
Bath
PO
Montague
Marine
7

Worthing
Borough
Council
Pavilion Theatre

F **G** **H** 56 **J** **K**

Mouse

Wiston
Barn

A   **B**   **C**   **D**

1

Pepperscoo

2

South Downs Way

3

Bostal Road

Monarch's Way

4

No Man's Land

New Hill
Barn

Steyning
Bowl

5

South Downs Way

Sopers Lane

Park
Brow

south

A   **B**   **20**   **C**   **D**

1 grid square represents 500 metres

STEYNING

Bramber

UPPER BEED

Botolphs

Steyning Sports Centre

E1 1 Sir George's Pl

F1 1 Tunsgate

Kings Barn Farm

Coxham Lane

Steyning Grammar School

Steyning Football Field

Shooting Field

Shooting Field

Canons Way

Bowmans Cl

Abbey Rd

Church Md

Church Rd

BY-PASS

I
F2 1 Coombe Dro

Penns Ct

Sir George's Pl

Breach Close

Tanyard Lane

Brook Gv

Town Field

Church Lane

Market Fd

Station Rd

Rosemary Close

Rosemary Av

Saxon Road

Stone Avenue

Mill Road

Charlton St

Steyning Health Centre

Elm Lane

Museum

Church St

vicarage La

Kg Afred Chps

King's Barn Ws

Castle Way

Bramber Castle

Steyning Athletic Club

Charlton Street

High Street

Bank Passage

School Lane

Grammar School

Holland Rd

De Braose Way

Roman Road

King's Stone

King's Barn Ws

2
G1 1 Southdown Ter

Sheep Pen La

Dog Lane

Jarvis Street

Wykeham

Clivedale Gdns

Castle La

Castle Lane

Bramber

Lane Chandler's Way

Hills Road

Goodstalls La

Perrots La

Newmans

Penfold Way

College Hill

Goring

Bramber Rd

The Crescent

3

8
G2 1 Castle Cl

Laines Road

Ingram

Portway

Penland's Rise

The Furlongs

Penland Way

Andrew Cres

Penland's

Clays

Hill

Hotel

The Street

UPPER BEED

Coombe Rd

Penlands

Penlands

Little Drove

Combe Drive

Maudlyn Park

Maudlyn Close

Monarchs Way

A283

4

Bostal Road

The Ridings

Maudlyn Parkway

Maudlin Lane

Sopers

Kingsmead Close

Annington Road

STEYNING BY-

Downs

Annington Farm

Link

Sopers Lane

Upper Maudlin Farm

Annington

Botolphs

5

South Downs Way

Annington Rd

Annington Hill Barn

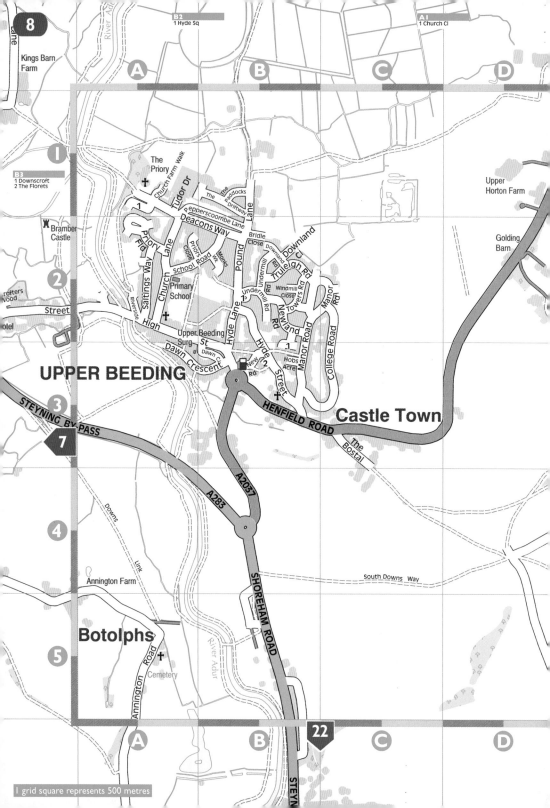

HENFIELD

Tottington
Manor
Farm

E

F

G
Manor Farm

H

Edburt

I

2

213
▲
Truleigh
Hill

South Downs Way

Tottington
Barn

Freshcombe
Farm

3

10

4

The
Warren

Bushy
Bottom

5

Monarchs Way

E

F

23

G

H

A   B   C   D

Edburton   ✝   Perching Manor Farm   Fu**D**ing   ✝

Drove

Stammers Hill

South

1

2

South Downs Way

3

▶ 9

West Sussex County
Brighton and Hove

4

Bushy
Bottom

5

A   B   **24**   C   D

West Sussex County
East Sussex County

r Path

E

Wickhurst
Barns

F

G

H

S

I

Devil's
Dyke

2

Devil's Dyke Road

South Downs Way

Border Path

3

12

Devil's

Dyke

Road

Devil's
Dyke Farm

4

5

Skeleton
Hovel

E

F

25

G

Monarchs Way

H

Brighton & Hove
Golf Course

12

A **B** **C** **D**

Saddlescombe

West Sussex County
Brighton and Hove

1

Sussex Border Path

2

3

11

Sussex Border Path

4

Brighton and Hove
West Sussex County

5

Skeleton
Hovel

Waterhall
Golf Course

A **B** **26** **C** **D**

Brighton & Hove
Golf Course

Devil's Dyke Road

Brighton
Rugby Club

1 grid square represents 500 metres

E F G H

1

2

3

14

4

Pangdean Farm

South Hill Farm

West Sussex County
Brighton and Hove

Sussex Border Path

Sussex Border Path

A23(T)

LONDON ROAD

Braypool Lane

Waterhall

Waterhall Road

Hill Road

A27(T)

A23(T)

LONDON ROAD

PATCHAM

27

Court Close

Church Hill

Vale

The Village Barn

Ashley Cl

Highview Av North

Highview Way

Highview Av

Old Patcham Mews

PO

Brangwyn

Ladies' Mile Road

Winfield

Braeside

Craignair Avenue

Barrhill Avenue

Solway Av

Sanyhils Av

Heston Av

Thornhill Av

Branscraig Av

Avenue

Bengairn Av

Kenilw

Plainfields

Mackie Avenue

Ladies

Mile Cl

Warmdene

Patcham CP School

Stoneleigh Close

Stoneleigh Av

Sunnyvale Av

Sunnyvale Close

Carden Close

Ladies' Mile Road

Single Road

Hay

14

A   B   C   D

Lower
Standean

1

New
Barn

Ditchling   Road

2

3

13

Ditchling

4

Ditchling   Road

Coldean Lane

A27

Eastwick Cl

Mackie Avenue

Avenue

Kenmure Av

Bengairn Av

Glenfalls Av

Estbank Av

Lomond Av

The Deeside

BN1

Carden Avenue

Crowhurst Road

Saunders Hill

Brimside

Heston Av

Baranscraig Av

Thornhill Av

Plainfields Av

PO

Clovers
End

Old Boat
Wk

Beatty Av

Kenwards

5

Solway Av

Sanyhils Av

Mackie Avenue

Windmill
Vw

Buttercup
Wk

Crawley
Road

Beatty Av

Cold
Junic
Infan

Ladies' Mile

Ladies'
Mile
Cl

Singleton
Road

Portfield

Tangmere
Rd

Morecambe Rd

Sunnydale Cl

Haywards

Petworth Road

Midhurst Rise

Callers Cl

28

Orchid Vw

Elwood Cl

Cuckmere Way

Sedgewick

Elsted Cre

The
Surger

Hawkhurst

Waldron Av

PO

Drive

A   B   C   D

stoneleigh
close

Darcey Dr

Avenue

Col

field

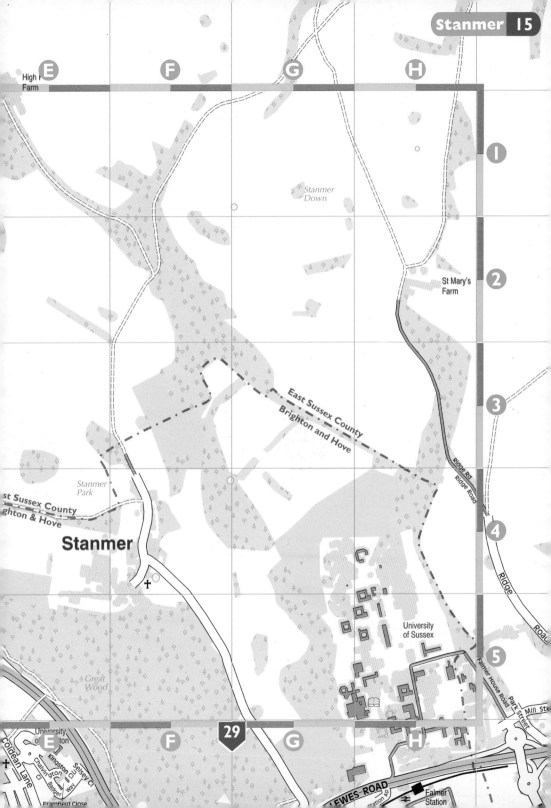

E High Farm
F
G
H

I

Stanmer Down

St Mary's Farm

2

East Sussex County
Brighton and Hove

3

st Sussex County
ghton & Hove

Stanmer Park

Ridge Rd
Ridge Road

Stanmer

✝

4

University of Sussex

Ridge ROAD

5

Falmer House Road

Park Street

Mill St

Great Wood

University of ... ton

E

F

29

G

H

Coldean Lane

Kingston ...

Chalvin ...

Badger Way

Selsey Cl

✝

Framfield Close

LEWES ROAD

Falmer Station

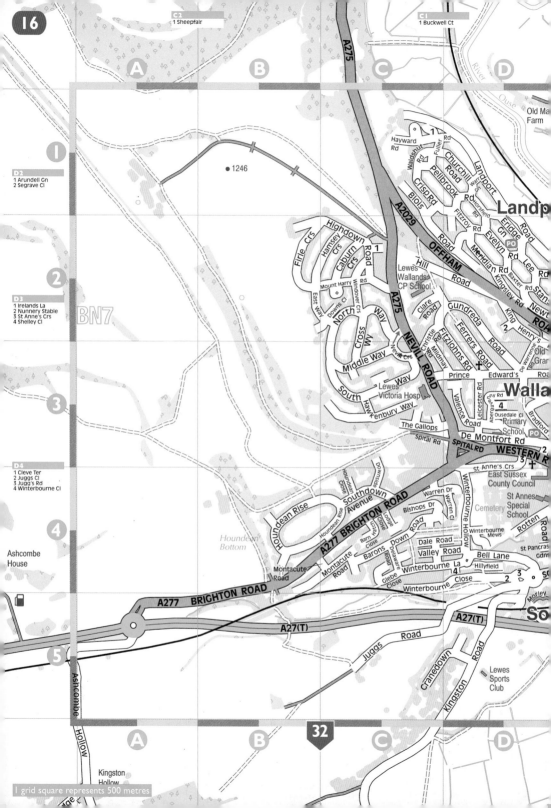

16

C2
1 Sheepfair

C1
1 Buckwell Ct

A   B   C   D

●1246

D2
1 Arundell Gn
2 Segrave Cl

D3
1 Irelands La
2 Nunnery Stable
3 St Anne's Crs
4 Shelley Cl

BN7

D4
1 Cleve Ter
2 Juggs Cl
3 Jugg's Rd
4 Winterbourne Cl

Ashcombe
House

Houndean
Bottom

Hayward Rd

Waldshut Rd
Watt Cl

Fuller Rd
Crisp Rd
Pellbrook Rd
Churchill Road
Bois
Mansfield

A2029
Blois

OFFHAM
A275

Hill Road

Lewes Wallands
CP School

Fitzroy Rd

Evelyn Rd
Endd Road
Meridian Rd
Kingsley Rd
Baxter Rd
Lee Rd
Stan...
Newt

Landp

Landp

Firle Crs
Highdown Crs
Hamsey Crs
Cabourn Crs

Road

Mount Harry
Windover Crs
Rd

Downs Cl
East Way

North Way

Cross Wy

Middle Way

South Way

Lewes Way

Hawkenbury Way

The Gallops

Spital Rd

Clare Road
Gundreda Road
Christie Rd
Millmay
Fitzjohns Rd
Ferrers Road

King Henry's
Old Gran

De Warenne Rd

Nevil Crs

NEVIL ROAD
A275

Valence Road

Lewes
Victoria Hosp

Prince Edward's

Walla

Walla

Leicester Rd
Abergav Rd
Ousedale Cl

4
Primary
School
PO

De Montfort Rd

SPITAL RD   WESTERN R

St Anne's Crs

East Sussex
County Council

St Annes
Special
School

Cemetery

3

Houndean Rise

Southdown
Avenue

A277 BRIGHTON ROAD

Downside Close

Bishops Dr
Warren Dr
Warren Rd

Lodge Cl
Barn Cl

Dale Road
Barons Down
Delaware Road
Montacute Road

Glebe Close

Down Valley Road

Winterbourne La

Winterbourne Hollow

Winterbourne Mews

Hillyfield
Bell Lane

St Pancras Gdns

Rotten Road

Winterbourne Close

Morley

Montacute
Road

A277   BRIGHTON ROAD

A27(T)
Road

Juggs Road

Cranedown

Kingston Road

Lewes
Sports
Club

Ashcombe Hollow

A27(T)

So

So

Kingston
Hollow

32

A   B   C   D

1 grid square represents 500 metres

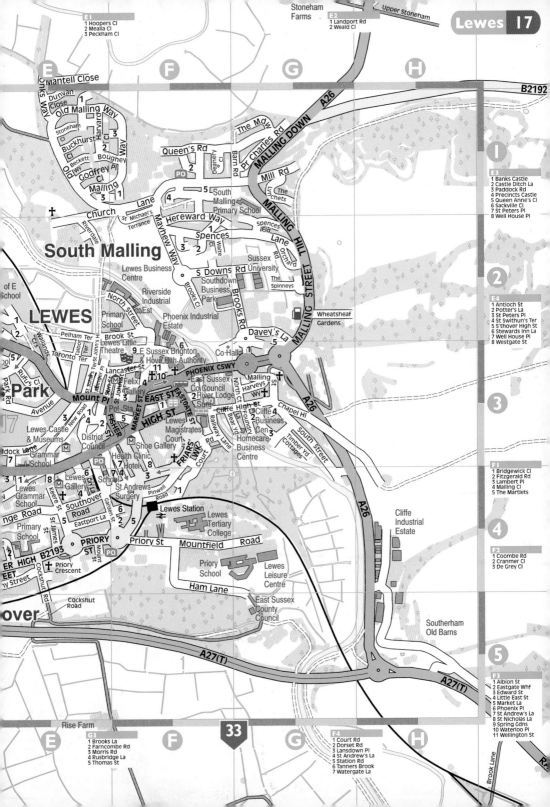

18

Findon

Nepcote

High Salving 36

D4
1 Downside Av

C5
1 Firsdown Cl
2 Furzeholme
3 West Hill Cl

Kingswood

LONG FURLONG A280

FINDON BY-PASS

FINDON BY-PASS

Monarch's Way

Monarch's Way

Findon Place

School Hill

Horsham Road

Homewood

Downview Rd

The Downs

Ivy Arch Close

Pony Farm

Lime Road

Elm Rise

Kilmore Lane

Beech Rd

Ash Cl

Stable

St John Baptist Primary School

Cemetery

Tudor Cl

Dowland

Summerfields

West Way Ter

Paddock Wy

Nepcote Lane

Holmcroft Gdns

Cross La

West La

Cross La

Hotel

High Street

Steep Lane

Lane

Monarch's Way

Steep Cl

Fox Lea

Nepfield Close

High St

The Chase

A24

The Quadrangle

Nepcote Lane Cissbury

Roger's Lane

Roger's Farm

The Vale

FINDON ROAD

Storrington Rise

Long

Sullington

May Tree Avenue

Hazelhurst

Bost Hill

Downside Close

Downside 7 Avenue

Findon Road

A24

Central

Marshall Av

Findon Road Avenue

Vale

Lime Tree

Cissbury

PO

Honeysuckle Lane

Honeysuckle Lane

Kinfauns Dr

Furze Close

Furze

Heather Lane

Gorse La 3

West Hill Road

2

Bost Hill

Vale Drive

Vale Dr

PO

Hillview Road

Vale Walk

Hillvie Rise

Clapham Wood

PO

1

Firsdown Road

Highlands Close

Vale CP School

High View

Newling Way

Mill Lane

Parhar

Palmers

Southwold Close

Cherry Tree Close

1

Cherry Walk

Oak Close

Chute Aver

Havling Gardens

Woodland

West Way

Maple Close

Street

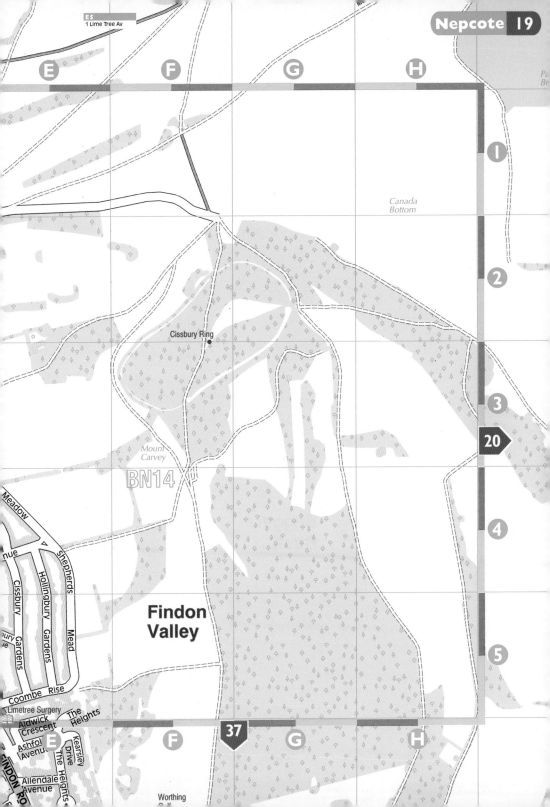

E5
1 Lime Tree Av

E

F

G

H

I

Canada
Bottom

2

Cissbury Ring

3

20

Mount
Carvey

BN14

4

Meadow

Cissbury Gardens

Hollingbury Gardens

Shepherds Mead

bury Gardens

**Findon
Valley**

5

Coombe Rise

Limetree Surgery

Aldwick
Crescent

The
Heights

E

Ashfol
Avenue

Kearsley
Drive

The Heights

F

37

G

H

FINDON RO

Allendale
Avenue

Worthing

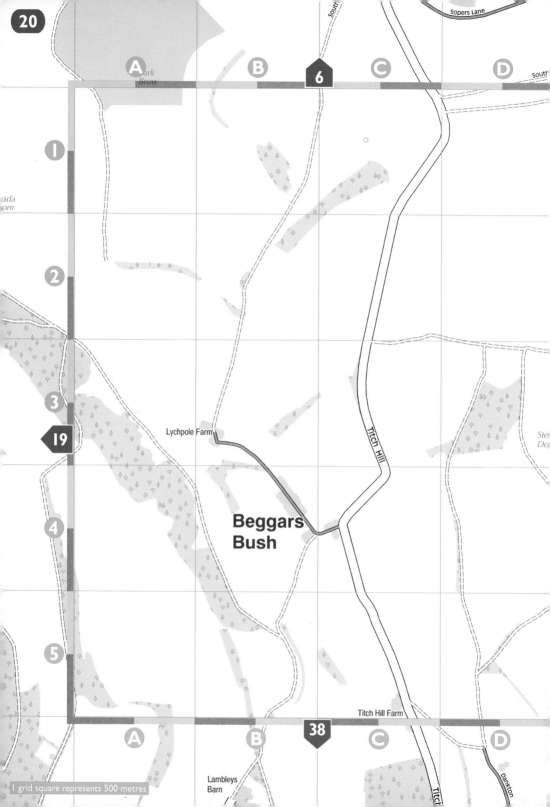

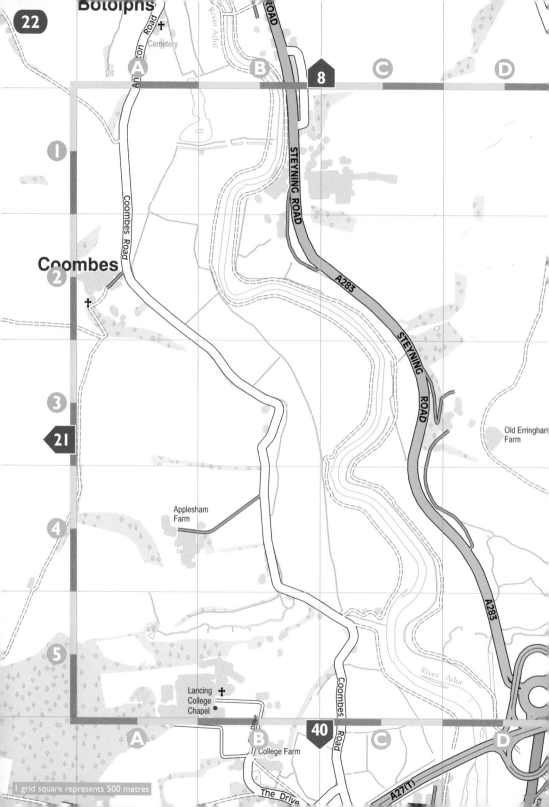

Botolphs

22

Alaston Road

Cemetery

A

River Adur

B

ROAD

8

C

D

1

STEYNING ROAD

Coombes Road

Coombes

2

A283

3

21

STEYNING ROAD

Old Erringham Farm

4

Applesham Farm

5

River Adur

Lancing College Chapel

A

B

40

Coombes Road

C

A283

D

College Farm

Drive

The Drive

A27(T)

1 grid square represents 500 metres

E F **9** G H

Monarchs Way

I

2

3

24

4

5

Mill Hill

New Erringham
Farm

BN43

Buckingham
Barn

Slonk Hill
Farm

E Mill HI
CI

Mill Hill Drive

Mill Hill Gdns

Chanctonbury Drive

Saxons

The Drive

Kingsway

Edburton Av

Gdns

F

The

Ravensbourne Av

Cypress CI

Downside CI

41

Slonk Hill Road

Truleigh Wy

Downside

G

Ashlings Wy

Greenways
Crescent

H

New Barn Rd

Rosemary Drive

Lavender HI

Valender Wy

Bergamot

Saffron

Tarragon Wy

Old
Shoreham
Street

24

A **B** **10** **C** **D**

D4
1 Foxhunters Rd

C3
1 Nursery Cl
2 Westway Cl

1

D5
1 Lodge Cl

West Sussex County
East Sussex County

Sussex Border Path

2

BN41

Mile Oak
Farm

3

23

Overdo

Gorse Cl

Graham

Gra

Westway Gdns

Aven

Cl

Heathfield

Dr

Heathfield

Oakdene

Crs

1

Stanley

Avenue

Junior
School

2

Oakdene
Ri

Chrisdory Rd

Sefton Rd

Beechers Rd

PO

Oakdene
Wy

Oakdene
Av

Oakdene
Gdns

Oakdene

Beech
Cl

Chalk

Mile Oak
Clinic

Wickhurs

4

Monarchs Way

Oakdene

Soulton

Mile Oak Road

Hillbank

Hillcroft

Wicl

Close

A27(T)

**Mile
Oak**

Hillcroft

Hill

The

Portslade
Community
College

Sidehill

Edgehi

Dr

Highdov

Edgem

Dr

1

5

Slonk Hill
Farm

Holmbush
Cl

Hawkins
Crs

Hill Farm Way

Oakd

Whitelot

Cromleigh
Way

Downsway

Summe

Aspen

Highdown
Cl

Highdow

Ridgew

A **B** **42** **C** **D**

2

3

Lavender

Saffron

New B
Rd

Rosemary Drive

Kingston Broadwa

Holmbush County
Infants School

Herons
Dale
School

Hawkins Road

Hawki

Mulb

erry
Cl

Upper Kingston Lane

Downland
Cl

Kings Road

bush Way

Queens
Rd

The Drive

Windmill
Rd

Wilby
Av

Overhill
Way

Hilcroft Gdns

Millcroft
Gdns

Cemetery

Church Ho
Cl

Upton Av

Eastbank

Gree

I grid square represents 500 metres

E3
1 Ridge Cl

E5
1 The Crossway

Skeleton Hovel

E   F   ‖   G   H

Monarchs Way

Brighton & Hove Golf Course

I

F4
1 Juniper Cl
2 The Parks

2

F5
1 Blackthorn Cl
2 Brackenbury Cl
3 Cornford Cl
4 Foredown Cl
5 Highways
6 Meadow Cl

A27(T)

SHOREHAM BY-PASS

Thornhill Rise

England

Broomfield Dr

Whitfield
Thornhill Wy

Northfield Rd

Honey Croft

Rushey Cl

West

3

26

Hard

G4
1 Meads Cl
2 Meyners Cl
3 Sycamore Cl

East Sussex County Counc

4

1 Cottage Bush Cl

Har

Foredown Road

Thornbush Crs

Benfield Valley Golf Course

Warenne Road

Drive

The Down

Cowdens

Valley

Lynchets Crescent

Broad Rig Avenue

Northfield Rd

Sherbourne Road

Spencer Avenue

Sherbourne

Hangleton

Clark Hill

Crs

Park Hill

Hamilton Cl

Foxway

Crest

Wy

Hazel Cl

Sheepbell Cl

Meads Av

Downsview

St Helen's Crs

St Helen's Dr

Sylvester Way

The H Mdw

Pipers Cl

Hangleton

Northease

Summerdale Rd

Gleton Avenue

Hangleton County Junior & Infant School

Kingston

Hawthorn Wy

Shepard Wy

Farm Cl

Crover Wy

Badger

Hangleton Lane

Hangleton Mnr

Hangleton Way

West

Hangleton Cl

Hove Medical Centre

Welfare Clinic

5

slade mmunity lege

Harebell Dr

Landridge

North Lane

Southdown

Downsview Rd

Henge Wy

Elder Wy

Anvil

Downs Park Sch

Flint

Forge

Warrior Cl

Barn Cl

Hangleton La

Dean Gdns

Dean

Farmway

Greenleas

Hangleton Gdns

Dale View Cl

A203

Portslade Village

Valley Road

North Rd

Drove Crescent

Stonery Rd

Foredown Rd

Fairway Crs

Deacons Dr

Valerie Cl

Helena Cl

Mill Lane

Sharon

Cliffe

Burlington Gdns

PeterGladwin School

Hillside School

Easthill Drive

Elm Drive

Rowan Av

Maytree Wk

Brighton & Hove Counc.

Mile Oak Rd

E

H5
1 Dale View Gdns
2 Northease Cl

Easthill Wy

Lucern

F

43

A293

G

H4
1 The Dene

H

Martin Road

Twin Rd

Millcros

Fairfield Rd

Foredown

Mill Lane

Gorne

Hillside

South St

Portslade Community College

PO

High St

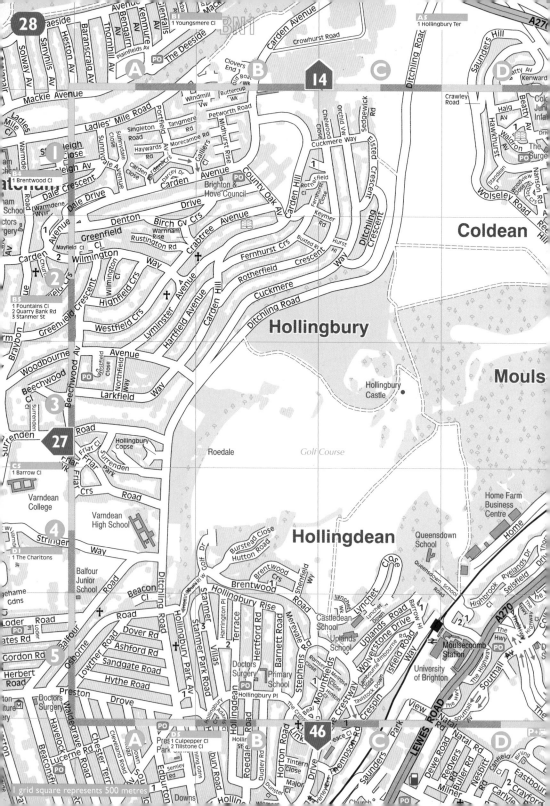

Varndean College
Varndean High School
Balfour Junior School

Coldean

Mouls

Hollingbury

Hollingbury Castle

Golf Course

Roedale

Hollingbury Copse

Hollingdean

Queensdown School

Home Farm Business Centre

Moulsecoomb Station

University of Brighton

A B **14** C D

A B **46** C D

B1
1 Youngsmere Cl

A5
1 Hollingbury Ter

B4
1 Brentwood Cl

B5
1 Fountains Cl
2 Quarry Bank Rd
3 Stanmer St

C5
1 Barrow Cl

D1
1 The Charltons

D5
1 Culpepper Cl
2 Tillstone Cl

of Sussex

E1
1 Selham Cl

E2
1 Arlington Crs
2 Ashburnham Cl

E   F   G   H

15

Great
Wood

Park Street

Mill St

University
of Brighton

Kingston
Charlvin gton
Selsey Cl
Way
Badger

Framfield Close

LEWES ROAD

Station

Falmer
Station

I

E4
1 Broadfields
2 Broadfields Rd

Village Way

Coldean Lane

Monk

Rushlake
Rd

m Dr
The Byway
Walton
Bank

Middleton
Rd
Ridge VW
Rushlake
Cl

Forest
Road
Road

Coldean Lane

A27(T)

A270

University of Brighton

University of Brighton

2

Roundway
Highfields

Park
Close

Park Road

Woburn
Pl

LEWES ROAD

Eggington
Close

PO

Road

Barcombe Rd

Rd

Road

Lucraft Road

Eggington Road

Newick
Rd

Chailey Road

Ringmer
Road

Ringmer

Ashurst Road

orth
omb

Barcombe
Rd

Newick Rd

Ringmer Rd

Ringmer
Cl

Friston

Halland Road

Bolney Rd

Stonecross Rd

3

Barcombe Rd

Eastergate
Road

Appledore

Sullington Cl

shortgate
Rd

Way

**East
Moulsecoomb**

30

Road

Westergate
Road

Moulsecoomb

Goodwood Wy

Wheatfield
Wy

Brighton
& Hove
Council

4

Moulsecoomb
County Junior
School

Clinic

Hodshrove
Road

Birdham
Road

Stapleford

Drive

Hillside

Beech
GV

Selba Dr

Moulsecoomb

Hillside

Bevendean Way

Nyetimber
Hill

Medmerry
Hill

Bevendean Crs

Bevendean

5

Kenilworth
Close

Norwich

Norwich
Close

Norwich
Drive

Bamford
Close

Bodiam
Close

PO
Crs

Knepp
Cl

Heath Hill Avenue

Bodiam Avenue

Avenue

Upr Bevendean Av

Lower
Bevendean Av

Leybourne
Road

PO

Bevendean
Primary S

47

Rd

Durham
d

1

Walmer
Crs

H

Willingt

Manton Rd

E

The Willow
Surgery

Plymouth Av

Fitch Drive

th Cl

Dartmouth
Close

F
Hi Av

Taunton

Hornby

2

Auckland

Midway

Drive

G

Durham

Drive

H

Upper
Bevendea

Sussex

30

Farm

Falmer House Road

Park Street

A Mill Street **B** A27(T) **C** **D**

Middle Street

Ne
Ba

Falmer

South St

B2123

Falmer Station **I** East St

Village Way

2 THE DROVE

3

29

South Downs Wa

B2123

East Sussex County
Brighton & Hove

4 FALMER ROAD

197 ▲
Newmarket Hill

5 Drove Avenue

A **B** **C** **D**
Norton Drive

48

Bexhill Road Norton Drive

Upper SuttonCl Treyford Cl

Road Langley

A27(T)

E   F   G   H

Ashcombe Hollow

Kingston Hollow

I

South Downs Way

Kingston Ridge

Ridgway Paddock

Ashcombe

The Avenue

The Flints

Church La

Lockitt Way

Monckton Way

Cordons

St Pancras

Bramley

Mushroom

2

Church Lane

Hyde

Bar Cl Stre

K
n

The

3

32

south Downs Way

South Downs Way

4

Dencher

Wildfowl
Reserve

5

E   F   G   H

49

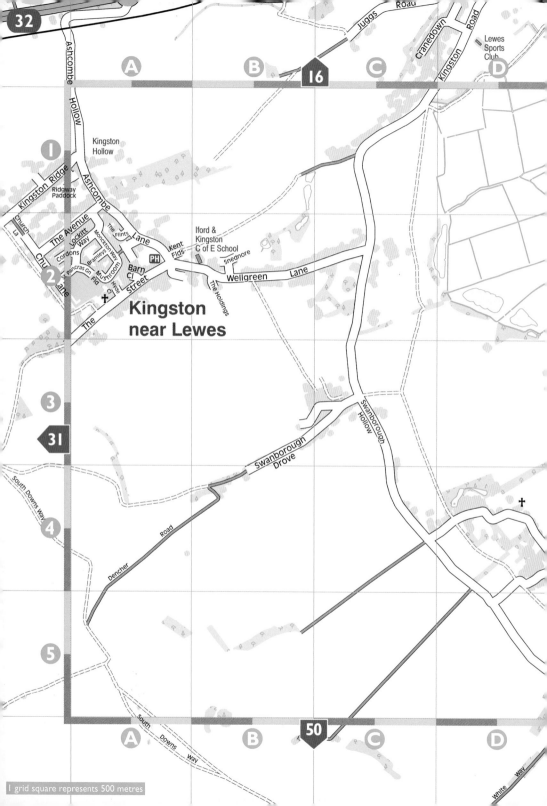

32

A **B** **16** **C** **D**

Ashcombe Hollow

Kingston Hollow

1

Kingston Ridge

Ashcombe Lane

Ridgway Paddock

The Avenue

Church La

Lockitt Way

Cordons

The Flints

Moneton Way

Bramley

Mushroom

Hyde Cl

St Pancras Gn Fld

2

Barn Cl

Kent Street

Flds

PH

Iford & Kingston C of E School

Snednore

Wellgreen Lane

The Holdings

Juggs Road

Cranedown

Kingston Road

Lewes Sports Club

Kingston near Lewes

The

3

31

South Downs Way

Swanborough Drove

Swanborough Hollow

4

Dencher Road

5

A **B** **50** **C** **D**

South Downs Way

White Way

A27(T)

Old Barns

A27(T)

E   F   **I7**   G   H

Rise Farm

Brook Lane

R

I

2

River Ouse

Rise
Barn

The
Brooks

3

ord

4

5

Northease
Manor
School

E   F   **5I**   G   H

Northease Farm

Rodmell
Primary School

A5
1 Cumberland Crs
2 Highfield Cl

A4
1 Brambletyne Cl
2 Ferndale Wk

A   B   C   D

The Street

Pat

I

Norfolk House

Selden Lane

Selden Farm

Coldharb

France Lane

Selden

2   Ham erpot
PH

Arundel Road

ARUNDEL

WATER LANE   A280

B2225

ARUNDEL

3   St Ma s C of E School

Lane

Dappers

Furzefield   Pine Trees Cl
Cl   Woodlands
Chantryfield Road   Garden Cl   Cl

Shardeloes Rd

Lloyd
Goring
Close

Meadowside

Elmhurst Cl
Ashleigh Cl

Beech View

1

2

Cres Ring
Crescent   Mertyfel
Plat

WATER LANE   A280

Ecclesden Farm

4   Lansdowne y

ROAD

Greena   Cres Ring

Lansdowne Road

7

Cumberland Rd

Weavers Hill

1
2

Hillside Crs

The Avenals

HIGH STREET   B2225

Weavers Ring

PO

Honey La

ctrells

5   Mill Road   e

Old Darlington Mushroom Farm Industrial Estate

A   B   C   D

52

ROUNDSTONE LANE

Mill Road Avenue

Foxdale Drive
Briar Cl   Birch
Dell Drive

Close

Worthing Rugby Club

leton Lane

1 grid square represents 500 metres

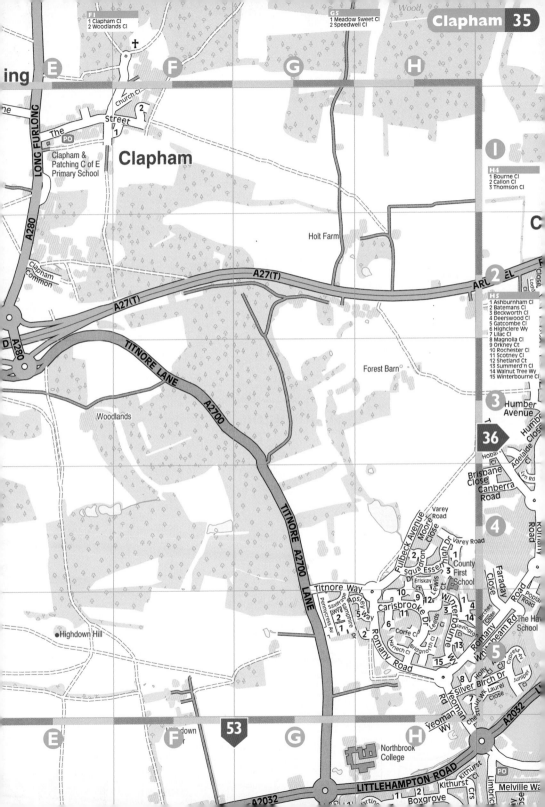

F1
1 Clapham Cl
2 Woodlands Cl

G5
1 Meadow Sweet Cl
2 Speedwell Cl

H4
1 Bourne Cl
2 Callon Cl
3 Thomson Cl

H5
1 Ashburnham Cl
2 Batemans Cl
3 Beckworth Cl
4 Deerswood Cl
5 Gatcombe Cl
6 Highclere Wy
7 Lilac Cl
8 Magnolia Cl
9 Orkney Ct
10 Rochester Cl
11 Scotney Cl
12 Shetland Ct
13 Summerd'n Cl
14 Walnut Tree Wy
15 Winterbourne Cl

E F G H I

Church Cl
Street
The
PO

Clapham & Patching C of E Primary School

Clapham

LONG FURLONG

A280

Clapham Common

A280

Holt Farm

A27(T)

A27(T)

ARUNDEL

2

TITNORE LANE

A2700

Woodlands

Forest Barn

Humber Avenue

36

Brisbane Close

Canberra Road

Highdown Hill

TITNORE LANE A2700

Titnore Way

Varey Road

Moore Close

Varey Road

Fulbeck Avenue

Squadron

High Dr

Essex

County First School

Eriskav

Lewis Cl

4

Winterbourne

Faraday Road

Poplar Road

Carisbrooke Dr

Leeds

Corfe Cl

Bridgnth

Hriech Cl

Romany Road

Romany

Wintheam Rd

The Haven School

5

15

Silver Birch Dr

Yeoman Rd

Laurel Close

Juniper

Yeoman Wy

A2032

53

E F G H

Northbrook College

LITTLEHAMPTON ROAD

Kithurst

Boxgrove

Melville Wa

A2032

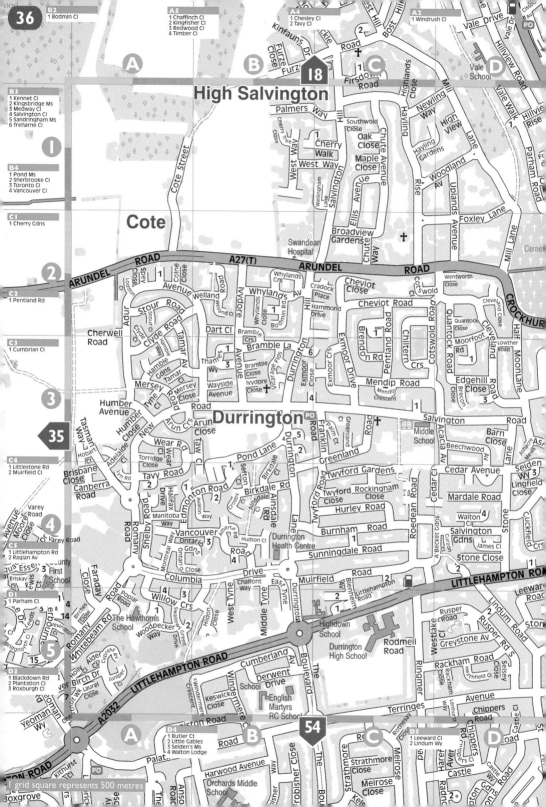

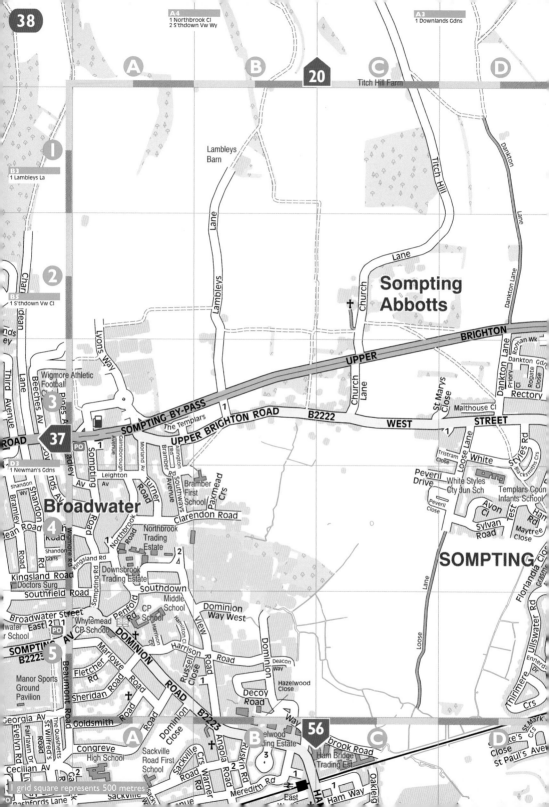

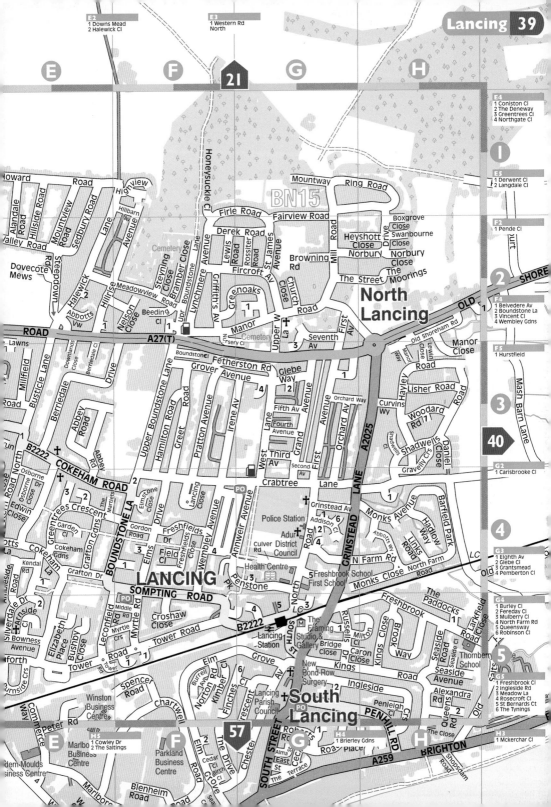

40

C5
1 Wenceling Cots
2 Widewater Cl
3 Willow Cl

A2
1 Old Shoreham Rd

A

B

22

C

D

River Adur

Lancing
College
Chapel

The Drive

Coombes Road

College Farm

I

The Drive

A27(T)

D5
1 Fishermans Wk
2 Mariners Cl
3 Seahaven Gdns

Hoe Court

Old Shoreham Road

st Nicolas

ove

The Paddock

Lesser F

bourne

PO

OLD SHOR

ury

ngs

2

OLD SHOREHAM ROAD A27(T)

Cecil Pashley Way

7

Old Shoreham Rd

Manor Close

Lewin Close

Road

Mash Barn Lane

sher Road

3

Museum

Woodard Rd 7

Chelsea College

39

adwell's Close

evly Cs

Cecil Pashley Way

Nature Reserv

Barfield Park

Hadlow Way

4

North Farm Road

LC

New Salts Farm Road

BRIGHTON

Old Salts Farm Road

ormonde

The Paddocks

Larkfield Close

Windsor Regent Millennium Cl

PO

Road

1

W Cl

Downs Cl

Abbey Cl

Manor Cl

Kings Gap

Woodards View

Seaside Road

Old Salts Farm Road

Drakes

Haigh Cl

Broadway

The

Sussex Rd

Orient Rd

Swallows Cl

Adur Cl

3 2 7

King

emberley Middle School

George V Avenue

Bristol Avenue

Boundary Road

2 3

Kings Drs

5

Seaside Avenue

West Avenue

Prince Way

West Avenue

PO

A259

West Beach Road

Alexandra Rd

Queens Rd

2

West

The Fairway

BRIGHTON ROAD

ok

The Close

Shopsdam Road

A

B

C

D

I grid square represents 500 metres

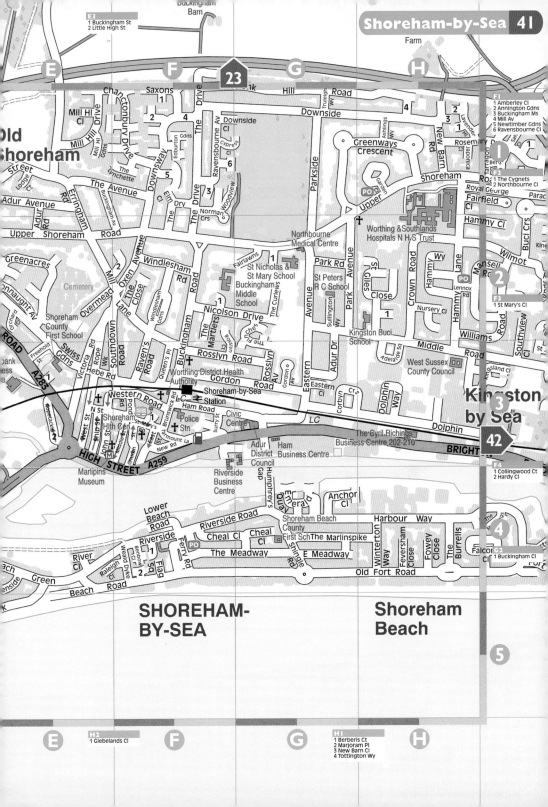

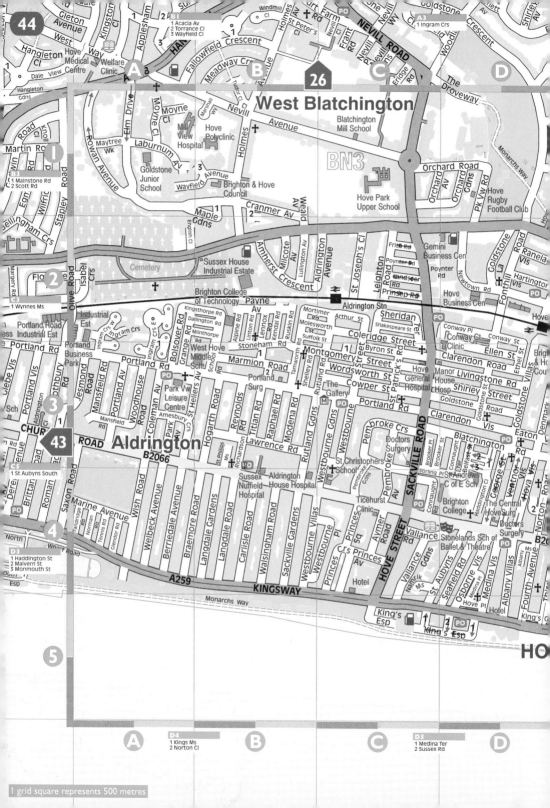

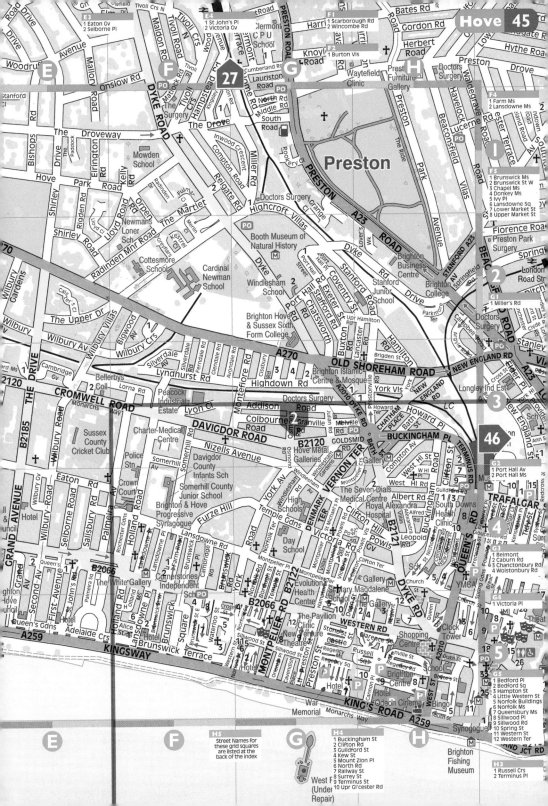

Preston

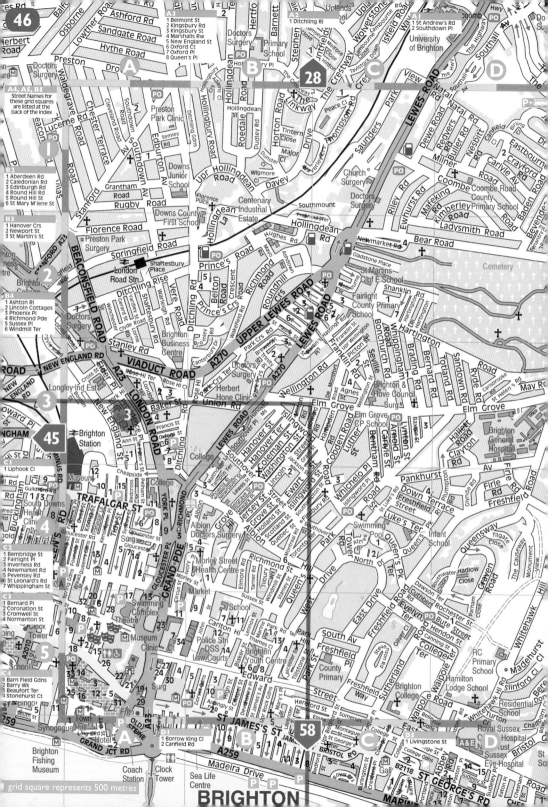

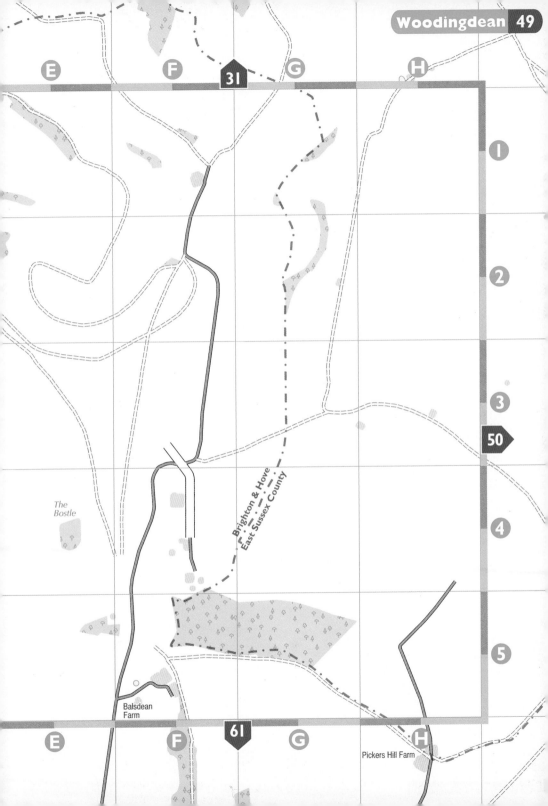

E   F   **31**   G   H

I

2

3

50

4

The Bostle

Brighton & Hove
East Sussex County

5

Balsdean
Farm

E   F   **61**   G   H

Pickers Hill Farm

50

A　　　　　B　　32　　C　　　　　D

South Downs Way

1

South Downs Way

White Way

2

Whiteway
Bottom

3

49

Breaky
Bottom

4

5

A　　　　　B　　62　　C　　　　　D

1 grid square represents 500 metres

E F 33 G H

Northease
Manor
School

Northease Farm

✝
Rodmell
Primary School

I

Rodmell

The
Dicklands

Badgers
Dene

The
Paddocks

Mill Lane

2

Itford F

LC

▪ Southease
Station

3

✝ ▽

Southease

River Ouse

4

5

Durham Farm

E F 63 G H

Dean's Farm

Money Burgh

FERRING

BN12

E2
1 Brookside Cl
2 Hangleton Gra
3 Middle Onslow Cl
4 Rifeside Gdns
5 West Onslow Cl

E3
1 Colindale Rd N
2 East Onslow Cl
3 Ferr'g G'ge Gdns
4 Greystoke Ms
5 The Grove

E4
1 Letchworth Cl

E5
1 April Cl
2 Chalet Cl
3 Ingle Green Cl

F4
1 Beehive Cl
2 Laburnum Cl

F5
1 Chalet Gdns
2 Doone End
3 Florida Gdns
4 Guernsey Rd
5 Lamorna Gdns
6 Milbury Cl

G
1 Lavant Cl

G3
1 Thakeham Cl

H3
1 Aldsworth Ct

H2
1 Denton Cl
2 Galsworthy Cl
3 Southwater Cl
4 Steyning Cl

H1
1 Boxgrove
2 Ditchling Cl
3 Fittleworth Cl

Highdown Hill

Highdown Tower

Northbrook College

LITTLEHAMPTON ROAD A2032

LITTLEHAMPTON ROAD A259 A2032

GORING STREET

Goring-by-Sea Station

GORING WAY A259

Northbrook College

Ferring Football Club

Primary School

Goring Cricket Club

Peregrine Gallery

West Sussex Co Council

Marine Drive

Marine Drive

West Sussex C of E School

Bowness
Avenue

Elizabeth
Place

Bush

Tower

1 Bessborough Ter
2 Laburnum Cl

Lancing
Station

Studio &
Gallery

Bridge
Close

Caron
Close

Kings

Grove

New
Pond-Row
Surgery

Ingleside

Seaside
Avenue

Alexandra
Rd

The Fairway

Winston
Business
Centre

Spencer
Road

Burrell
Av

Elm
Norton Rd

Kimber Rd

6

Lancing
Parish
Council

South
Lancing

Penleigh
Crs

Queens

The Close

Peter Rd

Marlborough
Business
Centre

Parkland
Business
Centre

Elm
Road

Cedar
Cl

The Drive

Chester

The

South STREET

Roberts
Road

Alma
East
St

Cecil
Road

Beachcroft
Place

A259

BRIGHTON

Shopsdam
Road

Old Salts

Western
Close

Blenheim
Road

Marlborough
Road

Birch
Cl

The Grove

The Terrace

Western

Winston Road

W End Way

Lancing Park

Seaview
Court

A259

G1
1 The Grovelands

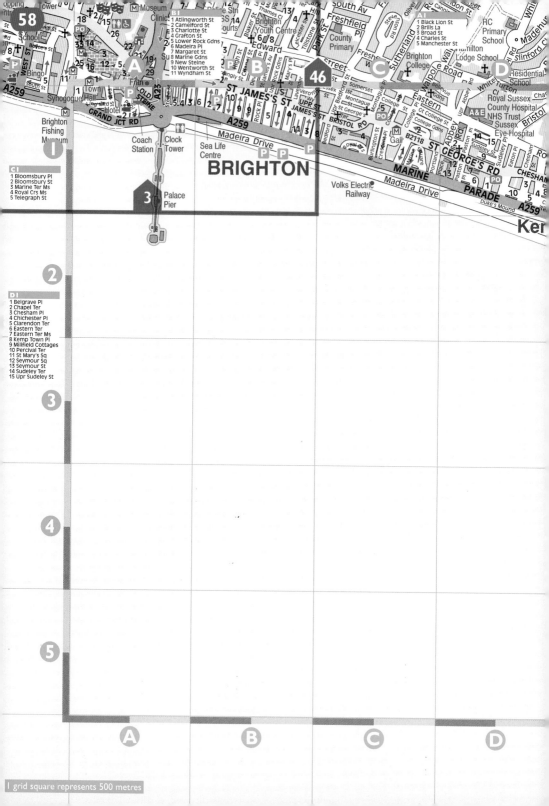

46

3

BRIGHTON

Brighton
Fishing
Museum

Coach
Station

Clock
Tower

Sea Life
Centre

Palace
Pier

Madeira Drive

Volks Electric
Railway

Madeira Drive

MARINE   PARADE

Duke's Mound

Ker

B1
1 Atlingworth St
2 Camelford St
3 Charlotte St
4 Grafton St
5 Lower Rock Gdns
6 Madeira Pl
7 Margaret St
8 Marine Gdns
9 New Steine
10 Wentworth St
11 Wyndham St

A1
1 Black Lion St
2 Brills La
3 Broad St
4 Charles St
5 Manchester St

C1
1 Bloomsbury Pl
2 Bloomsbury St
3 Marine Ter Ms
4 Royal Crs Ms
5 Telegraph St

D1
1 Belgrave Pl
2 Chapel Ter
3 Chesham Pl
4 Chichester Pl
5 Clarendon Ter
6 Eastern Ter
7 Eastern Ter Ms
8 Kemp Town Pl
9 Millfield Cottages
10 Percival Ter
11 St Mary's Sq
12 Seymour Sq
13 Seymour St
14 Sudeley Ter
15 Upr Sudeley St

A259
GRAND JCT RD
OLD STEINE
ST JAMES'S ST
UPR ST JAMES'S ST
A259
BRISTOL RD
ST GEORGE'S RD
A259

Royal Sussex
County Hospital
NHS Trust
Sussex
Eye Hospital
A&E

RC
Primary
School

Brighton
College

Lodge School

Residential
School

County
Primary

Freshfield

Eastern Road

Museum

School

Bingo

A   B   C   D

1   2   3   4   5

Black Rock

Brighton Marina

Virgin Cinemas

Trafalgar Gate

Victory Mews

The Strand

Marina Way

MARINE DRIVE

A259

MARINE

B2118

ROEDEAN ROAD

The Cliff

Roedean Hts

Roedean Path

Roedean Road

Roedean Vale

Crescent

Roedean Road

Roedean School

Roed

Stanley Deason Leisure Centre

Broadway Surgery

Bell Tower Ind Est

BRISTOL GDNS

Henley Rd

Marlow Rd

Peel Rd

Reading Rd

Whitehawk Road

Rugby Pl

Bennett Rd

St Faith Clinic

Bristol Rd

Bristol Pl

Manor Rd

Prince's Ter

Regent's Cl

Robin Dene

Playden

Paddock

CHURCH PLACE

Eastern Rd

Lewes Crs

Arundel Ter

Arundel Pl

Arundel Rd

Arundel Street

Boundary rd

Marina Drive

Cliff Way

Cliff Rd

Cliff Apt

Marina Way

Marina St

Eastern Pl

Eastern Rd

Town

deira Drive

Manor Way

Manor

Findon Road

Wilson Avenue

Maresfield

Cowfold

Manor

Manor Hall

Marks of E im Sch

Hall Girls

B2118

B2137

PO

47

E1 1 Eastern Rd

E2 1 De Courcel Rd

E   F   G   H

I

2

3

60

4

5

E   F   G   H

60

48

59

D4
1 Vicarage La
2 Vicarage Ter
3 Whipping Post La

A B C D

I

Ovingdean Road

Wanderdown Road

Vale

Longhill School

Woodland Walk

Ovingdean Hall School

PO

Longhill Road

Wanderdown Way

Wanderdown drive

Wanderdown Close

Martyns Cl

Longhill Close

Rowan Way

Rowan Wy

Elvin Crescent

Eley

New Barn Road

B2123

Court Farm Rd

Dower Close

Ainsworth Close

Ainsworth Avenue

Greenways

Eley Crs

Eley Drive

Court Ord Rd

FALMER ROAD

Meadow Cl

Meadow Pde

Rottingdean Surgery

Wilkinson Close

Rottingdean Football Cl

2

Roedean School

Roedean

Beacon Hill

Ovingdean

Greenways

MARINE

DRIVE

A259

3

The Rotyngs

Challoners Ms

Our Lady of Lourdes School

Sheep Wk

Nevill Road

Olde Pl Ms

Nevill Road

Nevill Road

Park Crs

Park Cl

Crs

Park Rd

West St

The Gn

THE GREEN

Nort Close

HIGH STREET

M

MARINE

4

5

A B C D

I grid square represents 500 metres

E
F
G
H
I

49

F4
1 Abbotsbury Cl

Balsdean Farm

Pickers Hill Farm

2

Coombe Vale
Coombe Vale North
Westfield Av
Westfield Av S
Westfield
Av
Westfield Rise
Stanmer Av
Stanmer Av
Coombe Rise

Bazehill Road
Welesmere Rd
Gorham Avenue
Road
Lustrells Road
Court Road
Whiteway Lane
Falmer Av
Wivelsfield Road
Perry Hill Road
Ridgewood Avenue
Tumulus
Winton Av
Saxon Close
Vale Rd
Hailsham Av
Hailsham Av
Edward
Hilgrove Rd
Hempstead Road
Berwick
Arlington Gdns
Gorham Close
Dean
Bishopstone Dr
Crescent
Chiltington Way
Chiltington
Efingham
Heathfield Av
Mount Dr
Vale Av
Glynde Av

ROTTINGDEAN
thfield Rd
Doyles
Westmeston Avenue
Lindfield Cl
Chorley Av
Lustrells Av
Lustrells
Falmer Av
Tremola Avenue
Saltdean County School
School Lane
PO
Hawthorn Close
Saltdean
Greenbank
Saltdean
Shepham Av
Saltdean

Ashdown Avenue
Founthill Road
Hill Rd
Saltdean Dr West
Glyndebourne Av
Homebush Avenue
Rodmell
Cissbury
Crescent
Findon Avenue North Av
venue

62
3

ttingdean mary School
Whiteway Lane
ning Road
Newlands Road
Chailey Av
Knole Rd
Grand Crescent
Cranleigh Avenue
Lenham Rd E
Lenham Av
Saltdean
Chichester D
Linchmere Av
Arundel Drive East
Oaklands
Wicklands Av
Bevendean Avenue
Avenue
Avenue
Ashurst

Aubyns ool
St Aubyns Md
The Park Tree Pk
Little W Crs
Eileen Av
Romney Rd
Marine Cl
Founthill Av
Arundel Drive West
Saltdean Park Rd
Arundel Drive
Withynham Av
Lynwood Rd
Doctors Surgery
PO
Crowborough Rd
Walesbeech Rd
Brambletyne Avenue
Nutley Avenue
Cowden Rd
Ardingly Rd
Bannings Vale
Hamsey Rd
Tye Close
4

Marine Clinic
DRIVE
1
Longridge
A259 SOUTH COAST ROAD
5

E
F
G
H

E3
1 Greenhill Wy
2 Mt Caburn Crs
3 Telscombe Pk

E4
1 The Cedars
2 Collingwood Cl
3 Trafalgar Cl

E · F · 51 · G · H

Durham Farm

Dean's Farm

Money Burgh

I

E5
1 Bramber Cl

Bullock Down

The Lookout

2

F3
1 Crocks Dean
2 Downs Vw
3 Linthouse Cl
4 Shepherds Cot

Halcombe Farm

Piddin

3

Roderick Avenue North

Valley Road

Gold Lane

Avenue

Heathdown Close

Wendale Drive

Highsted Park

Greenacres

Telscombe Road

64

F4
1 Pelham Cl
2 The Sparrows
3 Swannee Cl
4 The Sycamores

Down

4

scombe Oval

Johns Cl

Bretts Field

Road

Green Ga

Ashmore Cl

Coney Furlong

Morestead

Tor Road

Anzac Cl

Roderick

Badgers Field

Meridian CP School

Pelham Av

Rise

Cripps Av

skyline Vw

Hoddern Farm

nn Road

Glynn

Abbey Cl

Brow

Road

Pelham Rise

Hairpin Croft

Avenue

Turnpike Cl

Rosemary Close

Cinquefoil

The Bricky

5

BN10

well Av

North Roderick

Edith Av N

Horsham Av

Dorothy Av

Bramber Av N

View Road

Bee Raod

Southview Avenue

Dorothy Avenue North

Road

Peacehaven Town Council

East Sussex Cou Council

Meridian Leisure Centre

E · F · 67 · G · H

nwich

haven School

Hoyle Road

Way

Jason Cl

Damon Cl

Arundel

enue

Peacehaven Sports Centre

Cliff Pk Close

venue

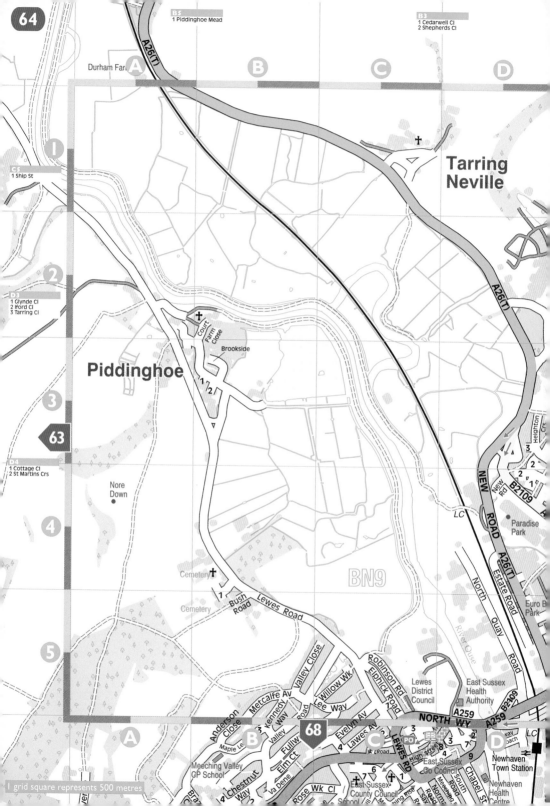

64

B5
1 Piddinghoe Mead

B3
1 Cedarwell Cl
2 Shepherds Cl

A B C D

A26(T)

Durham Far.

1

C5
1 Ship St

✝

**Tarring
Neville**

2

D3
1 Glynde Cl
2 Iford Cl
3 Tarring Cl

✝
Court
Farm
Close

Brookside

Piddinghoe

1 2

▽

3

63

D4
1 Cottage Cl
2 St Martins Crs

Nore
Down

A26(T)

NEW ROAD

Heighton Crs

3

2 1

B2109

New
Way

4

LC

Paradise
Park

Euro B
Park

Cemetery ✝

BN9

River Ouse

North Quay Road

Estate Road

5

Cemetery

7

Bush
Road

Lewes Road

Robinson Rd

Valley Close

Willow Wk

Elphick Road

Lewes
District
Council

East Sussex
Health
Authority

Euro B
Coach

LC

Mercalfe Av

Kennedy
Way

Valley
Road

Lee Way

Anderson
Close

Maple Le

A B 68 C D

Chestnut
Way

Fullw
Elm Ct

Va Dene

Evelyn Av

Lawes Av

L Road

PO

High Street

LEWES RD

East Sussex
Co Council

NORTH WY

A259 A259

B2109

Chapel St

South
Road

Newhaven
Town Station

Meeching Valley
CP School

Rose Wk Cl

6

East Sussex
County Council
School

7

Meeching
Road

Newhaven
Health
Centre

1 grid square represents 500 metres

E

F

G

H

I

2

3

4

5

N

South Heighton

Harfield Close

Harfield Road

The Close

Wellington Road

St Leonards Road

Cantercrow Hill

Cantercrow Hill

Denton

Thompson Road

Rookery Way

Lewis Cl

Heighton Road

PO

Port Vw

Denton Rise

The Grove

Acacia Road

Rectory Road

Hill Rise

Denton Rd

Denton Drive

Park Drive

St Leonards Cl

Hill Road

Denton

Denton County Primary School

King's Avenue

Fairholme Road

Crest Road

Palmerston Road

Palmerston Rd

Mount Pleasant

Beresford

Arundel Road

Station Road

Seaview Road

Claremont Road

Road

Howey Close

Holmdale Road

Falaise Road

Avis Close

Avis Rd

Mount

Mount Close

Rich Industrial Est

Way

East Sussex Co Council

THE DROVE

ROAD

A259

GROVE RD

A259

Poverty Bottom

Bishopstone Road

69

E

F

SEAFORD

G

H

Stud Farm

tbridge Rd

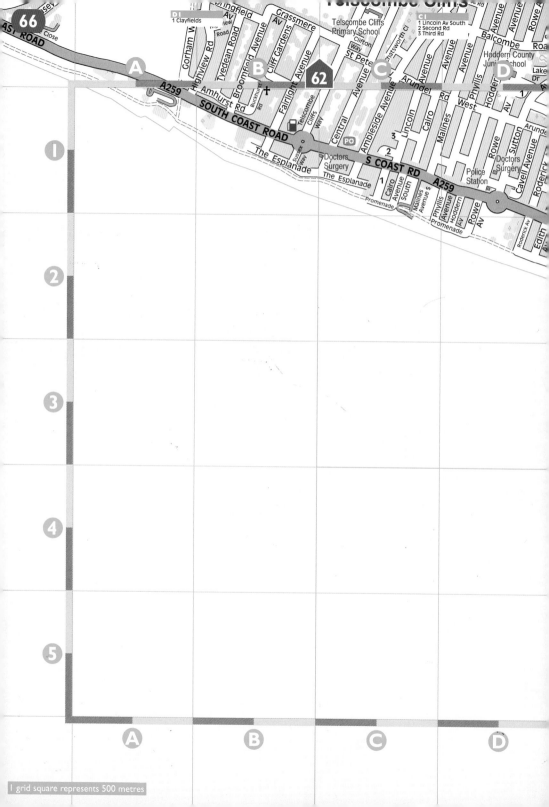

Telscombe Cliffs

AST ROAD

A259

SOUTH COAST ROAD

Gorham W

Highview Rd

Tyedean Road

Bloomfield Avenue

Amhurst Rd

Buckhurst Rd

Cliff Gardens

Fairlight Avenue

Cliffs Way

Sussex Way

Telscombe

Grassmere Av

ingfield Rd

Third Road

Grassmere Av

D1
1 Clayfields

Telscombe Cliffs
Primary School

Clifton
Way

St Pete

Chatsworth Cl

C1
1 Lincoln Av South
2 Second Rd
3 Third Rd

Balcombe

Avenue

Rowe A

Roa

Hoddern County
Jun School

Lake
Dr

62

Central Avenue

Ambleside Avenue

Lincoln Avenue

Cairo Rd West

Malines

Arundel Rd

Phyllis

Hodder

Av

Arunde

Sutton

Cavell Avenue

Roderick

The Esplanade

S COAST ROAD

PO

3

2

1

Doctors
Surgery

The Esplanade

Promenade

Cairo
Avenue
South

Malines
Avenue S

Phyllis
Avenue

Hoddern
Avenue

Rowe
Av

Promenade

Doctors
Surgery

Police
Station

Roderick Av

Edith

1

A259

1 grid square represents 500 metres

PEACEHAVEN

BN10

Peacehaven
Town Council

East
Sussex County
Council

Meridian
Leisure
Centre

Greenwich

Hoyle
Road

Jason Cl

Haven
School

E1
1 Newton Rd
2 Rayford Cl

E2
1 Aquarius Cl

G1
1 Headlands Cl

G2
1 Roundhay Av
2 Wellington Rd

Peacehaven
Sports
Centre

Dorothy Avenue
Bramber Av
Steyning Av
Victoria Av
Bolney Av
Arundel Road
Capel Av
Keymer Av
Slindon Av
Mayfield Av
Piddinghoe Av
Gladys Av
Sunview Av
Vernon Av
Southdown Avenue
Seaview Av
Friars' Av
Cornwall Av
Searle Av

Piddinghoe
Close

Arundel Road

Cornwall
Avenue

Cissbury Avenue

Downland Av

Cliff Pk
Close

Chichester
Close

East Sussex Co
Council

Ashington
Gdns

Links
Rd

Cresta
Road

Blakeney
Avenue

Outlook Avenue

Chene Road

SOUTH COAST ROAD

Cottage
Surgery

Promenade
Bramber Av
Steyning Av
Victoria Av
Bolney Av
Capel Avenue
Keymer Av
Slindon Av
Mayfield Av
Piddinghoe Avenue
Gladys Av
Sunview Av
Vernon Av
Southdown Av
Seaview Av
Friars' Av
Cornwall Av

Neville Rd

Jay
Rd

Seaview Road

Bayview
Road

York Rd

Cliff Av

Doctors Surgery

Promenade

Park
Road

The
Leas

The
Leas

**Peacehaven
Heights**

Friars'
Bay

63

68

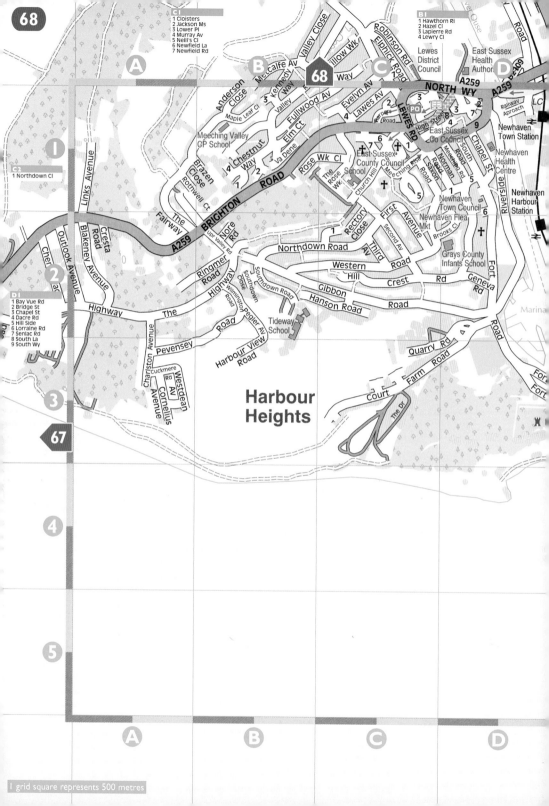

A

B

68

C

D

I

2

3

67

4

5

A

B

C

D

Lewes District Council

East Sussex Health Author

East Sussex District Council

NORTH WY

A259

LEWES RD

PO

East Sussex Go Council

Newhaven Town Station

Newhaven Health Centre

Newhaven Harbour Station

East Sussex County Council

Meeching Valley CP School

BRIGHTON ROAD

A259

Rose Wk Cl

The Rose Wk

Church Hill

Newhaven Town Council

Newhaven Flea Mkt

Brooks Cl

Grays County Infants School

Northdown Road

Western Hill

Crest

Gibbon

Hanson Road

Road

Geneva Rd

Marina

The Fairway

Links Avenue

Outlook Avenue

Blakeney Avenue

Cresta Road

Cher

Ringmer Road

Highway

Nore Rd

Southdown Close

Southdown Road

Wilmington Close

Pegler Av

Tideway School

Harbour View Road

The

Pevensey

Road

Charlston Avenue

Cuckmere Rd

Westdean Av

Cornelius Avenue

Hill Side

Quarry Rd

Court

Farm Road

The Dr

Fort Road

Fort

Harbour Heights

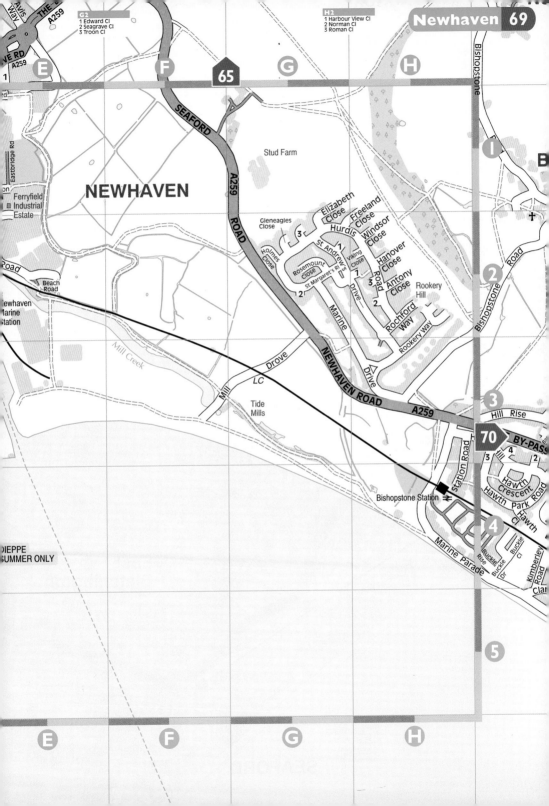

G2
1 Edward Cl
2 Seagrave Cl
3 Troon Cl

H2
1 Harbour View Cl
2 Norman Cl
3 Roman Cl

E
1

65

F

G

H

I

B

SEAFORD ROAD A259

NEWHAVEN

Stud Farm

Ferryfield
Industrial
Estate

Eastbridge Rd

Elizabeth Close

Freeland Close

Windsor Close

Hanover Close

Gleneagles Close

Hurdis

St Andrew's

Holmes Close

Rosemount Close

St Margaret's Rd

Viking Close

Antony Close

Rookery Hill

Marine Drive

Rochford Way

Rookery Way

Beach Road

Newhaven Marine Station

Mill Creek

Mill Drive

LC

Tide Mills

Drive

NEWHAVEN ROAD A259

Hill Rise

70

BY-PASS

Bishopstone Road

2

3

Hawth Crescent

Hawth Park Road

Station Road

Hawth Cl

Bishopstone Station

4

Marine Parade

Buckle Rise

Buckle Dr

Buckle Cl

Kimberley Road

Clar

5

DIEPPE
SUMMER ONLY

E

F

G

H

Rathfinny Farm

The Comp

E2
1 Normansal Cl
2 Sandringham Cl

E3
1 Jubilee Gdns
2 Monarch Gdns
3 The Peverells
4 Sovereign Cl

E F G H

Cradle Hill

1

E4
1 Benenden Cl
2 Hindover Crs
3 Lexden Ct
4 Roadean Cl
5 Sandore Cl

White Horse

2

E5
1 Aquila Pk
2 Went Hill Pk

Alfriston Road

3

1 Hillside Av
2 Landsdown Rd
3 Seafield Cl
4 Upr Chyn'n Gdns

Hythe Cl

BN25

4

F4
1 Dulwich Cl

Dymock Farm

Balmoral Close
Belvedere Gdns
Barn
Argent Close
Pitt Dr
Raymond Close
Cemetery
Quarry Drive
Valley
Vale Road
Vale
West Dean Rd
East Dean Rd
Kammond Avenue
Cradle Hill Road
Rise
Alfriston Road
Richington Way
Upr Chynton Garden
Landsdown Rd
Hastings Avenue
Battle Cl
Deal Av
Dymchurch
Hythe Crs
Hythe Way
Hythe Crescent
Hythe Avenue
Hillside Av
Sandore Rd
Eton Cl
Harrow Cl
Bromley Rd
Rigby Cl
Millfield
Blue Haze Av
Green Well
Pevensey Garden
Millberg Road
Rye Close
The Shepway
Chyngton Gardens
Saltwood Road
Chyngton Av
Warner Road
Unique Ports
Bodiam Close
PO

5

Dymock Farm

Sutton

Downs Leisure Centre
A259 ROAD
Downs Rd
Wellington Road
Sheep Pen La
Meadow Wy
Stoke Cl
Stoke Mnr Cl
Stoke Rd North
Chesterton Av
Chesterton Drive
Perth Close
Stirling Avenue
Elgin Gardens
Ash Drive
Chyngton Lane North
A259 EASTBOURNE ROAD

Arundel Rd
Manor Cl
Hazeldene
Manor
Manor Rd
Kingston Gn
Kingston Cl
Kingston Av
May Av
Badgers Copse
Juniper Close
Willow Drive
Barcombe Avenue
Headland Avenue
Downsview Road
Hartfield Rd
Links Cl
Darwall Dr
Seaford Head Community College
St Wilfred's
Kingston Way
Kingston Lane
Rother Road
Links Rd

E F 73 G H

G5
1 Barcombe Cl
2 Buckthorn Cl
3 Elm Cl
4 Findon Cl
5 Ladycross Cl
6 Romney Cl
7 Rowan Cl
8 Stirling Cl
9 Sycamore Cl

G4
1 Bodiam Cl
2 Dymock Cl
3 Hythe Crs
4 Hythe Vw
5 Stonewood Cl

G3
1 Folkestone Cl
2 Winchelsea Cl

Blackmere Road
Rodmell Rd
Fairways Road
Chyngton Pl
Chyngton Road
Steyning Road
Fld Avenue
Hamsey Lane
Chyngton Lane
Chyngton Farm
PO

SEAFORD

Seaford
Bay

A   **B**   **C**   **D**

1   2   3   4   5

Seaford Station

70

D1
1 Bramber Cl
2 Steyne Cl

C
1 Chatham Pl
2 Church La
3 Maliett Cl
4 Pelham Yd
5 West St

A   **B**   **C**   **D**

I grid square represents 500 metres

G1
1 Fairways Cl
2 Mark Cl
3 Newick Cl
4 Poynings Cl
5 Steyning Cl

1 Sunningdale Cl

Chesterton Drive

Badgers Copse

Headland Avenue

Manor Rd

Kingston Gn

Kingston Cl

King Way

Field Cl

May A

Willow Drive

Junipers Close

Ash Drive

Barcombe Avenue

E

F

G

H

71

Datwell Dr

St. Wilfrid's Pl

Green Wk

Sutton Avenue

Links Rd

Rundel Avenue

Hazeldene

Haz

Arundel Road

Bracken Road

Rother Road

Seaford Head Community College

Cuckmere Road

Chyngton Pl

Chyngton Road

Fairways Road

Roadmell Rd

Lindfield Avenue

Steyning Road

Hamsey Lane

Chyngton Lane

Chyngton Farm

PO

Chyngton Way

Lullington Cl

South Way

South Hill

Golf Course

Hill Fort

Vanguard Way

Seaford Head

Vanguard Way

Nature Rese

Southdown

I

2

3

4

5

E

F

G

H

Aldrington	44 A3	Findon Valley	19 F5	North Moulsecoomb	28 D3	South Heighton	65
Beggars Bush	20 B4	Fishersgate	42 D3	Old Shoreham	41 E1	South Lancing	39
Bevendean	29 G5	Goring-by-Sea	54 A2	Ovingdean	60 C2	South Malling	17
Bishopstone	70 A1	Hangleton	26 A5	Patcham	27 H1	Southover	16
Black Rock	59 G2	Hangleton	52 C1	Peacehaven	67 E1	Southwick	42
Botolphs	7 H5	Harbour Heights	68 B3	Peacehaven Heights	67 G3	Stanmer	15
Bramber	7 H2	High Salvington	36 A1	Piddinghoe	64 A3	Steyning	7
Brighton	3 G6	Hollingbury	28 B2	Portslade-by-Sea	43 F4	Sutton	71
Broadwater	37 H4	Hollingdean	28 B4	Portslade Village	25 E5	Tarring Neville	64
Castle Town	8 C3	Hove	44 D5	Preston	45 G1	Telscombe	62
Clapham	35 F1	Iford	32 D4	Rodmell	51 F2	Telscombe Cliffs	62
Coldean	28 D2	Kemp Town	58 D2	Roedean	60 A2	Upper Beeding	7
Coombes	21 H2	Kingston by Sea	41 H3	Rottingdean	61 E3	Wallands Park	16
Cote	36 A2	Kingston near Lewes	32 A2	Saddlescombe	12 A1	West Blatchington	44
Denton	65 F4	Lancing	39 F4	Saltdean	61 H3	Westdene	26
Durrington	36 B3	Landport	16 D1	Salvington	37 E3	West Kingston	52
East Blatchington	70 C4	Lewes	17 E2	Seaford	72 B1	West Tarring	55
East Kingston	52 C4	Mile Oak	24 D4	Shoreham Beach	41 H5	West Worthing	54
East Moulsecoomb	29 F3	Moulsecoomb	29 F4	Shoreham-by-Sea	41 F5	Whitehawk	47
East Preston	52 B3	Mount Pleasant	65 G4	Sompting	38 D4	Withdean	27
East Worthing	56 D2	Nepcote	18 D2	Sompting Abbotts	38 C2	Woodingdean	48
Falmer	30 B1	Newhaven	69 E1	Southease	51 G3	Worthing	4
Ferring	53 F3	North Lancing	39 H2	Southern Cross	43 E2	Worthing	55

USING THE STREET INDEX

Street names are listed alphabetically. Each street name is followed by its postal town or area locality, the Postcode District, the page number, and the reference to the square in which the name is found.

Example: Abbotsbury Cl *ROTT* BN2 .... 61 F4 ▣

Some entries are followed by a number in a blue box. This number indicates the location of the street within the referenced grid square. The full street name is listed at the side of the map page.

GENERAL ABBREVIATIONS

ACC	ACCESS	E	EAST	LDG	LODGE	R	RIVE
ALY	ALLEY	EMB	EMBANKMENT	LGT	LIGHT	RBT	ROUNDABOU
AP	APPROACH	EMBY	EMBASSY	LK	LOCK	RD	ROA
AR	ARCADE	ESP	ESPLANADE	LKS	LAKES	RDG	RIDG
ASS	ASSOCIATION	EST	ESTATE	LNDG	LANDING	REP	REPUBLI
AV	AVENUE	EX	EXCHANGE	LTL	LITTLE	RES	RESERVOI
BCH	BEACH	EXPY	EXPRESSWAY	LWR	LOWER	RFC	RUGBY FOOTBALL CLU
BLDS	BUILDINGS	EXT	EXTENSION	MAG	MAGISTRATE	RI	RIS
BND	BEND	F/O	FLYOVER	MAN	MANSIONS	RP	RAMI
BNK	BANK	FC	FOOTBALL CLUB	MD	MEAD	RW	ROV
BR	BRIDGE	FK	FORK	MDW	MEADOWS	S	SOUT
BRK	BROOK	FLD	FIELD	MEM	MEMORIAL	SCH	SCHOO
BTM	BOTTOM	FLDS	FIELDS	MKT	MARKET	SE	SOUTH EAS
BUS	BUSINESS	FLS	FALLS	MKTS	MARKETS	SER	SERVICE ARE
BVD	BOULEVARD	FLS	FLATS	ML	MALL	SH	SHOR
BY	BYPASS	FM	FARM	ML	MILL	SHOP	SHOPPIN
CATH	CATHEDRAL	FT	FORT	MNR	MANOR	SKWY	SKYWA
CEM	CEMETERY	FWY	FREEWAY	MS	MEWS	SMT	SUMMI
CEN	CENTRE	FY	FERRY	MSN	MISSION	SOC	SOCIET
CFT	CROFT	GA	GATE	MT	MOUNT	SP	SPUI
CH	CHURCH	GAL	GALLERY	MTN	MOUNTAIN	SPR	SPRIN
CHA	CHASE	GDN	GARDEN	MTS	MOUNTAINS	SQ	SQUAR
CHYD	CHURCHYARD	GDNS	GARDENS	MUS	MUSEUM	ST	STREE
CIR	CIRCLE	GLD	GLADE	MWY	MOTORWAY	STN	STATION
CIRC	CIRCUS	GLN	GLEN	N	NORTH	STR	STREAM
CL	CLOSE	GN	GREEN	NE	NORTH EAST	STRD	STRAND
CLFS	CLIFFS	GND	GROUND	NW	NORTH WEST	SW	SOUTH WES
CMP	CAMP	GRA	GRANGE	O/P	OVERPASS	TDG	TRADINC
CNR	CORNER	GRG	GARAGE	OFF	OFFICE	TER	TERRACI
CO	COUNTY	GT	GREAT	ORCH	ORCHARD	THWY	THROUGHWAY
COLL	COLLEGE	GTWY	GATEWAY	OV	OVAL	TNL	TUNNEI
COM	COMMON	GV	GROVE	PAL	PALACE	TOLL	TOLLWA
COMM	COMMISSION	HGR	HIGHER	PAS	PASSAGE	TPK	TURNPIKE
CON	CONVENT	HL	HILL	PAV	PAVILION	TR	TRACI
COT	COTTAGE	HLS	HILLS	PDE	PARADE	TRL	TRAII
COTS	COTTAGES	HO	HOUSE	PH	PUBLIC HOUSE	TWR	TOWEI
CP	CAPE	HOL	HOLLOW	PK	PARK	U/P	UNDERPASS
CPS	COPSE	HOSP	HOSPITAL	PKWY	PARKWAY	UNI	UNIVERSITY
CR	CREEK	HRB	HARBOUR	PL	PLACE	UPR	UPPEI
CREM	CREMATORIUM	HTH	HEATH	PLN	PLAIN	V	VALE
CRS	CRESCENT	HTS	HEIGHTS	PLNS	PLAINS	VA	VALLEY
CSWY	CAUSEWAY	HVN	HAVEN	PLZ	PLAZA	VIAD	VIADUCT
CT	COURT	HWY	HIGHWAY	POL	POLICE STATION	VIL	VILLA
CTRL	CENTRAL	IMP	IMPERIAL	PR	PRINCE	VIS	VISTA
CTS	COURTS	IN	INLET	PREC	PRECINCT	VLG	VILLAGE
CTYD	COURTYARD	IND EST	INDUSTRIAL ESTATE	PREP	PREPARATORY	VLS	VILLAS
CUTT	CUTTINGS	INF	INFIRMARY	PRIM	PRIMARY	VW	VIEW
CV	COVE	INFO	INFORMATION	PROM	PROMENADE	W	WEST
CYN	CANYON	INT	INTERCHANGE	PRS	PRINCESS	WD	WOOD
DEPT	DEPARTMENT	IS	ISLAND	PRT	PORT	WHF	WHARF
DL	DALE	JCT	JUNCTION	PT	POINT	WK	WALK
DM	DAM	JTY	JETTY	PTH	PATH	WKS	WALKS
DR	DRIVE	KG	KING	PZ	PIAZZA	WLS	WELLS
DRO	DROVE	KNL	KNOLL	QD	QUADRANT	W	WAY
DRY	DRIVEWAY	L	LAKE	QU	QUEEN	YD	YARD
DWGS	DWELLINGS	LA	LANE	QY	QUAY	YHA	YOUTH HOSTEL

OSTCODE TOWNS AND AREA ABBREVIATIONS

G/EP ....Angmering/East Preston
R.............Brighton
R ....Ferring
/BW ....Findon/Broadwater
..............Henfield

HOVE..............Hove
LAN/SOMP..............Lancing/Sompting
LEW..............Lewes
NEWHV..............Newhaven
PEAHV..............Peacehaven

POY/PYE..............Poynings/Pyecombe
PTSD..............Portslade
RING/NEW..............Ringmer/Newick
ROTT..............Rottingdean
SALV..............Salvington

SEAF..............Seaford
SHOR..............Shoreham
STEY/UB..............Steyning/Upper Beeding
STHW..............Southwick
WTHG..............Worthing

Index - streets

Abb - Bel

A

...bey Cl LAN/SOMP BN15 ...... 40 B4
...PEAHV BN10 ...... 63 E4
...bey Rd LAN/SOMP BN15 ...... 39 E3
...OTT BN2 ...... 58 D1
.... 4 B7
...botsbury Cl ROTT BN2 ...... 61 F4
...botts Cl WTHG BN11 ...... 4 D4
...botts Vw LAN/SOMP BN15 ...... 39 E2
...botts Wy LAN/SOMP BN15 ...... 39 H4
...becket Gdns SALV BN13 ...... 36 D4
...ergavenny Rd LEW BN7 ...... 16 D3
...nger Pl LEW BN7 ...... 17 E5
...nger Rd PTSD BN41 ...... 43 F2
...OTT BN2 ...... 48 C4
...acia Av HOVE BN3 ...... 44 B1
...SALV BN13 ...... 36 D3
...acia Rd NEWHV BN9 ...... 65 E3
...e Acre Cl WTHG BN11 ...... 4 A5
...ams Cl BRI BN1 ...... 28 B5
...dison Cl LAN/SOMP BN15 ...... 39 G4
...dison Rd HOVE BN3 ...... 2 C1
...elaide Cl SALV BN13 ...... 36 A4
...SEAF BN25 ...... 70 C3
...elaide Crs HOVE BN3 ...... 45 E5
...elaide Sq SHOR BN43 ...... 41 H3
...ur Av SALV BN13 ...... 36 A2
...HOR BN43 ...... 41 E1
...ur Cl LAN/SOMP BN15 ...... 40 C5
...ur Dr SHOR BN43 ...... 41 G3
...ur Rd FERR BN12 ...... 41 E2
...versane Rd FIN/BW BN14 ...... 37 F5
...laia Rd WTHG BN11 ...... 54 D4
...nes St ROTT BN2 ...... 46 C3
...asdale Cl SALV BN13 ...... 36 B4
...asdale Rd SALV BN13 ...... 36 B4
...nsworth Av ROTT BN2 ...... 60 B2
...nsworth Cl ROTT BN2 ...... 60 B1
...andale Rd LAN/SOMP BN15 ...... 39 E2
...an Wy ROTT BN2 ...... 47 F4
...bany Cl WTHG BN11 ...... 55 E4
...bany Ms HOVE BN3 ...... 44 D4
...bany Rd SEAF BN25 ...... 70 A5
...bany Vls HOVE BN3 ...... 44 D5
...berta Rd SALV BN13 ...... 36 B4
...bert Ms HOVE BN3 ...... 44 D4
...bert Rd BRI BN1 ...... 2 E2
...STHW BN42 ...... 42 B3
...bion Hl ROTT BN2 ...... 3 K3
...bion St LEW BN7 ...... 17 F3
...PTSD BN41 ...... 42 B4
...PTSD BN41 ...... 43 F3
...ROTT BN2 ...... 3 J2
...STHW BN42 ...... 43 E3
...bourne Ct ROTT BN2 ...... 47 E3
...der Cl SALV BN13 ...... 36 A5
...derney Rd FERR BN12 ...... 53 F5
...drich Cl ROTT BN2 ...... 47 F4
...drington Av HOVE BN3 ...... 44 C2
...drington Cl HOVE BN3 ...... 43 H3
...dsworth Av FERR BN12 ...... 53 H3
...dsworth Ct FERR BN12 ...... 53 H3
...dwick Crs FIN/BW BN14 ...... 37 E1
...exandra Cl SEAF BN25 ...... 70 C3
...exandra Ct FERR BN12 ...... 54 A2
...exandra Rd LAN/SOMP BN15 ...... 39 H5
...WTHG BN13 ...... 5 K4
...exandra Vls BRI BN1 ...... 2 E2
...ford Cl FIN/BW BN14 ...... 37 E3
...fred Pl WTHG BN11 ...... 5 H5
...fred Rd BRI BN1 ...... 2 E2
...friston Cl FIN/BW BN14 ...... 37 F5
...ROTT BN2 ...... 47 F4
...friston Pk SEAF BN25 ...... 71 G3
...friston Rd FIN/BW BN14 ...... 37 F5
...ROTT BN2 ...... 47 F4
...friston Rd FIN/BW BN14 ...... 37 F5
...SEAF BN25 ...... 71 F3
...ice St HOVE BN3 ...... 2 A4
...inora Av FERR BN12 ...... 54 A4
...inora Cl FERR BN12 ...... 54 A4
...inora Crs FERR BN12 ...... 54 A4
...inora Dr FERR BN12 ...... 54 A4

Allendale Av FIN/BW BN14 ...... 37 E1
Allington Rd FIN/BW BN14 ...... 38 A3
Alma St LAN/SOMP BN15 ...... 57 G1
Alpine Rd HOVE BN3 ...... 44 B2
Alverstone Rd WTHG BN11 ...... 5 J2
Amberley Cl SHOR BN43 ...... 41 F1
Amberley Dr FERR BN12 ...... 53 H4
   HOVE BN3 ...... 26 A4
Ambleside Av PEAHV BN10 ...... 66 C1
Ambleside Rd LAN/SOMP BN15 ...... 39 E5
Ambrose Pl WTHG BN11 ...... 4 E4
Amelia Rd WTHG BN11 ...... 4 D4
Amesbury Crs HOVE BN3 ...... 44 A3
Amherst Crs HOVE BN3 ...... 44 B2
Amhurst Rd PEAHV BN10 ...... 66 B1
Anchor Cl SHOR BN43 ...... 41 G4
Ancren Cl FERR BN12 ...... 53 F1
Anderson Cl NEWHV BN9 ...... 68 B1
Andrew Cl STEY/UB BN44 ...... 7 F2
Anglesea St WTHG BN11 ...... 4 C3
Angola Rd FIN/BW BN14 ...... 56 B1
Angus Rd FERR BN12 ...... 54 C3
Annington Gdns SHOR BN43 ...... 41 F1
Annington Rd LAN/SOMP BN15 ...... 22 A1
   STEY/UB BN44 ...... 7 G3
Ann St BRI BN1 ...... 3 G1
   WTHG BN11 ...... 5 F5
Annweir Av LAN/SOMP BN15 ...... 39 G4
Anscombe Cl WTHG BN11 ...... 54 D4
Anscombe Rd WTHG BN11 ...... 54 D4
Ansisters Rd FERR BN12 ...... 53 E4
Anson Rd FERR BN12 ...... 54 A1
Ansty Cl ROTT BN2 ...... 47 E5
Antioch St LEW BN7 ...... 17 E4
Antony Cl SEAF BN25 ...... 69 H2
Anvil Cl PTSD BN41 ...... 25 F5
Anzac Cl PEAHV BN10 ...... 63 E4
Appledore Rd ROTT BN2 ...... 29 F5
Applesham Av HOVE BN3 ...... 26 A5
Applesham Wy PTSD BN41 ...... 43 E1
Appletrees ANG/EP BN16 ...... 52 B5
The Approach BRI BN1 ...... 27 G4
April Cl FERR BN12 ...... 53 E5
Apsley Wy SALV BN13 ...... 35 G5
Aquarius Cl PEAHV BN10 ...... 67 E2
Aquila Pk SEAF BN25 ...... 71 E5
Archibald Rd WTHG BN11 ...... 56 C2
Ardale Cl WTHG BN11 ...... 54 D3
Ardingly Dr FERR BN12 ...... 53 H2
Ardingly Rd ROTT BN2 ...... 61 H5
Ardingly St ROTT BN2 ...... 3 J5
Ardsheal Cl FIN/BW BN14 ...... 37 G5
Ardsheal Rd FIN/BW BN14 ...... 37 G4
Argent Cl SEAF BN25 ...... 71 E3
Argyle Rd BRI BN1 ...... 45 H2
Ariadne Rd WTHG BN11 ...... 4 A7
Arlington Av FERR BN12 ...... 53 H5
Arlington Cl FERR BN12 ...... 53 H4
Arlington Crs ANG/EP BN16 ...... 52 B2
   BRI BN1 ...... 29 E2
Arlington Gdns ROTT BN2 ...... 61 H3
Arnold St ROTT BN2 ...... 46 C3
Arnside Cl LAN/SOMP BN15 ...... 39 E5
Arthur St HOVE BN3 ...... 44 C2
Arun Cl LAN/SOMP BN15 ...... 39 E3
   SALV BN13 ...... 36 B3
Arun Crs SALV BN13 ...... 36 A3
Arundel Cl SHOR BN43 ...... 42 A2
Arundel Dr East ROTT BN2 ...... 61 G4
Arundel Dr West ROTT BN2 ...... 61 F4
Arundell Gn LEW BN7 ...... 16 D2
Arundel Pl ROTT BN2 ...... 59 E1
Arundel Rd ANG/EP BN16 ...... 34 C2
   NEWHV BN9 ...... 65 E4
   PEAHV BN10 ...... 67 E1
   ROTT BN2 ...... 59 E2
   SALV BN13 ...... 35 H2
   SEAF BN25 ...... 71 E5
Arundel Road Central
   PEAHV BN10 ...... 66 D1
Arundel Rd West PEAHV BN10 ...... 62 C5
Arundel St ROTT BN2 ...... 59 E2
Arundel Ter ROTT BN2 ...... 59 E2
Ashacre La SALV BN13 ...... 36 D3
Ashacre Ms SALV BN13 ...... 36 D3

Ashacre Wy SALV BN13 ...... 36 D3
Ashburnham Cl BRI BN1 ...... 29 E2
   SALV BN13 ...... 35 H5
Ashburnham Dr BRI BN1 ...... 28 D1
Ash Cl FIN/BW BN14 ...... 18 C1
   HOVE BN3 ...... 27 E4
Ashcombe La LEW BN7 ...... 32 A1
Ashcroft Cl SHOR BN43 ...... 42 B3
Ashdown Av ROTT BN2 ...... 61 F4
Ashdown Rd ROTT BN2 ...... 46 B2
   WTHG BN11 ...... 5 F2
Ash Dr SEAF BN25 ...... 71 G5
Ashfold Av FIN/BW BN14 ...... 37 E1
Ashford Rd BRI BN1 ...... 28 A5
Ash Gv WTHG BN11 ...... 5 G4
Ashington Gdns PEAHV BN10 ...... 67 G2
Ashley Cl BRI BN1 ...... 13 G5
Ashlings Wy HOVE BN3 ...... 26 A5
   SHOR BN43 ...... 41 H1
Ashmore Cl PEAHV BN10 ...... 63 F3
Ashton Ri ROTT BN2 ...... 3 J3
Ashurst Av ROTT BN2 ...... 62 A5
Ashurst Cl FERR BN12 ...... 53 H4
Ashurst Dr FERR BN12 ...... 53 H4
Ashurst Rd ROTT BN2 ...... 29 F2
   SEAF BN25 ...... 72 D1
Ashwood Cl WTHG BN11 ...... 5 K1
Athelstan Rd SALV BN13 ...... 55 E1
Atlingworth St ROTT BN2 ...... 3 K6
Attree Dr ROTT BN2 ...... 46 C4
Auckland Dr ROTT BN2 ...... 47 F1
Audrey Cl BRI BN1 ...... 27 G2
   SEAF BN25 ...... 70 B3
Augusta Pl WTHG BN11 ...... 4 E6
Avalon Wy SALV BN13 ...... 36 B4
The Avenals ANG/EP BN16 ...... 34 A5
The Avenue FERR BN12 ...... 53 H2
   LEW BN7 ...... 16 D3
   LEW BN7 ...... 31 H2
   ROTT BN2 ...... 28 D5
   SHOR BN43 ...... 41 E1
Avery Cl PTSD BN41 ...... 24 D3
Avis Cl NEWHV BN9 ...... 65 E4
Avis Rd NEWHV BN9 ...... 64 D4
Avis Wy NEWHV BN9 ...... 65 E4
Avon Cl LAN/SOMP BN15 ...... 38 D4
Avondale Cl FERR BN12 ...... 54 B2
Avondale Rd HOVE BN3 ...... 45 F3
   SEAF BN25 ...... 70 D5
Aymer Rd HOVE BN3 ...... 44 C4

B

Baden Rd ROTT BN2 ...... 46 D2
Badger Cl PTSD BN41 ...... 25 F5
Badgers Copse SEAF BN25 ...... 71 G5
Badgers Dene LEW BN7 ...... 51 F2
Badgers Fld PEAHV BN10 ...... 63 E4
Badger Wy BRI BN1 ...... 29 E1
Bainbridge Cl SEAF BN25 ...... 72 D1
Baker St BRI BN1 ...... 3 H1
Balcombe Av FIN/BW BN14 ...... 37 G5
Balcombe Rd PEAHV BN10 ...... 62 D5
Balfour Rd BRI BN1 ...... 27 H5
Balmoral Cl SEAF BN25 ...... 71 H5
Balsdean Rd ROTT BN2 ...... 48 B1
Bamford Cl ROTT BN2 ...... 29 G5
Bampfield St PTSD BN41 ...... 43 F2
Bank Pas STEY/UB BN44 ...... 7 F1
Banks Castle LEW BN7 ...... 17 E5
Bankside BRI BN1 ...... 27 E2
Bannings V ROTT BN2 ...... 61 H5
Banstead Cl FERR BN12 ...... 54 A4
Baranscraig Av BRI BN1 ...... 14 A5
Barbary La FERR BN12 ...... 53 E4
Barcombe Av SEAF BN25 ...... 71 G5
Barcombe Cl SEAF BN25 ...... 71 G5
Barcombe Rd BRI BN1 ...... 29 F2
Barfield Pk LAN/SOMP BN15 ...... 39 H4
Barley Cl PEAHV BN10 ...... 62 D3
Barn Cl LEW BN7 ...... 32 A2
   SALV BN13 ...... 36 D3
   SEAF BN25 ...... 71 E2

Barnes Rd PTSD BN41 ...... 43 F2
Barnett Rd BRI BN1 ...... 28 B5
Barnet Wy HOVE BN3 ...... 26 A4
Barn Field Gdns ROTT BN2 ...... 46 C4
Barn Hatch Cl LEW BN7 ...... 16 C4
Barn Ri BRI BN1 ...... 27 F2
   SEAF BN25 ...... 71 E3
Barn Rd LEW BN7 ...... 17 G1
Barons Cl SEAF BN25 ...... 70 A3
Barons Down Rd LEW BN7 ...... 16 C4
Barrhill Av BRI BN1 ...... 13 H5
Barrington Cl FERR BN12 ...... 54 A3
Barrington Rd FERR BN12 ...... 54 A3
Barrow Cl BRI BN1 ...... 28 C5
Barrowfield Cl HOVE BN3 ...... 27 E4
Barrowfield Dr HOVE BN3 ...... 27 E5
Barrow Hl BRI BN1 ...... 28 C5
Barry Wk ROTT BN2 ...... 46 C4
Bartholomews BRI BN1 ...... 3 G5
Barton Cl SALV BN13 ...... 37 E5
Bashfords La FIN/BW BN14 ...... 5 F1
Basin Rd South PTSD BN41 ...... 42 D4
Batemans Cl SALV BN13 ...... 35 H5
Batemans Rd ROTT BN2 ...... 48 C3
Bates Rd BRI BN1 ...... 27 H5
Bath Pl WTHG BN11 ...... 5 F6
Bath Rd WTHG BN11 ...... 4 A7
Bath St BRI BN1 ...... 2 E1
Battle Cl SEAF BN25 ...... 71 G3
Bavant Rd BRI BN1 ...... 27 G5
Baxter Rd LEW BN7 ...... 16 D2
Baxter St ROTT BN2 ...... 46 C3
Bay Tree Cl SHOR BN43 ...... 42 A1
Bayview Rd PEAHV BN10 ...... 67 G3
Bay Vue Rd NEWHV BN9 ...... 68 D1
Baywood Gdns ROTT BN2 ...... 48 A1
Bazehill Rd ROTT BN2 ...... 61 E2
Beach Cl SEAF BN25 ...... 70 B5
Beachcroft Pl LAN/SOMP BN15 ...... 57 G1
Beach Gn SHOR BN43 ...... 40 D4
Beach Pde WTHG BN11 ...... 5 H5
Beach Rd NEWHV BN9 ...... 69 E2
   SHOR BN43 ...... 41 E5
Beachside Cl FERR BN12 ...... 54 C4
Beacon Cl BRI BN1 ...... 28 A5
   SEAF BN25 ...... 70 B3
Beacon Dr SEAF BN25 ...... 70 B3
Beacon Hl ROTT BN2 ...... 60 C2
Beacon Rd SEAF BN25 ...... 70 B4
Beaconsfield Rd BRI BN1 ...... 46 A2
   PTSD BN41 ...... 43 F2
Beaconsfield Vls BRI BN1 ...... 45 H1
Beal Crs BRI BN1 ...... 28 B5
Bear Rd ROTT BN2 ...... 46 C2
Bear Yd LEW BN7 ...... 17 F3
Beatty Av BRI BN1 ...... 14 D5
Beaufort Ter BRI BN1 ...... 46 C4
Beaumont Rd FIN/BW BN14 ...... 37 H5
Beccles Rd WTHG BN11 ...... 4 B4
Becket Rd FIN/BW BN14 ...... 55 E2
Beckett Wy LEW BN7 ...... 17 E1
Beckley Cl ROTT BN2 ...... 47 E5
Beckworth Cl SALV BN13 ...... 35 H5
Bedford Pl BRI BN1 ...... 2 C4
Bedford Rw WTHG BN11 ...... 5 G5
Bedford Sq BRI BN1 ...... 2 C5
Bedford St ROTT BN2 ...... 58 C1
Beech Cl PTSD BN41 ...... 24 D4
Beechers Rd PTSD BN41 ...... 24 D4
Beeches Av FIN/BW BN14 ...... 37 H3
The Beeches BRI BN1 ...... 27 F4
Beech Gv ROTT BN2 ...... 29 E4
Beechlands Cl ANG/EP BN16 ...... 52 A4
Beech Rd FIN/BW BN14 ...... 18 C1
Beech Vw ANG/EP BN16 ...... 34 A3
Beechwood Av BRI BN1 ...... 27 H3
   SALV BN13 ...... 36 D3
Beechwood Cl BRI BN1 ...... 27 H3
Beeding Av HOVE BN3 ...... 26 B4
Beeding Cl LAN/SOMP BN15 ...... 39 F2
Beehive Cl FERR BN12 ...... 53 F4
Beehive La FERR BN12 ...... 53 E4
Bee Rd PEAHV BN10 ...... 63 E5
Belfast St HOVE BN3 ...... 44 D4
Belgrave Crs SEAF BN25 ...... 70 D3

Belgrave Pl *ROTT* BN2 .... 58 D1
Belgrave Rd *SEAF* BN25 .... 70 B4
Belgrave St *ROTT* BN2 .... 3 J2
Bellevue Gdns *ROTT* BN2 .... 46 C5
Bellingham Crs *HOVE* BN3 .... 43 H2
Bell La *LEW* BN7 .... 16 D4
Bellview Rd *SALV* BN13 .... 37 E5
Belmont *BRI* BN1 .... 45 G3
Belmont St *BRI* BN1 .... 3 H1
Belsize Cl *WTHG* BN11 .... 4 A3
Belsize Rd *WTHG* BN11 .... 4 A3
Belton Rd *ROTT* BN2 .... 46 B2
Belvedere Av *LAN/SOMP* BN15 .. 39 F4
Belvedere Gdns *SEAF* BN25 ...... 71 E3
Bembridge Rd *ROTT* BN2 .... 46 C2
Benbow Cl *SHOR* BN43 .... 41 F4
Benedict Cl *WTHG* BN11 .... 56 D2
Benedict Dr *WTHG* BN11 .... 56 C2
Benenden Cl *SEAF* BN25 .... 71 E4
Benett Av *HOVE* BN3 .... 26 D5
Benett Dr *HOVE* BN3 .... 26 D5
Benfield Cl *PTSD* BN41 .... 43 G2
Benfield Crs *PTSD* BN41 .... 43 G1
Benfield Wy *PTSD* BN41 .... 43 G2
Bengairn Av *BRI* BN1 .... 14 A5
Bennett Rd *ROTT* BN2 .... 59 E1
Bentham Rd *ROTT* BN2 .... 46 B2
Berberis Ct *SHOR* BN43 .... 41 H1
Beresford Rd *NEWHV* BN9 .... 65 E4
   ROTT BN2 .... 46 D5
Bergamot Crs *SHOR* BN43 .... 42 A1
Berkeley Sq *WTHG* BN11 .... 55 E3
Bernard Pl *ROTT* BN2 .... 46 C3
Bernard Rd *ROTT* BN2 .... 46 C3
   WTHG BN11 .... 54 D4
Berriedale Av *HOVE* BN3 .... 44 A4
Berriedale Cl *LAN/SOMP* BN15 ... 39 E3
Berriedale Dr *LAN/SOMP* BN15 .. 39 E3
Berry Cl *PEAHV* BN10 .... 62 C4
Berwick Cl *SEAF* BN25 .... 70 B4
Berwick Rd *ROTT* BN2 .... 61 H2
Bessborough Ter
   LAN/SOMP BN15 .... 57 F1
Bevendean Av *ROTT* BN2 .... 61 H4
Bevendean Crs *ROTT* BN2 .... 29 E5
Bevendean Rd *ROTT* BN2 .... 46 D2
Bexhill Rd *ROTT* BN2 .... 48 B1
Bigwood Av *HOVE* BN3 .... 45 F3
Birch Cl *LAN/SOMP* BN15 .... 57 F1
Birches Cl *SALV* BN13 .... 36 A5
Birch Grove Crs *BRI* BN1 .... 28 A2
Birdham Rd *ROTT* BN2 .... 29 E4
Birkdale Cl *SALV* BN13 .... 36 B4
Birkdale Rd *SALV* BN13 .... 36 B4
Birling Cl *ROTT* BN2 .... 46 D1
   SEAF BN25 .... 70 B4
Bishops Cl *SALV* BN13 .... 55 E1
   SEAF BN25 .... 70 A4
Bishops Dr *LEW* BN7 .... 16 C4
Bishops Rd *HOVE* BN3 .... 45 E1
Bishopstone Dr *ROTT* BN2 .... 61 F3
Bishopstone Rd *SEAF* BN25 ...... 70 A2
Blackdown Rd *SALV* BN13 .... 36 D3
Black Lion St *BRI* BN1 .... 3 G6
Blackman St *BRI* BN1 .... 3 G2
Blacksmiths Crs
   LAN/SOMP BN15 .... 38 D4
Blackthorn Cl *BRI* BN1 .... 27 F4
   PTSD BN41 .... 25 F5
Blakeney Av *NEWHV* BN9 .... 68 A2
Blaker St *ROTT* BN2 .... 3 J5
Blatchington Cl *SEAF* BN25 .... 70 D4
Blatchington Hl *SEAF* BN25 .... 70 C4
Blatchington Rd *HOVE* BN3 .... 44 D3
   SEAF BN25 .... 70 C5
Blenheim Av *SALV* BN13 .... 36 A5
Blenheim Pl *BRI* BN1 .... 3 H3
Blenheim Rd *LAN/SOMP* BN15 .. 57 F1
Blois Rd *LEW* BN7 .... 16 C1
Bloomsbury Pl *ROTT* BN2 .... 58 C1
Bloomsbury St *ROTT* BN2 .... 58 C1
Blue Haze Av *SEAF* BN25 .... 71 F4
Bodiam Av *FERR* BN12 .... 53 C3
   ROTT BN2 .... 47 H1
Bodiam Cl *ROTT* BN2 .... 29 H5
   SEAF BN25 .... 71 G4
Bodmin Cl *SALV* BN13 .... 36 B2
Bodmin Rd *SALV* BN13 .... 36 B2
Bolney Av *PEAHV* BN10 .... 67 E2
Bolney Rd *ROTT* BN2 .... 29 F3
Bolsover Rd *HOVE* BN3 .... 44 A3
   SALV BN13 .... 54 C2
Bonchurch Rd *ROTT* BN2 .... 46 C2
Bond St *BRI* BN1 .... 3 G4
Borough St *BRI* BN1 .... 2 C4
Borrow King Cl *ROTT* BN2 .... 46 D1
Bostal Rd *STEY/UB* BN44 .... 6 D3
The Bostal *STEY/UB* BN44 .... 8 C3

Bost Hl *FIN/BW* BN14 .... 18 C4
   SALV BN13 .... 18 C5
Boston St *BRI* BN1 .... 46 A3
Boughey Pl *LEW* BN7 .... 17 E1
The Boulevard *FERR* BN12 .... 54 C1
   SALV BN13 .... 36 B5
Boundary & Station Roads
   PTSD BN41 .... 43 G4
Boundary Cl *WTHG* BN11 .... 4 A6
Boundary Rd *LAN/SOMP* BN15 .. 40 B5
   ROTT BN2 .... 59 E2
   WTHG BN11 .... 55 E4
The Boundary *SEAF* BN25 .... 72 C1
Boundary Wy *ANG/EP* BN16 ..... 52 B5
Boundstone Cl
   LAN/SOMP BN15 .... 39 F3
Boundstone La
   LAN/SOMP BN15 .... 39 F4
Bourne Cl *SALV* BN13 .... 35 H4
Bowden Ri *SEAF* BN25 .... 70 C2
Bowness Av *LAN/SOMP* BN15 .. 39 E5
Bowring Wy *ROTT* BN2 .... 58 D1
Boxgrove *FERR* BN12 .... 53 H1
Boxgrove Cl *LAN/SOMP* BN15 .. 39 H2
Boyce's St *BRI* BN1 .... 3 F5
Brackenbury Cl *PTSD* BN41 ...... 25 F5
Bracken Rd *SEAF* BN25 .... 73 E1
Bradford Rd *LEW* BN7 .... 16 D3
Brading Rd *ROTT* BN2 .... 46 C3
Braemore Rd *HOVE* BN3 .... 44 A4
Braeside Av *BRI* BN1 .... 13 H5
Bramber Av *HOVE* BN3 .... 26 B4
   PEAHV BN10 .... 67 E1
Bramber Av North *PEAHV* BN10 .. 63 E5
Bramber Cl *LAN/SOMP* BN15 .... 39 F2
   PEAHV BN10 .... 63 E5
   SEAF BN25 .... 72 D1
Bramber La *SEAF* BN25 .... 72 D1
Bramber Rd *FIN/BW* BN14 .... 38 A3
   SEAF BN25 .... 72 D1
   STEY/UB BN44 .... 7 F2
Bramble Cl *SALV* BN13 .... 36 B3
Bramble Crs *SALV* BN13 .... 36 B2
Brambledean Rd *PTSD* BN41 .... 43 F3
Bramble La *SALV* BN13 .... 36 B3
Bramble Ri *BRI* BN1 .... 27 E2
Brambletyne Av *ROTT* BN2 .... 61 H4
Brambletyne Cl
   ANG/EP BN16 .... 34 A4
Bramley Cl *FIN/BW* BN14 .... 37 H4
Bramley Rd *FIN/BW* BN14 .... 37 H4
Bramleys *LEW* BN7 .... 32 A2
Brands Cl *NEWHV* BN9 .... 64 D3
Brangwyn Av *BRI* BN1 .... 27 G1
Brangwyn Crs *BRI* BN1 .... 27 G1
Brangwyn Dr *BRI* BN1 .... 27 F1
Brangwyn Wy *BRI* BN1 .... 27 G2
Brasslands Dr *PTSD* BN41 .... 42 D1
Braybon Av *BRI* BN1 .... 27 H3
Braypool La *BRI* BN1 .... 13 F4
Brazen Cl *NEWHV* BN9 .... 68 A1
Breach Cl *STEY/UB* BN44 .... 7 F1
Bread St *BRI* BN1 .... 3 G4
Brecon Cl *SALV* BN13 .... 36 D3
Brede Cl *ROTT* BN2 .... 47 E5
Brendon Rd *SALV* BN13 .... 36 C2
Brentwood Cl *BRI* BN1 .... 28 B4
Brentwood Crs *BRI* BN1 .... 28 B4
Brentwood Rd *BRI* BN1 .... 28 B4
Bretts Fld *PEAHV* BN10 .... 63 E3
Brewer St *ROTT* BN2 .... 46 B3
Briar Cl *ROTT* BN2 .... 48 B2
Briarcroft Rd *ROTT* BN2 .... 48 B3
The Bricky *PEAHV* BN10 .... 63 F5
Bridge Cl *FERR* BN12 .... 54 A2
   LAN/SOMP BN15 .... 39 G5
Bridge Rd *FIN/BW* BN14 .... 4 E2
Bridge St *NEWHV* BN9 .... 68 D1
Bridgewick Cl *LEW* BN7 .... 17 F1
Bridgnorth Cl *SALV* BN13 .... 35 H5
Bridle Cl *STEY/UB* BN44 .... 8 B2
Bridle Wy *PEAHV* BN10 .... 62 C4
Brierley Gdns
   LAN/SOMP BN15 .... 39 H4
Brigden St *BRI* BN1 .... 45 H3
Brighton Pl *BRI* BN1 .... 3 G5
Brighton Rd *LAN/SOMP* BN15 .. 57 H1
   LEW BN7 .... 16 A5
   NEWHV BN9 .... 68 B2
   SHOR BN43 .... 40 D4
   WTHG BN11 .... 5 G5
Brills La *BRI* BN1 .... 3 G6
Brisbane Cl *SALV* BN13 .... 35 H4
Bristol Av *LAN/SOMP* BN15 ...... 40 B5
Bristol Gdns *ROTT* BN2 .... 59 E1
Bristol Ga *ROTT* BN2 .... 58 D1
Bristol Ms *ROTT* BN2 .... 59 E1
Bristol Pl *ROTT* BN2 .... 59 E1

Bristol Rd *ROTT* BN2 .... 58 C1
Bristol St *ROTT* BN2 .... 59 E1
Brittany Rd *FIN/BW* BN14 .... 55 C1
   HOVE BN3 .... 43 H4
Broadfields *ROTT* BN2 .... 29 E4
Broadfields Rd *ROTT* BN2 .... 29 E4
Broad Gn *ROTT* BN2 .... 48 C4
Broad Rig Av *HOVE* BN3 .... 25 H3
Broad St *ROTT* BN2 .... 3 H6
   SEAF BN25 .... 70 C5
Broadview Gdns *SALV* BN13 ..... 36 C2
Broadwater Rd *FIN/BW* BN14 ... 37 H5
Broadwater St East
   FIN/BW BN14 .... 37 H5
Broadwater St West
   FIN/BW BN14 .... 37 H5
Broadwater Wy *FIN/BW* BN14 .. 37 H4
The Broadway *LAN/SOMP* BN15 .. 40 B5
Brockley Cl *FIN/BW* BN14 .... 4 C1
Bromley Rd *ROTT* BN2 .... 46 B3
   SEAF BN25 .... 71 F4
Brompton Cl *BRI* BN1 .... 27 G1
Brook Barn Wy *FERR* BN12 .... 54 C4
Brook Cl *WTHG* BN11 .... 56 C1
Brookdean Rd *WTHG* BN11 .... 56 D2
Brooker Pl *HOVE* BN3 .... 44 C3
Brooker St *HOVE* BN3 .... 44 C3
Brook La *FERR* BN12 .... 53 E4
Brooklyn Av *WTHG* BN11 .... 54 D3
Brooklyn Rd *SEAF* BN25 .... 70 C5
Brooks Cl *LEW* BN7 .... 17 F2
   NEWHV BN9 .... 68 C2
Brookside *NEWHV* BN9 .... 64 B3
Brookside Cl *FERR* BN12 .... 53 E2
Brookside Rd *ANG/EP* BN16 ..... 52 D5
Brooks La *LEW* BN7 .... 17 G3
Brooks Rd *LEW* BN7 .... 17 F2
Brook St *LEW* BN7 .... 17 F2
Brook Wy *LAN/SOMP* BN15 ...... 39 H5
Broomfield Av *FIN/BW* BN14 ..... 37 F5
   PEAHV BN10 .... 66 B1
Broomfield Dr *PTSD* BN41 .... 25 E3
Brou Cl *ANG/EP* BN16 .... 52 B4
Brougham Rd *WTHG* BN11 .... 56 C2
Browning Rd *LAN/SOMP* BN15 .. 39 G2
   WTHG BN11 .... 4 B3
Brownleaf Rd *ROTT* BN2 .... 48 C4
The Brow *ROTT* BN2 .... 48 B2
Bruce Av *WTHG* BN11 .... 54 D3
Bruce Wy *WTHG* BN11 .... 54 D2
Brunswick Ms *HOVE* BN3 .... 2 A4
Brunswick Pl *HOVE* BN3 .... 2 B3
Brunswick Rd *HOVE* BN3 .... 2 B3
   SHOR BN43 .... 41 F3
   WTHG BN11 .... 4 C7
Brunswick Sq *HOVE* BN3 .... 2 A4
Brunswick St East *HOVE* BN3 ..... 2 B3
Brunswick St West *HOVE* BN3 ... 2 A4
Brunswick Ter *HOVE* BN3 .... 2 A4
Buci Crs *SHOR* BN43 .... 42 A2
Buckhurst Cl *LEW* BN7 .... 17 E1
Buckhurst Rd *PEAHV* BN10 .... 66 B1
Buckingham Av *SHOR* BN43 ..... 41 E1
Buckingham Cl *SEAF* BN25 .... 70 C4
   SHOR BN43 .... 41 G2
Buckingham Ms *SHOR* BN43 .... 41 F1
Buckingham Pl *BRI* BN1 .... 2 E1
Buckingham Rd *BRI* BN1 .... 3 F2
   SHOR BN43 .... 41 F3
   WTHG BN11 .... 4 B3
Buckingham St *BRI* BN1 .... 3 F2
   SHOR BN43 .... 41 F3
Buckland Rd *SEAF* BN25 .... 70 D3
Buckle By-pass *SEAF* BN25 ...... 70 A3
Buckle Cl *SEAF* BN25 .... 70 A4
Buckle Dr *SEAF* BN25 .... 70 A4
Buckle Ri *SEAF* BN25 .... 70 A4
Buckler St *PTSD* BN41 .... 43 F2
Buckley Cl *HOVE* BN3 .... 26 A3
Buckthorn Cl *SEAF* BN25 .... 71 G5
Buckwell Ct *LEW* BN7 .... 16 C1
Buckingham Av *FIN/BW* BN14 .... 4 B1
Buller Rd *ROTT* BN2 .... 46 D1
Burford Cl *SALV* BN13 .... 37 E3
Burley Cl *LAN/SOMP* BN15 .... 39 G4
Burlington Gdns *PTSD* BN41 ..... 43 G1
Burlington Rd *FERR* BN12 .... 54 B2
Burlington St *ROTT* BN2 .... 58 C1
Burlow Cl *ROTT* BN2 .... 47 E5
Burnham Cl *ROTT* BN2 .... 48 D3
Burnham Rd *SALV* BN13 .... 36 C4
Burnside Crs *LAN/SOMP* BN15.. 39 E5
Burrell Av *LAN/SOMP* BN15 ...... 39 F5
The Burrells *SHOR* BN43 .... 41 H4
Burstead Cl *BRI* BN1 .... 28 B4
Burton Vls *HOVE* BN3 .... 45 F2
Burwash Cl *ANG/EP* BN16 .... 52 B2
Burwash Rd *HOVE* BN3 .... 26 A4

Bury Dr *FERR* BN12 53
Bushby Cl *LAN/SOMP* BN15 39
Bush Cl *PEAHV* BN10 62
   ROTT BN2 48
Bush Rd *NEWHV* BN9 64
Busticle La *LAN/SOMP* BN15 39
Bute St *ROTT* BN2 46
Butler Ct *SALV* BN13 .... 36 D
Buttercup Wk *BRI* BN1 28
Butts Rd *STHW* BN42 42
Buxted Ri *BRI* BN1 28
Buxton Rd *BRI* BN1 45
Bydown *SEAF* BN25 71
The Byeways *SEAF* BN25 70
Byron Rd *WTHG* BN11 4
Byron St *HOVE* BN3 44
The Byway *BRI* BN1 29
Byworth Cl *ROTT* BN2 47

C

Caburn Crs *LEW* BN7 16
Caburn Rd *HOVE* BN3 .... 45 G
Cairo Av *PEAHV* BN10 66
Cairo Av South *PEAHV* BN10 66
Caister's Cl *HOVE* BN3 45
Caledonian Rd *ROTT* BN2 .... 46 B
Callon Cl *SALV* BN13 .... 35 H
Cambridge Gv *HOVE* BN3 45
Cambridge Rd *HOVE* BN3 2
   WTHG BN11 4
Camden St *PTSD* BN41 .... 43 G
Camelford St *ROTT* BN2 3
Campbell Rd *BRI* BN1 45
Canada Cl *PEAHV* BN10 .... 62 D
Canberra Rd *SALV* BN13 36
Canfield Cl *ROTT* BN2 46
Canfield Rd *ROTT* BN2 .... 46 D
Canning St *ROTT* BN2 46
Cannon Pl *BRI* BN1 2
Canterbury Ct *SALV* BN13 .... 54 D
Canterbury Dr *ROTT* BN2 46
Canterbury Rd *SALV* BN13 54
Cantercrow Hl *NEWHV* BN9 65
Capel Av *PEAHV* BN10 67
Carden Av *BRI* BN1 27
Carden Cl *BRI* BN1 28
Carden Crs *BRI* BN1 28
Carden Hl *BRI* BN1 28
Carey Down *PEAHV* BN10 .... 62 D
Carisbrooke Cl
   LAN/SOMP BN15 .... 39 G
Carisbrooke Dr *SALV* BN13 35
Carisbrooke Rd *ROTT* BN2 46
Carlisle Rd *HOVE* BN3 44
Carlton Cl *SEAF* BN25 70
Carlton Hl *ROTT* BN2 3
Carlton Ms *WTHG* BN11 55
Carlton Pl *ROTT* BN2 .... 3 K
Carlton Rd *SEAF* BN25 70
Carlton Ter *HOVE* BN3 45
Carlyle Av *ROTT* BN2 46
Carlyle St *ROTT* BN2 46
Carnegie Cl *FIN/BW* BN14 37
Carnegie Gdns *FIN/BW* BN14 ... 37
Carnegie Rd *FIN/BW* BN14 37
Carnforth Rd *LAN/SOMP* BN15 .. 38
Carol Cl *BRI* BN1 27
Caroline Cl *SEAF* BN25 .... 70 B
Caron Cl *LAN/SOMP* BN15 39
Castle Cl *SALV* BN13 54
   STEY/UB BN44 .... 7 G
Castle Ditch La *LEW* BN7 .... 17 E
Castle La *STEY/UB* BN44 7
Castle Rd *SALV* BN13 54
Castle Sq *BRI* BN1 3
Castle St *BRI* BN1 2
Castle Wy *SALV* BN13 54
   STEY/UB BN44.......................... 7
Catherine V *ROTT* BN2 48
The Causeway *FERR* BN12 54
   ROTT BN2 46
   SEAF BN25 72
Cavell Av *PEAHV* BN10 66
Cavell Av North *PEAHV* BN10.. 63
Cavendish Cl *FERR* BN12 54
   PEAHV BN10 62
Cavendish Pl *BRI* BN1 2
Cavendish St *ROTT* BN2 .... 3 J
Cecilian Av *FIN/BW* BN14 55
Cecil Rd *LAN/SOMP* BN15 57
Cedar Av *SALV* BN13 36
Cedar Cl *FERR* BN12 53
   LAN/SOMP BN15..................... 57
   SALV BN13 36

ars Gdns *BRI* BN1 .... 27 F4
Cedars *PEAHV* BN10 .... 63 E4
arwell Cl *NEWHV* BN9 ...... 64 B3
tral Av *FIN/BW* BN14 .... 18 D4
EAHV BN10 .... 66 C1
trecourt Cl *FIN/BW* BN14....... 4 D1
trecourt Rd *FIN/BW* BN14....... 4 D1
turion Rd *BRI* BN1 .... 3 F3
dborn Cl *ROTT* BN2............. 58 D1
ffinch Cl *SALV* BN13 .... 36 A5
iley Av *ROTT* BN2 .... 61 E4
iley Crs *ROTT* BN2 .... 62 A4
iley Rd *BRI* BN1 .... 29 E3
let Cl *FERR* BN12 .... 53 E5
let Gdns *FERR* BN12 .... 53 F5
let Rd *FERR* BN12 .... 53 E4
lfont Dr *HOVE* BN3 .... 27 E4
lfont Wy *SALV* BN13 .... 36 B4
kland Ri *ROTT* BN2 .... 48 C2
lky Rd *PTSD* BN41 .... 24 D4
lloners Cl *ROTT* BN2 .... 60 D3
lloners Ms *ROTT* BN2 .... 60 D3
lvington Cl *BRI* BN1 .... 29 E1
EAF BN25 .... 70 D2
anctonbury Dr *SHOR* BN43 .... 41 E1
anctonbury Rd *HOVE* BN3 .. 45 G3
ancton Cl *WTHG* BN11 .... 54 D2
ancton View Rd
THG BN11 .... 54 D2
andlers Wy *STEY/UB* BN44 ...... 7 E1
andos Rd *WTHG* BN11 .... 4 E6
annel View Rd *ROTT* BN2..... 47 H2
antry Rd *SALV* BN13 .... 37 E4
apel Cl *SEAF* BN25 .... 70 C4
apel Hl *LEW* BN7 .... 17 G3
apel Ms *BRI* BN1 .... 2 B4
apel Pl *PTSD* BN41 .... 43 F3
apel Rd *PTSD* BN41 .... 43 E3
THG BN11 .... 4 E3
apel St *NEWHV* BN9 .... 68 D1
OTT BN2 .... 3 J5
apel Ter *ROTT* BN2 .... 58 D1
arlecote Rd *WTHG* BN11 .... 5 G4
arles Cl *HOVE* BN3 .... 26 C4
EAF BN25 .... 70 B3
arles St *ROTT* BN2 .... 3 H6
arlotte St *ROTT* BN2 .... 3 K6
ariston Av *NEWHV* BN9 ...... 68 A3
e Charltons *BRI* BN1 .... 28 D1
ariton St *STEY/UB* BN44 .... 7 E1
armandean La *FIN/BW* BN14 .... 37 H2
armandean Rd *FIN/BW* BN14 .... 37 H1
artfield *HOVE* BN3 .... 26 C5
artwell Cl *SEAF* BN25 .... 70 C2
artwell Rd *LAN/SOMP* BN15 .... 39 F5
e Chase *FIN/BW* BN14 .... 18 C2
atham Pl *BRI* BN1 .... 2 E1
EAF BN25 .... 72 C1
atham Rd *WTHG* BN11 .... 56 C2
atsmore Crs *FERR* BN12..... 53 G2
atsworth Av *PEAHV* BN10 .. 62 C4
atsworth Cl *PEAHV* BN10... 62 C5
atsworth Pk *PEAHV* BN10 .. 62 D4
atsworth Rd *BRI* BN1 .... 45 G2
THG BN11 .... 5 F5
aucer Rd *WTHG* BN11 .... 4 B3
eal Cl *SHOR* BN43 .... 41 G4
eapside *BRI* BN1 .... 3 G2
elston Av *HOVE* BN3 .... 43 H3
eltenham Pl *BRI* BN1 .... 3 H3
elwood Av *FERR* BN12 .... 54 A4
elwood Cl *BRI* BN1 .... 28 C1
ene Rd *PEAHV* BN10 .... 67 H2
erry Gdns *SALV* BN13 .... 36 C1
erry Tree Cl *SALV* BN13 .... 36 B1
erry Wk *SALV* BN13 .... 36 C1
erwell Rd *SALV* BN13 .... 36 A2
esham Ct *ANG/EP* BN16 ..... 52 A4
esham Pl *ROTT* BN2 .... 58 D1
esham Rd *ROTT* BN2 .... 58 D1
esham St *ROTT* BN2 .... 58 D1
esley Cl *SALV* BN13 .... 36 A4
esswood Cl *WTHG* BN11..... 5 K1
esswood Rd *WTHG* BN11 .... 5 H2
ester Av *LAN/SOMP* BN15 .. 57 C1
NTHG BN11 .... 5 K2
esterfield Rd *FERR* BN12 .... 54 B2
ester Ter *FERR* BN12 .... 46 A1
esterton Av *SEAF* BN25 .... 71 F5
esterton Dr *SEAF* BN25 ...... 71 F5
estnut Ct *ANG/EP* BN16 .... 52 A4
estnut Wk *SALV* BN13 .... 53 H1
estnut Wy *NEWHV* BN9 ..... 68 B1
eviot Cl *ANG/EP* BN16 .... 52 A3
SALV BN13 .... 36 C2
eviot Rd *SALV* BN13 .... 36 C2
ichester Cl *HOVE* BN3 ...... 26 A3
EAHV BN10 .... 67 H1

Chichester Dr East *ROTT* BN2 .... 61 G5
Chichester Dr West *ROTT* BN2 .. 61 F4
Chichester Pl *ROTT* BN2 ... 58 D1
Chichester Rd *SEAF* BN25 .... 70 C5
Chichester Ter *ROTT* BN2 .. 58 D1
Chiddingley Cl *ROTT* BN2 .. 47 F5
Chilgrove Cl *SALV* BN13 .... 36 A5
Chiltern Cl *ANG/EP* BN16 .. 52 A3
SHOR BN43 .... 42 A2
Chiltern Crs *SALV* BN13 ..... 36 C2
Chiltington Cl *ROTT* BN2 ... 61 G3
Chiltington Wy *ROTT* BN2 .. 61 G3
Chippers Cl *SALV* BN13 ..... 54 D1
Chippers Rd *SALV* BN13 .... 36 D5
Chippers Wk *SALV* BN13 ... 54 D1
Chorley Av *ROTT* BN2 .... 61 F3
Chrisdory Rd *PTSD* BN41 ... 24 C4
Christchurch Rd *WTHG* BN11 .... 4 E3
Christie Rd *LEW* BN7 .... 16 C3
Church Cl *BRI* BN1 .... 27 H2
LAN/SOMP BN15 .... 39 G2
SALV BN13 .... 35 F1
STEY/UB BN44 .... 8 A1
Church Farm Wk *STEY/UB* BN44.. 8 A1
Church Gn *SHOR* BN43 .... 42 A3
Church Hl *BRI* BN1 .... 27 G1
NEWHV BN9 .... 68 C1
Church House Cl *STHW* BN42 .. 42 C1
Churchill Rd *LEW* BN7 .... 17 E4
SEAF BN25 .... 70 B3
Church La *FERR* BN12 .... 53 E3
LAN/SOMP BN15 .... 38 C3
LEW BN7 .... 31 H2
ROTT BN2 .... 72 C1
STEY/UB BN44 .... 7 F1
STEY/UB BN44 .... 42 B3
STHW BN42 .... 42 B3
Church Pl *ROTT* BN2 .... 59 E1
Church Rd *HOVE* BN3 .... 44 D4
PTSD BN41 .... 43 F3
SALV BN13 .... 37 E5
Church St *BRI* BN1 .... 2 E3
PTSD BN41 .... 43 F3
SEAF BN25 .... 70 C5
SHOR BN43 .... 41 F3
STEY/UB BN44 .... 7 F1
Church Wk *WTHG* BN11 .... 5 K4
Church Wy *SALV* BN13 .... 37 E5
Church Way Cl *SALV* BN13 .... 37 E5
Chute Av *SALV* BN13 .... 36 C1
Chute Wy *SALV* BN13 .... 36 C2
Chyngton Av *SEAF* BN25 ... 71 F4
Chyngton Gdns *SEAF* BN25 .. 71 F4
Chyngton La *SEAF* BN25 .... 71 G5
Chyngton La North *SEAF* BN25 .. 71 G5
Chyngton Pl *SEAF* BN25 .... 73 E1
Chyngton Rd *SEAF* BN25 ... 73 E1
Chyngton Wy *SEAF* BN25 .. 73 E1
Cinquefoil *PEAHV* BN10 .... 63 E5
Cinque Ports Wy *SEAF* BN25 .... 71 F4
The Circle *ANG/EP* BN16 .... 52 A5
Circus St *ROTT* BN2 .... 3 H4
Cissbury Av *FIN/BW* BN14 .. 18 D5
PEAHV BN10 .... 67 G2
Cissbury Crs *ROTT* BN2 ..... 62 A4
Cissbury Dr *FIN/BW* BN14 .. 18 D4
Cissbury Gdns *FIN/BW* BN14 .. 19 E4
Cissbury Rd *FERR* BN12 ..... 53 G2
FIN/BW BN14 .... 37 U4
HOVE BN3 .... 44 B5
Clapham Cl *BRI* BN1 .... 28 C1
Clapham Common *SALV* BN13.. 35 E2
Claremont Rd *NEWHV* BN9 .. 68 C4
SEAF BN25 .... 70 A5
Clarence Sq *BRI* BN1 .... 2 D5
Clarendon Pl *PTSD* BN41 .... 43 G4
Clarendon Rd *FERR* BN12 ... 38 A4
HOVE BN3 .... 44 D3
SHOR BN43 .... 42 A2
Clarendon Ter *ROTT* BN2 ... 58 D1
Clarendon Vls *HOVE* BN3 ... 44 C3
Clare Rd *LEW* BN7 .... 16 C2
Clarke Av *HOVE* BN3 .... 26 B4
Clayfields *PEAHV* BN10 ...... 66 D1
Clays Hl *STEY/UB* BN44 .... 7 G2
Clayton Rd *ROTT* BN2 .... 46 D5
Clayton Wy *HOVE* BN3 .... 26 B4
Clementine Av *SEAF* BN25 .. 70 B3
Clermont Rd *BRI* BN1 .... 27 F5
Clermont Ter *BRI* BN1 .... 27 G5
Cleveland Cl *SALV* BN13 .... 36 D2
Cleveland Rd *BRI* BN1 .... 46 A1
SALV BN13 .... 36 D2
Cleve Ter *LEW* BN7 .... 16 D4
Cliff Ap *ROTT* BN2 .... 59 F1
Cliff Av *PEAHV* BN10 .... 67 G3
Cliff Cl *SEAF* BN25 .... 72 D2

Cliffe High St *LEW* BN7 .... 17 F3
Cliff Gdns *PEAHV* BN10 ...... 62 B5
SEAF BN25 .... 72 D2
Cliff Park Cl *PEAHV* BN10 .. 67 H1
Cliff Rd *ROTT* BN2 .... 59 F2
SEAF BN25 .... 72 D2
The Cliff *ROTT* BN2 .... 59 F1
Clifton Hl *BRI* BN1 .... 2 D2
Clifton Pl *BRI* BN1 .... 2 D2
Clifton Rd *BRI* BN1 .... 2 E2
NEWHV BN9 .... 68 D1
WTHG BN11 .... 4 D3
Clifton St *BRI* BN1 .... 3 F2
Clifton Ter *BRI* BN1 .... 2 E3
Clifton Wy *PEAHV* BN10 ..... 62 C5
Clinton La *SEAF* BN25 .... 70 C5
Clinton Pl *SEAF* BN25 .... 70 C5
Clive Av *SALV* BN13 .... 54 B3
Clivedale Gdns *STEY/UB* BN44 .. 7 F1
Cloisters *NEWHV* BN9 .... 68 C1
The Close *BRI* BN1 .... 27 F2
LAN/SOMP BN15 .... 57 H1
NEWHV BN9 .... 65 F3
SEAF BN25 .... 72 D1
SHOR BN43 .... 41 F2
Clover La *FERR* BN12 .... 53 E4
Clovers End *BRI* BN1 .... 14 B5
Clover Wy *PTSD* BN41 .... 25 F5
Club Wk *ANG/EP* BN16 .... 52 A5
Cluny St *LEW* BN7 .... 17 E4
Clyde Cl *SALV* BN13 .... 36 A2
Clyde Rd *BRI* BN1 .... 46 A2
SALV BN13 .... 36 A3
Coach House Ms *WTHG* BN11 .. 4 D5
Coastal Rd *ANG/EP* BN16 ... 52 B5
Cobden Rd *ROTT* BN2 .... 46 C3
WTHG BN11 .... 4 C4
Cobton Dr *HOVE* BN3 .... 26 C4
Cockshut Rd *LEW* BN7 .... 17 E5
Cokeham Gdns *LAN/SOMP* BN15 .. 39 E4
Cokeham La *LAN/SOMP* BN15 .. 39 E4
Cokeham Rd *LAN/SOMP* BN15 .. 39 E3
Colbourne Av *ROTT* BN2 .... 28 D5
Colbourne Rd *HOVE* BN3 ...... 2 C1
Coldean La *BRI* BN1 .... 14 C4
Coldharbour La *SALV* BN13 .. 34 D1
Colebrook Cl *WTHG* BN11 ... 5 K2
Colebrook Rd *BRI* BN1 .... 27 F3
STHW BN42 .... 42 D3
Coleman Av *HOVE* BN3 ...... 44 A3
Coleman St *ROTT* BN2 .... 3 K1
Coleridge Cl *FERR* BN12 .... 53 H2
Coleridge Crs *FERR* BN12 .. 53 G2
Coleridge Rd *FERR* BN12 ... 53 H2
Coleridge St *HOVE* BN3 ...... 44 C2
Colgate Cl *ROTT* BN2 .... 47 F4
Colindale Rd *FERR* BN12 .... 53 E3
Colindale Rd North
FERR BN12 .... 53 E3
College Cl *PTSD* BN41 .... 24 D4
College Gdns *ROTT* BN2 ..... 58 C1
WTHG BN11 .... 55 E3
College Hl *STEY/UB* BN44 ..... 7 F2
College Pl *ROTT* BN2 .... 58 C1
College Rd *ROTT* BN2 .... 58 C1
SEAF BN25 .... 72 C1
STEY/UB BN44 .... 8 C3
College St *ROTT* BN2 .... 58 C1
College Ter *ROTT* BN2 .... 46 C5
Cullingworth Cl *PEAHV* BN10 .. 63 F3
Cullingworth Ct *SHOR* BN43 .. 41 F4
Cullingwood Rd *FERR* BN12 .. 54 A1
Colne Cl *SALV* BN13 .... 36 A2
Columbia Dr *SALV* BN13 .... 36 A4
Colvill Av *SHOR* BN43 .... 40 D2
Combe Dr *STEY/UB* BN44 ..... 7 F2
Commerce Wy *LAN/SOMP* BN15 .. 39 E5
Compton Av *BRI* BN1 .... 2 E2
FERR BN12 .... 53 H3
Compton Rd *BRI* BN1 .... 45 F1
The Compts *PEAHV* BN10 ... 62 D4
Coney Furlong *PEAHV* BN10 .. 63 F4
Congreve Rd *FIN/BW* BN14 .. 56 A1
Coniston Cl *LAN/SOMP* BN15 .. 39 E4
Coniston Rd *FERR* BN12 ..... 54 A1
Connaught Av *SHOR* BN43 .. 41 E2
Connaught Rd *HOVE* BN3 ... 44 C4
SEAF BN25 .... 70 A5
Connaught Ter *HOVE* BN3 ... 44 D3
Connell Dr *ROTT* BN2 .... 48 C3
Conway Pl *HOVE* BN3 .... 44 D1
Conway St *HOVE* BN3 .... 44 D2
Cooksbridge Rd *ROTT* BN2 .. 47 E4
Coolham Dr *ROTT* BN2 .... 47 E4
Coombe Dro *STEY/UB* BN44 .. 7 F2
Coombe Ri *FIN/BW* BN14 .... 19 E5
ROTT BN2 .... 61 H2
Coombe Rd *LEW* BN7 .... 17 F2

ROTT BN2 .... 46 D1
STEY/UB BN44 .... 7 E2
Coombes Rd *LAN/SOMP* BN15 .. 22 A1
Coombe V *ROTT* BN2 .... 61 H2
Copse Hl *BRI* BN1 .... 27 F2
Copthorne Cl *SALV* BN13 ... 37 E2
Copthorne Hl *SALV* BN13 ... 36 D3
Corbyn Crs *SHOR* BN43 ...... 41 G3
Cordons *LEW* BN7 .... 31 H2
Corfe Cl *SALV* BN13 .... 35 H5
Cornelius Av *NEWHV* BN9 .. 68 A3
Corner Garth *FERR* BN12 ... 53 F4
Cornfield Cl *SEAF* BN25 ..... 70 D5
Cornfield Rd *SEAF* BN25 .... 70 D5
Cornford Cl *PTSD* BN41 ...... 25 F5
Cornwall Av *PEAHV* BN10 .. 67 G2
Cornwall Gdns *BRI* BN1 ...... 27 G4
Coronation St *ROTT* BN2 .... 46 C3
Corsica Cl *SEAF* BN25 .... 72 D2
Corsica Rd *SEAF* BN25 .... 72 D2
Cortis Av *FIN/BW* BN14 ...... 37 G5
Cote St *SALV* BN13 .... 36 A1
Cotswold Cl *SALV* BN13 ..... 36 C2
Cotswold Rd *SALV* BN13 .... 36 D3
The Cotswolds *STHW* BN42 .. 42 C3
Cotswold Wy *ANG/EP* BN16 .. 52 A3
Cottage Bush Cl *PTSD* BN41 .. 25 G5
Cottage Cl *NEWHV* BN9 ...... 64 D4
Cottenham Rd *WTHG* BN11 .. 5 J2
County Oak Av *BRI* BN1 ...... 28 B1
The Course *LEW* BN7 .... 16 D4
Court Cl *BRI* BN1 .... 13 G5
Court Farm Cl *NEWHV* BN9 .. 64 C3
Court Farm Rd *HOVE* BN3 .. 26 B5
NEWHV BN9 .... 68 C3
ROTT BN2 .... 60 C2
Courtlands Cl *FERR* BN12 .. 54 C4
Courtlands Wy *FERR* BN12 .. 54 C4
Court Ord Rd *ROTT* BN2 ..... 60 C2
Court Rd *LEW* BN7 .... 17 F4
Coventry St *BRI* BN1 .... 45 G2
The Covers *SEAF* BN25 .... 72 D1
Cowden Rd *ROTT* BN2 .... 61 H5
Cowdens Cl *HOVE* BN3 ...... 25 H3
Cowdray Cl *FERR* BN12 ...... 54 B4
Cowdray Dr *FERR* BN12 ...... 54 B4
Cowfold Rd *ROTT* BN2 .... 47 E5
Cowley Dr *LAN/SOMP* BN15 .. 39 H5
ROTT BN2 .... 48 D3
Cowper Rd *WTHG* BN11 .... 4 B4
Cowper St *HOVE* BN3 .... 44 C3
Crabtree Av *BRI* BN1 .... 28 A2
Crabtree La *LAN/SOMP* BN15 .. 39 G4
Cradle Hill Rd *SEAF* BN25 .. 71 E2
Cradock Pl *SALV* BN13 .... 36 B2
Craignair Av *BRI* BN1 .... 13 H5
Cranedown *LEW* BN7 .... 16 C5
Cranleigh Av *ROTT* BN2 ..... 61 F4
Cranleigh Rd *FIN/BW* BN14 .. 37 F5
Cranmer Av *HOVE* BN3 ...... 44 B1
Cranmer Cl *LEW* BN7 .... 17 F2
Cranmer Rd *SALV* BN13 ..... 55 E2
Cranworth Rd *WTHG* BN11 ... 5 J2
Craven Rd *ROTT* BN2 .... 46 D4
Crawley Rd *BRI* BN1 .... 28 D1
Crayford Rd *ROTT* BN2 .... 46 D1
Crescent Cl *ROTT* BN2 .... 48 C2
Crescent Dr North *ROTT* BN2 .. 48 C2
Crescent Dr South *ROTT* BN2 .. 48 C4
Crescent Pl *ROTT* BN2 .... 58 C1
Crescent Rd *ROTT* BN2 .... 46 D2
WTHG BN11 .... 4 D5
The Crescent *LAN/SOMP* BN15 .. 57 G1
ROTT BN2 .... 29 E5
STEY/UB BN44 .... 7 F2
STHW BN42 .... 42 D2
Crespin Wy *BRI* BN1 .... 46 C1
Cresta Rd *NEWHV* BN9 .... 68 A2
Crest Rd *NEWHV* BN9 .... 65 F4
Crest Wy *PTSD* BN41 .... 25 F4
The Crestway *BRI* BN1 .... 46 C1
Cricketfield Rd *SEAF* BN25 .. 72 D1
Cripps Av *PEAHV* BN10 ...... 63 F4
Cripps La *STEY/UB* BN44 ...... 7 G1
Crisp Rd *LEW* BN7 .... 16 C1
Crockhurst Hl *SALV* BN13 ... 36 D2
Crocks Dean *PEAHV* BN10 .. 63 F3
Croft Av *STHW* BN42 .... 42 C3
Croft Ct *SEAF* BN25 .... 70 C5
Croft Dr *PTSD* BN41 .... 25 E4
Crofters Wd *STEY/UB* BN44 .. 7 H1
Croft La *SEAF* BN25 .... 70 C5
Croft Rd *BRI* BN1 .... 27 F3
The Croft *ANG/EP* BN16 ..... 52 A4
Cromleigh Wy *STHW* BN42 .. 24 C5
Cromwell Rd *HOVE* BN3 ..... 45 E3
Cromwell St *ROTT* BN2 .... 46 C3
Crooked La *SEAF* BN25 .... 72 D1

Crosby Cl *SALV* BN13 .... 36 B4
Croshaw Cl *LAN/SOMP* BN15 ...... 39 F5
Crossbush Rd *ROTT* BN2 .... 47 E4
Cross La *FIN/BW* BN14 .... 18 C1
Cross Rd *STHW* BN42 .... 42 B2
Crossroad Cl *STHW* BN42 .... 42 B2
Cross St *BRI* BN1 .... 46 A3
  HOVE BN3 .... 2 B4
  WTHG BN11 .... 4 D2
Cross Wy *LEW* BN7 .... 16 C3
Crossways *ANG/EP* BN16 .... 52 B3
Crossways Av *FERR* BN12 .... 53 C1
The Crossway *BRI* BN1 .... 28 B5
  PTSD BN41 .... 25 E5
Crouch La *SEAF* BN25 .... 72 C1
Crowborough Dr *FERR* BN12 ...... 53 H3
Crowborough Rd *ROTT* BN2 ...... 61 H5
Crown Hl *SEAF* BN25 .... 70 C2
Crown Rd *PTSD* BN41 .... 43 E2
  SHOR BN43 .... 41 H2
Crown St *BRI* BN1 .... 2 E4
Cuckfield Crs *SALV* BN13 .... 36 D4
Cuckmere Rd *NEWHV* BN9 .... 68 A3
  SEAF BN25 .... 73 F1
Cuckmere Wy *BRI* BN1 .... 28 B1
Culpepper Cl *ROTT* BN2 .... 28 D5
Culver Rd *LAN/SOMP* BN15 .... 39 G4
Cumberland Av *FERR* BN12 .... 36 B5
Cumberland Crs *ANG/EP* BN16 .. 34 A5
Cumberland Dr *BRI* BN1 .... 27 C5
Cumberland Rd *ANG/EP* BN16 .... 34 A5
  BRI BN1 .... 27 C5
Cumbrian Cl *SALV* BN13 .... 36 C3
The Curlews *SHOR* BN43 .... 41 G2
Curvins Wy *LAN/SOMP* BN15 ..... 39 H3
Curwen Pl *BRI* BN1 .... 27 G4
Curzon Cl *SALV* BN13 .... 36 D4
Cuthbert Rd *ROTT* BN2 .... 46 C4
The Cygnets *SHOR* BN43 .... 41 F2
Cypress Av *SALV* BN13 .... 36 A5
Cypress Cl *SHOR* BN43 .... 41 F1

D

Dacre Rd *NEWHV* BN9 .... 68 D1
Dagmar St *WTHG* BN11 .... 5 F2
Dale Av *BRI* BN1 .... 27 H2
Dale Crs *BRI* BN1 .... 27 H1
Dale Dr *BRI* BN1 .... 27 H1
Dale Rd *LEW* BN7 .... 16 C4
  WTHG BN11 .... 56 D1
Dale Vw *HOVE* BN3 .... 25 H5
Dale View Gdns *HOVE* BN3 .... 25 H5
Dallington Rd *HOVE* BN3 .... 44 A2
Damon Cl *PEAHV* BN10 .... 67 E1
Dane Cl *SEAF* BN25 .... 72 B1
Danehill Rd *ROTT* BN2 .... 47 F5
Dane Rd *SEAF* BN25 .... 72 B1
Daniel Cl *LAN/SOMP* BN15 .... 39 H3
Dankton Gdns *LAN/SOMP* BN15 .. 38 D3
Dankton La *LAN/SOMP* BN15 ..... 38 D2
Dapper's La *ANG/EP* BN16 .... 34 A4
Darcey Dr *BRI* BN1 .... 28 A1
Dart Cl *SALV* BN13 .... 36 B2
Dartmouth Cl *ROTT* BN2 .... 47 F1
Dartmouth Crs *ROTT* BN2 .... 47 E1
Darwall Dr *SEAF* BN25 .... 71 E5
Davey Dr *BRI* BN1 .... 46 B1
Davey's La *LEW* BN7 .... 17 G2
Davigdor Rd *HOVE* BN3 .... 2 B1
Dawes Av *WTHG* BN11 .... 5 K2
Dawes Cl *WTHG* BN11 .... 5 K2
Dawlish Cl *ROTT* BN2 .... 47 E1
Dawn Cl *STEY/UB* BN44 .... 8 B3
Dawn Crs *STEY/UB* BN44 .... 8 A3
Dawson Ter *ROTT* BN2 .... 46 C4
Deacons Dr *PTSD* BN41 .... 25 F5
Deacons Wy *STEY/UB* BN44 ...... 8 A2
Deal Av *SEAF* BN25 .... 71 G3
Dean Cl *PTSD* BN41 .... 25 G5
Dean Court Rd *ROTT* BN2 .... 61 E3
Deanery Cl *LEW* BN7 .... 17 F1
Dean Gdns *PTSD* BN41 .... 25 G5
Dean Rd *SEAF* BN25 .... 72 D1
Deans Cl *ROTT* BN2 .... 48 C2
Dean St *BRI* BN1 .... 2 D4
Deanway *HOVE* BN3 .... 26 D4
De Braose Wy *STEY/UB* BN44 ... 7 G2
De Courcel Rd *ROTT* BN2 .... 59 E2
Decoy Rd *FIN/BW* BN14 .... 38 B5
Deerswood Cl *SALV* BN13 .... 35 H5
The Deeside *BRI* BN1 .... 14 A5
De Grey Cl *LEW* BN7 .... 17 F2
Delaware Rd *LEW* BN7 .... 16 C4
De Montfort Rd *LEW* BN7 .... 16 D3

  ROTT BN2 .... 46 C3
Dencher Rd *LEW* BN7 .... 32 A4
Deneside *BRI* BN1 .... 27 F2
The Dene *HOVE* BN3 .... 25 H4
Dene V *BRI* BN1 .... 27 F2
The Deneway *BRI* BN1 .... 27 F3
  LAN/SOMP BN15 .... 39 E4
Denmark Rd *PTSD* BN41 .... 43 G3
Denmark Ter *BRI* BN1 .... 2 D2
Denmark Vls *HOVE* BN3 .... 44 D3
Dennis Hobden Cl *ROTT* BN2 .. 47 E1
Denton Cl *FERR* BN12 .... 53 H2
Denton Dr *BRI* BN1 .... 28 A2
  NEWHV BN9 .... 65 E4
Denton Ri *NEWHV* BN9 .... 65 E3
Denton Rd *NEWHV* BN9 .... 65 E4
Derek Av *HOVE* BN3 .... 43 H4
Derek Rd *LAN/SOMP* BN15 .... 39 F2
Derwent Cl *LAN/SOMP* BN15 .... 39 E5
Derwent Dr *FERR* BN12 .... 36 B5
Desmond Wy *ROTT* BN2 .... 47 F4
Devil's Dyke Rd *HOVE* BN3 ...... 26 B1
  POY/PYE BN45 .... 11 F2
  PTSD BN41 .... 11 G3
Devonport Pl *WTHG* BN11 .... 56 C2
Devonport Rd *WTHG* BN11 .... 56 C2
Devonshire Pl *ROTT* BN2 .... 3 J6
De Warrenne Rd *LEW* BN7 .... 16 B3
Dewe Rd *ROTT* BN2 .... 46 C1
The Dewpond *PEAHV* BN10 ...... 62 D4
Ditchling Cl *FERR* BN12 .... 53 H1
Ditchling Crs *BRI* BN1 .... 28 C2
Ditchling Gdns *BRI* BN1 .... 46 A1
Ditchling Ri *BRI* BN1 .... 46 A2
Ditchling Rd *BRI* BN1 .... 14 C1
  ROTT BN2 .... 3 H1
  ROTT BN2 .... 46 B2
Dog La *STEY/UB* BN44 .... 7 F1
Dolphin Rd *SHOR* BN43 .... 41 H3
Dolphin Wy *SHOR* BN43 .... 41 H3
Dominion Cl *FIN/BW* BN14 .... 56 A1
Dominion Rd *FIN/BW* BN14 .... 38 A5
Dominion Wy *FIN/BW* BN14 ...... 38 B5
Dominion Wy West
  FIN/BW BN14 .... 38 B5
Donald Hall Rd *ROTT* BN2 .... 46 D5
Donkey Ms *HOVE* BN3 .... 2 B4
Donnington Rd *ROTT* BN2 .... 48 C4
Doone End *FERR* BN12 .... 53 F5
Dorchester Gdns *WTHG* BN11 .. 55 E3
Dorothy Av *PEAHV* BN10 .... 63 E5
  PEAHV BN10 .... 67 E2
Dorothy Av North *PEAHV* BN10 .. 63 E5
Dorothy Rd *HOVE* BN3 .... 43 H2
Dorset Gdns *ROTT* BN2 .... 3 J5
Dorset Pl *ROTT* BN2 .... 3 J5
Dorset Rd *LEW* BN7 .... 17 F4
Dorset St *ROTT* BN2 .... 3 H5
Douglas Av *WTHG* BN11 .... 54 D3
Douglas Cl *WTHG* BN11 .... 54 D3
Dovecote Ms *LAN/SOMP* BN15 .. 39 E2
Dover Cl *SEAF* BN25 .... 71 G3
Dover Rd *BRI* BN1 .... 28 A5
  WTHG BN11 .... 55 E4
Dower Cl *ROTT* BN2 .... 60 B2
Downash Cl *ROTT* BN2 .... 47 E4
Downland Av *PEAHV* BN10 ...... 67 G2
  STHW BN42 .... 42 B1
Downland Cl *FIN/BW* BN14 .... 18 C1
  ROTT BN2 .... 47 H2
  STEY/UB BN44 .... 8 B2
  STHW BN42 .... 42 B1
Downland Crs *HOVE* BN3 .... 26 B4
Downland Dr *HOVE* BN3 .... 26 B4
Downland Rd *ROTT* BN2 .... 47 H2
  STEY/UB BN44 .... 8 B2
Downlands Av *FIN/BW* BN14 ..... 37 H3
Downlands Cl *LAN/SOMP* BN15 .. 39 E2
Downlands Gdns *FIN/BW* BN14 .. 38 A3
Downs Cl *LAN/SOMP* BN15 .... 40 B4
  LEW BN7 .... 16 C2
Downscroft *STEY/UB* BN44 .... 8 B3
Downside *BRI* BN1 .... 27 F2
  HOVE BN3 .... 26 D4
  LEW BN7 .... 16 C3
  SHOR BN43 .... 41 G1
Downside Av *FIN/BW* BN14 ...... 18 D4
Downside Cl *FIN/BW* BN14 .... 18 C4
  SHOR BN43 .... 41 F1
Downs Link *STEY/UB* BN44 .... 8 A4
Downs Md *LAN/SOMP* BN15 ..... 39 E2
Downs Rd *SEAF* BN25 .... 71 G5
Downs Valley Rd *ROTT* BN2 ..... 48 C2
Downsview *HOVE* BN3 .... 25 H4
Downs Vw *PEAHV* BN10 .... 63 F3
Downsview Av *ROTT* BN2 .... 48 A1
Downsview Rd *ANG/EP* BN16 ... 52 D5
  PTSD BN41 .... 25 E5

SEAF BN25 .... 71 E5
Downs Wk *PEAHV* BN10 .... 62 D3
Downsway *ROTT* BN2 .... 48 B2
  SHOR BN43 .... 41 F1
  STHW BN42 .... 24 D5
Down Ter *ROTT* BN2 .... 46 C4
The Down *HOVE* BN3 .... 25 G3
Downview Av *FERR* BN12 .... 53 E2
Downview Rd *FERR* BN12 .... 53 E2
Down View Rd *WTHG* BN11 ...... 55 E2
Drake Av *FERR* BN12 .... 54 B1
Drakes Cl *LAN/SOMP* BN15 ..... 40 B4
Draxmont Wy *BRI* BN1 .... 27 H4
Draycliff Cl *FERR* BN12 .... 53 E4
The Driftway *STEY/UB* BN44 ...... 8 B1
The Drive *ANG/EP* BN16 .... 52 B5
  HOVE BN3 .... 45 E3
  LAN/SOMP BN15 .... 40 B1
  LAN/SOMP BN15 .... 57 F1
  NEWHV BN9 .... 68 C3
  SHOR BN43 .... 41 F2
  STHW BN42 .... 42 C1
  WTHG BN11 .... 54 D2
The Driveway *SHOR* BN43 .... 41 F2
Drove Av *ROTT* BN2 .... 30 B5
Drove Crs *PTSD* BN41 .... 25 E5
Drove Rd *NEWHV* BN9 .... 65 E5
  PTSD BN41 .... 43 E1
  ROTT BN2 .... 47 G2
Drovers Cl *PTSD* BN41 .... 25 G5
The Drove *BRI* BN1 .... 30 A2
  BRI BN1 .... 45 F1
  NEWHV BN9 .... 65 E5
The Droveway *HOVE* BN3 .... 45 E1
Drummond Rd *FERR* BN12 .... 54 C4
Duchess Dr *SEAF* BN25 .... 70 C2
Dudley Rd *BRI* BN1 .... 46 B1
Dudwell Rd *ROTT* BN2 .... 48 C3
Dukes Cl *SEAF* BN25 .... 70 B3
Duke's Mound *ROTT* BN2 .... 58 D1
Duke St *BRI* BN1 .... 3 F5
Dukes Yd *STEY/UB* BN44 .... 7 F1
Dulwich Cl *SEAF* BN25 .... 71 F4
Dunster Cl *BRI* BN1 .... 46 B1
Dunvan Cl *LEW* BN7 .... 17 E1
Durham Cl *ROTT* BN2 .... 47 G1
Durrington Hl *SALV* BN13 .... 36 B3
Durrington La *SALV* BN13 .... 36 B3
Dyke Cl *HOVE* BN3 .... 26 D3
Dyke Rd *BRI* BN1 .... 26 D3
  BRI BN1 .... 3 F4
Dyke Road Av *HOVE* BN3 .... 26 D3
Dyke Road Dr *BRI* BN1 .... 45 G2
Dyke Road Pl *HOVE* BN3 .... 27 E4
Dymchurch Cl *SEAF* BN25 .... 71 F3
Dymock Cl *SEAF* BN25 .... 71 G4

E

Earls Cl *SEAF* BN25 .... 70 A3
East Albany Rd *SEAF* BN25 ...... 70 D4
East Av *FERR* BN12 .... 54 D4
Eastbank *STHW* BN42 .... 42 D1
Eastbourne Rd *ROTT* BN2 .... 46 D1
  SEAF BN25 .... 71 G5
Eastbridge Rd *NEWHV* BN9 ..... 69 E1
Eastbrook Rd *PTSD* BN41 .... 43 F3
Eastbrook Wy *STHW* BN42 ...... 43 E3
Eastcourt Rd *FIN/BW* BN14 .... 4 D1
East Dean Ri *SEAF* BN25 .... 71 E3
East Dr *ROTT* BN2 .... 46 C5
Eastergate Cl *FERR* BN12 .... 53 F3
Eastergate Rd *ROTT* BN2 .... 29 E3
Eastern Av *SHOR* BN43 .... 41 G3
Eastern Cl *ANG/EP* BN16 .... 52 B3
  SHOR BN43 .... 41 G3
Eastern Pl *ROTT* BN2 .... 59 E1
Eastern Rd *ROTT* BN2 .... 3 K5
  ROTT BN2 .... 59 E1
Eastern Ter *ROTT* BN2 .... 59 E1
Eastern Terrace Ms *ROTT* BN2 .. 58 D1
Eastgate St *LEW* BN7 .... 17 F3
Eastgate Whf *LEW* BN7 .... 17 F3
Easthill Dr *PTSD* BN41 .... 43 F1
Easthill Wy *PTSD* BN41 .... 43 F1
East Md *FERR* BN12 .... 53 F4
East Meadway *SHOR* BN43 ...... 41 G4
East Onslow Cl *FERR* BN12 ...... 53 E3
Eastport La *LEW* BN7 .... 17 E4
East St *BRI* BN1 .... 3 G5
  BRI BN1 .... 30 A1
  LAN/SOMP BN15 .... 57 G1
  LEW BN7 .... 17 F3
  PTSD BN41 .... 43 G4
  SEAF BN25 .... 70 C5
  SHOR BN43 .... 41 F3

East Tyne *SALV* BN13 3
East Wy *LEW* BN7 1
Eastwick Cl *BRI* BN1 1
Eaton Gdns *HOVE* BN3 4
Eaton Gv *HOVE* BN3 45
Eaton Pl *ROTT* BN2 4
Eaton Rd *HOVE* BN3 4
Eaton Vls *HOVE* BN3 4
Edburton Av *BRI* BN1 4
Edburton Gdns *SHOR* BN43 4
Edgehill Cl *SALV* BN13 3
Edgehill Wy *PTSD* BN41 2
Edinburgh Rd *ROTT* BN2 46
  SEAF BN25 7
Edith Av *PEAHV* BN10 6
Edith Av North *PEAHV* BN10 6
Edmonton Rd *SALV* BN13 3
Edward Av *HOVE* BN3 4
  ROTT BN2 6
Edward Cl *HOVE* BN3 2
  SEAF BN25 69
Edward St *LEW* BN7 17
  ROTT BN2 3
Edwin Cl *LAN/SOMP* BN15 3
Effingham Cl *ROTT* BN2 2
Egginton Cl *BRI* BN1 2
Egginton Rd *ROTT* BN2 2
Egmont Rd *HOVE* BN3 4
Egremont Pl *ROTT* BN2 3
Eighth Av *LAN/SOMP* BN15 39
Eileen Av *ROTT* BN2 6
Eirene Av *FERR* BN12 5
Eirene Rd *FERR* BN12 5
Elder Cl *PTSD* BN41 2
Elder Pl *BRI* BN1 4
Eldon Rd *WTHG* BN11 5
Eldred Av *BRI* BN1 2
Eleanor Cl *SEAF* BN25 70
Eley Crs *ROTT* BN2 6
Eley Dr *ROTT* BN2 6
Elgin Gdns *SEAF* BN25 7
Elgin Rd *FERR* BN12 5
Elizabeth Av *HOVE* BN3 2
Elizabeth Cl *HOVE* BN3 26
  SEAF BN25 69
Elizabeth Pl *LAN/SOMP* BN15 3
Elizabeth Rd *SHOR* BN43 4
  WTHG BN11 5
Ellen St *HOVE* BN3 4
  PTSD BN41 4
Ellis Av *SALV* BN13 3
Elm Av *ANG/EP* BN16 5
Elm Cl *HOVE* BN3 2
  SEAF BN25 71
  SHOR BN43 4
Elm Ct *NEWHV* BN9 68
Elm Dr *HOVE* BN3 2
Elm Gv *LAN/SOMP* BN15 39
  ROTT BN2 5
  WTHG BN11 5
Elm Grove La *STEY/UB* BN44 7
Elmhurst Cl *ANG/EP* BN16 3
Elmore Rd *ROTT* BN2 5
Elm Pk *FERR* BN12 5
Elm Ri *FIN/BW* BN14 5
Elm Rd *PTSD* BN41 4
  WTHG BN11 5
Elms Dr *LAN/SOMP* BN15 39
Elms Lea Av *BRI* BN1 2
Elmstone Cl *LAN/SOMP* BN15 3
Elphick Rd *NEWHV* BN9 64
Elrington Rd *HOVE* BN3 45
Elsie Rd *WTHG* BN11 4
Elsted Crs *BRI* BN1 28
Elverlands Cl *FERR* BN12 53
Elvin Crs *ROTT* BN2 5
Ely Cl *SALV* BN13 54
Ely Rd *SALV* BN13 54
Emerald Quay *SHOR* BN43 41
English Cl *HOVE* BN3 4
Ennerdale Dr *LAN/SOMP* BN15 ... 38
Eridge Gn *LEW* BN7 16
Eridge Rd *HOVE* BN3 26
Eriskay Ct *SALV* BN13 35
Eriswell Rd *WTHG* BN11 4
Erringham Rd *SHOR* BN43 41
Erroll Rd *HOVE* BN3 4
Esher Cl *SEAF* BN25 70
Eskbank Av *BRI* BN1 14
Esplanade *SEAF* BN25 72
Esplanade Ms *SEAF* BN25 72
The Esplanade *PEAHV* BN10 66
  WTHG BN11 5
Essenhigh Dr *SALV* BN13 35
Essex St *ROTT* BN2 3
Estate Rd *NEWHV* BN9 64
  NEWHV BN9 65
  NEWHV BN9 ....

elred Rd SALV BN13 55 E1
el St HOVE BN3 44 D3
elwulf Rd SALV BN13 55 E1
erton Wy SEAF BN25 71 E4
n Cl SEAF BN25 71 E4
n Rd WTHG BN11 55 E2
lyn Av NEWHV BN9 68 C1
lyn Rd FIN/BW BN14 55 H1
EW BN7 16 D2
lyn Ter ROTT BN2 46 C5
art St ROTT BN2 3 K2
hurst Rd ROTT BN2 46 C2
eat Cl ROTT BN2 47 E4 1
ter St BRI BN1 45 G2
moor Cl SALV BN13 36 B3
moor Crs SALV BN13 36 C3
moor Dr SALV BN13 36 C2

F

rdene STHW BN42 42 D1
rfield Cl SHOR BN43 41 H1
rfield Gdns PTSD BN41 43 F1
rholme Rd NEWHV BN9 65 F4
rlawn Dr FIN/BW BN14 55 H1
rlawns SHOR BN43 41 G2
rlie Gdns BRI BN1 27 G4
rlight Av PEAHV BN10 66 B1
rlight Pl ROTT BN2 46 C2 2
rview Av FERR BN12 54 A4
rview Ri BRI BN1 27 F2
rview Rd LAN/SOMP BN15 39 G2
rway Crs PTSD BN41 25 G5
rways Cl SEAF BN25 73 G1 1
rways Rd SEAF BN25 73 F1
e Fairway LAN/SOMP BN15 40 A5
NEWHV BN9 68 A2
aise Rd NEWHV BN9 65 F4
con Cl SHOR BN43 42 A4
lowfield Cl HOVE BN3 26 B5 1
lowfield Crs HOVE BN3 26 A5
mer Av FERR BN12 53 H4
ROTT BN2 61 F2
mer Cl FERR BN12 54 A4
mer Gdns ROTT BN2 48 B2
mer Rd ROTT BN2 30 B5
raday Cl SALV BN13 36 A4
rm Cl PTSD BN41 25 E5
SEAF BN25 71 F4
rm Hl ROTT BN2 48 A2
rm Ms HOVE BN3 2 A3
rm Rd HOVE BN3 2 B3
rm Wy STHW BN42 43 E3
rmway Cl HOVE BN3 25 H5
rncombe Rd LEW BN7 17 G3 2
WTHG BN11 5 J3
reday Cl LAN/SOMP BN15 39 G4 2
rndale Rd HOVE BN3 45 F3
rndale Wk ANG/EP BN16 34 A4 2
rnhurst Cl BRI BN1 28 C1
rnhurst Crs BRI BN1 28 B2
rnhurst Dr FERR BN12 53 G3
rnwood Ri BRI BN1 27 F2
rrers Rd LEW BN7 16 D2
rring Cl FERR BN12 53 E5
rring Grange Gdns
FERR BN12 53 E3 3
rringham La FERR BN12 53 E4
rringham Wy FERR BN12 53 E5
rring La FERR BN12 53 F2
rring Marine FERR BN12 53 F5
rring St FERR BN12 53 E3
rry Rd SHOR BN43 41 F4
therston Rd LAN/SOMP BN15 39 F3
versham Cl SHOR BN43 41 H4
eld Cl LAN/SOMP BN15 39 F4
SEAF BN25 73 F1
fth Av FIN/BW BN14 37 G2
LAN/SOMP BN15 39 G3
nches Cl LAN/SOMP BN15 39 F5
e Finches SHOR BN43 41 G3
ndon Av ROTT BN2 62 A4
ndon By-pass FIN/BW BN14 18 B1
ndon Cl HOVE BN3 26 B4 1
SEAF BN25 71 G5 4
ndon Rd FIN/BW BN14 18 D4
ROTT BN2 47 F5
nsbury Rd ROTT BN2 3 K2
Cl ROTT BN2 48 D3
rcroft Av LAN/SOMP BN15 39 F2
rcroft Cl BRI BN1 27 G4
le Cl SEAF BN25 70 C3
le Crs LEW BN7 16 B2
le Dr SEAF BN25 70 C3
le Gra SEAF BN25 70 C3
le Rd LAN/SOMP BN15 39 F1
PEAHV BN10 62 D4
ROTT BN2 46 D3
SEAF BN25 70 C4
Firsdown Cl SALV BN13 18 C5 1
Firsdown Rd SALV BN13 18 C5
First Av FIN/BW BN14 37 G2
HOVE BN3 45 E5
LAN/SOMP BN15 39 G4
NEWHV BN9 68 C2
Fishergate Cl PTSD BN41 43 E3 2
Fishermans Wk SHOR BN43 40 D5 1
Fishersgate Ter PTSD BN41 43 E3
Fisher St LEW BN7 17 E3
Fitch Dr ROTT BN2 47 E1
Fittleworth Cl FERR BN12 53 H1 3
Fitzgerald Av SEAF BN25 72 D1
Fitzgerald Pk SEAF BN25 72 D1
Fitzgerald Rd LEW BN7 17 F1 2
Fitzherbert Dr ROTT BN2 46 D2
Fitzjohns Rd LEW BN7 16 C2
Fitzroy Rd LEW BN7 16 D1
Flag Sq SHOR BN43 41 F4
Fletcher Rd FIN/BW BN14 38 A5
Fletching Cl ROTT BN2 47 F4
Flimwell Cl ROTT BN2 47 E5 1
Flint Cl PTSD BN41 25 F5
SEAF BN25 70 C2
The Flints LEW BN7 32 A2
Florence Av HOVE BN3 43 H2
Florence Pl BRI BN1 46 B1
Florence Rd BRI BN1 46 A2
The Florets STEY/UB BN44 8 B3 2
Florida Cl FERR BN12 53 F5
Florida Gdns FERR BN12 53 F5 3
Florida Rd FERR BN12 53 F5
Florlandia Cl LAN/SOMP BN15 38 D5
Foamcourt Waye FERR BN12 53 E4
Folkestone Cl SEAF BN25 71 G3 1
Fonthill Rd HOVE BN3 44 D2
Fontwell Cl FIN/BW BN14 37 E2
Foredown Cl PTSD BN41 25 F5 4
Foredown Dr PTSD BN41 43 F1
Foredown Rd PTSD BN41 25 F4
Forest Rd BRI BN1 29 E2
FIN/BW BN14 37 H4
Forge Cl PTSD BN41 25 F5
Fort Hvn SHOR BN43 42 A4
Fort Ri NEWHV BN9 68 D3
Fort Rd NEWHV BN9 68 D3
Forward Cl NEWHV BN9 65 E3
Foster Cl SEAF BN25 70 C4
Foundry La LEW BN7 17 G3
Foundry St BRI BN1 3 G3
Fountains Cl BRI BN1 28 B5 1
Founthill Av ROTT BN2 61 F4
Founthill Rd ROTT BN2 61 F4
Fourth Av FIN/BW BN14 37 H3
HOVE BN3 44 D5
LAN/SOMP BN15 39 G3
Fowey Cl SHOR BN43 41 H4
Foxdown Rd ROTT BN2 48 D3
Foxhill PEAHV BN10 63 E4
Foxhunters Rd PTSD BN41 24 D4 1
Fox Lea FIN/BW BN14 18 C2
Foxley La SALV BN13 36 D2
Fox Wy PTSD BN41 25 E4
Framfield Cl BRI BN1 29 E1
The Framptons ANG/EP BN16 52 B4
France La SALV BN13 34 D2
Francis St BRI BN1 3 H1
Franklands Cl FIN/BW BN14 36 D1
Franklin Rd PTSD BN41 43 G3
ROTT BN2 46 C3
SALV BN13 36 C3
SHOR BN43 42 A2
Franklin St ROTT BN2 46 C3
Frant Rd HOVE BN3 26 C5
Frederick Pl BRI BN1 3 G2
Frederick St BRI BN1 3 F3
Freehold St SHOR BN43 41 E3
Freehold Ter ROTT BN2 46 B2
Freeland Cl SEAF BN25 69 H2
Freemans Rd PTSD BN41 43 E2
Freshbrook Cl
LAN/SOMP BN15 39 G5 1
Freshbrook Rd LAN/SOMP BN15 39 H5
Freshfield Pl ROTT BN2 46 C5
Freshfield Rd ROTT BN2 46 C5
Freshfields Cl LAN/SOMP BN15 39 F4
Freshfields Dr LAN/SOMP BN15 39 F4
Freshfield St ROTT BN2 46 C4
Freshfield Wy ROTT BN2 46 C5
Friar Cl BRI BN1 28 A3
Friar Crs BRI BN1 27 H4
Friar Rd BRI BN1 28 A3
Friars' Av PEAHV BN10 67 G2
Friars' Wk LEW BN7 17 F3
Friar Wk BRI BN1 27 H3
SALV BN13 54 D2
Frimley Cl ROTT BN2 48 C3
Friston Cl ROTT BN2 29 F3
SEAF BN25 70 A4
Frith Rd HOVE BN3 44 C2
Frobisher Cl FERR BN12 54 B1
Frobisher Wy FERR BN12 54 B1
Fulbeck Av SALV BN13 35 H4
Fuller Rd LEW BN7 16 C1
Fullwood Av NEWHV BN9 68 B1
Fulmar Cl HOVE BN3 45 F1
The Furlongs STEY/UB BN44 7 F2
Furze Cl SALV BN13 18 B5
Furze Hl HOVE BN3 2 B2
Furzeholme SALV BN13 18 C5 2
Furze Rd SALV BN13 18 B5

G

Gableson Av BRI BN1 26 D3
Gainsborough Av FIN/BW BN14 38 A3
Gaisford Cl FIN/BW BN14 4 C1
Gaisford Rd FIN/BW BN14 55 F1
Galliers Cl BRI BN1 28 B1
The Gallops LEW BN7 16 C3
Galsworthy Cl FERR BN12 53 H2 2
Galsworthy Rd FERR BN12 53 H2
Gannon Rd WTHG BN11 5 K3
Garden Cl ANG/EP BN16 34 A3
LAN/SOMP BN15 39 E4
PTSD BN41 43 G2
SHOR BN43 41 H1
Gardener St PTSD BN41 43 E2
The Gardens PTSD BN41 43 G2
STHW BN42 42 D3
Garden St LEW BN7 17 E4
Gardner Rd PTSD BN41 43 E3
Gardner St BRI BN1 3 G4
Garrick Rd FIN/BW BN14 55 H1
Gatcombe Cl SALV BN13 35 H5 5
Geneva Rd NEWHV BN9 68 D2
George St HOVE BN3 44 D4
PTSD BN41 43 G3 1
PTSD BN41 43 E3
ROTT BN2 3 J5
George V Av FERR BN12 54 D3
LAN/SOMP BN15 40 B5
WTHG BN11 54 C2
Georgia Av FIN/BW BN14 55 H1
Gerald Rd SEAF BN25 72 D2
WTHG BN11 54 D4
Gerard St BRI BN1 46 A2
Ghyllside ROTT BN2 47 E1
Gibbon Rd NEWHV BN9 68 B2
Gildredge Rd SEAF BN25 70 D5
Gladstone Pl ROTT BN2 46 C2
Gladstone Rd PTSD BN41 43 F3
Gladys Av PEAHV BN10 67 F2
Gladys Rd HOVE BN3 43 H2
Glastonbury Rd HOVE BN3 43 H4
Glebe Cl LAN/SOMP BN15 39 G3 2
LEW BN7 16 C4
STHW BN42 42 D3
Glebe Dr SEAF BN25 70 C5
Glebelands Cl SHOR BN43 41 H2 1
Glebe Rd SALV BN13 37 E5
Glebeside Av FIN/BW BN14 37 E5
Glebeside Cl FIN/BW BN14 37 E5
Glebe Vls HOVE BN3 43 H3
Glebe Wy LAN/SOMP BN15 39 G3
Glenbarrie Wy FERR BN12 52 D2
Glendale Rd HOVE BN3 45 F3
Glendor Rd HOVE BN3 44 A4
Gleneagles Cl SEAF BN25 69 G2
Glenfalls Av BRI BN1 14 A5
Glen Gdns FERR BN12 53 F3
Glen Ri BRI BN1 26 D2
Glen Rise Cl BRI BN1 26 D2
The Glen SALV BN13 37 E3
Gleton Av HOVE BN3 25 H5
Gloucester Pas BRI BN1 3 H3 2
Gloucester Pl ROTT BN2 3 H3
Gloucester Rd BRI BN1 3 G3 1
Gloucester St BRI BN1 3 H3
Glynde Av FERR BN12 53 F3
ROTT BN2 61 G3
Glyndebourne Av ROTT BN2 61 G4
Glynde Cl FERR BN12 53 F3
NEWHV BN9 64 D3 1
Glynde Rd ROTT BN2 46 D4
Glynn Ri PEAHV BN10 62 D4
Glynn Rd PEAHV BN10 63 E4
Godfrey Cl LEW BN7 17 E1
Godstalls La STEY/UB BN44 7 E1
Godwin Rd HOVE BN3 43 H2
Golden Acre ANG/EP BN16 52 B5
Golden Av ANG/EP BN16 52 B4
Golden Avenue Cl ANG/EP BN16 52 B5
Gold La PEAHV BN10 63 E3
Goldsmid Rd HOVE BN3 2 D1
Goldsmith Rd FIN/BW BN14 56 A1
Goldstone Cl HOVE BN3 26 D4
Goldstone Crs HOVE BN3 26 C5
Goldstone La HOVE BN3 44 D2
Goldstone Rd HOVE BN3 44 C3
Goldstone St HOVE BN3 44 D3
Goldstone Vls HOVE BN3 44 D3
Goldstone Wy HOVE BN3 26 C5
Golf Dr BRI BN1 28 B4
Goodwood Rd SALV BN13 37 E3
Goodwood Wy ROTT BN2 29 E4
Gordon Av SHOR BN43 41 G3
Gordon Rd BRI BN1 27 H5
LAN/SOMP BN15 39 F4
PTSD BN41 43 E3
PTSD BN41 43 G3
SHOR BN43 41 F3
WTHG BN11 5 F3
Gorham Av ROTT BN2 61 E3
Gorham Cl ROTT BN2 61 E3
Gorham Wy PEAHV BN10 62 A5
Goring Cha FERR BN12 53 G1
Goring Rd FERR BN12 54 A3 2
STEY/UB BN44 7 F2
WTHG BN11 54 D3
Goring St FERR BN12 53 G1
Goring Wy FERR BN12 53 F3
Gorringe Cl SHOR BN43 42 B3
Gorse Av FIN/BW BN14 37 F4
Gorse Cl PTSD BN41 24 D3
Gorse Dr SEAF BN25 70 D2
Gorse La SALV BN13 18 C5
Graffham Cl ROTT BN2 47 E4
Grafton Dr LAN/SOMP BN15 39 E4
Grafton Gdns LAN/SOMP BN15 39 E4
Grafton Pl WTHG BN11 4 E5
Grafton Rd WTHG BN11 4 E5
Grafton St ROTT BN2 3 K6
Graham Av BRI BN1 27 G3
PTSD BN41 24 D3
Graham Crs PTSD BN41 24 D3
Graham Rd WTHG BN11 4 E5
Grand Av HOVE BN3 45 E4
LAN/SOMP BN15 39 G3
SEAF BN25 70 A3
WTHG BN11 55 E3
Grand Crs ROTT BN2 61 E4
Grand Junction Rd BRI BN1 3 G6
Grand Pde ROTT BN2 3 H3
Grand Parade Ms ROTT BN2 3 H4 1
Grange Cl BRI BN1 45 G1
FERR BN12 53 E4
Grange Park Rd FERR BN12 53 E4
Grange Rd HOVE BN3 44 A3
LEW BN7 17 E4
STHW BN42 42 C3
Grangeways BRI BN1 27 G2 1
Grantham Rd BRI BN1 46 A1
Grantsmead LAN/SOMP BN15 39 G3 3
Grant St ROTT BN2 3 K1
Granville Rd HOVE BN3 2 C1
Grasmere Av LAN/SOMP BN15 38 D4
Grassmere Av PEAHV BN10 62 B5
Gratwicke Rd WTHG BN11 4 D5
Gravelly Crs LAN/SOMP BN15 39 H4
Great College St ROTT BN2 58 C1
Greatham Rd FIN/BW BN14 36 D1
Greenacres PEAHV BN10 63 F3
SHOR BN43 41 E2
STEY/UB BN44 7 F2
Greenbank Av ROTT BN2 61 G4
Green Cl STHW BN42 42 C3 2
Greenfield Cl BRI BN1 28 A2
Green Field Cl STHW BN42 42 C2 1
Greenfield Crs BRI BN1 27 H2
Green Ga PEAHV BN10 63 E4
Greenhill Wy PEAHV BN10 63 E3 1
Greenland Cl SALV BN13 36 C3
Greenland Rd SALV BN13 36 C4
Green La LEW BN7 17 E4
ROTT BN2 48 C4
SEAF BN25 72 C1
Greenleas HOVE BN3 25 H5
Greenoaks LAN/SOMP BN15 39 F2
Green Pk FERR BN12 53 F2
Green Rdg BRI BN1 26 D2
The Green HOVE BN3 27 E5
ROTT BN2 60 D3
Greentrees Cl
LAN/SOMP BN15 39 E4 3
Greentrees Crs LAN/SOMP BN15 39 E4
Green Wk SEAF BN25 73 F1
Greenways ROTT BN2 60 B1
STHW BN42 42 D1

Greenways Crs *FERR* BN12 .... 53 F4
   SHOR BN43 .... 41 G1
The Green Wy *FERR* BN12 .... 53 H1
Greenwell Cl *SEAF* BN25 .... 71 F4
Greenwich Wy *PEAHV* BN10 .... 66 D1
Greet Rd *LAN/SOMP* BN15 .... 39 F3
Grenville Av *FERR* BN12 .... 54 B2 🔲
Grenville Cl *FERR* BN12 .... 54 A2
Grenville St *BRI* BN1 .... 2 E4
Greyfiars *HOVE* BN3 .... 45 F2
Greyfriars Cl *SALV* BN13 .... 37 E4
Greystoke Ms *FERR* BN12 .... 53 E3 🔲
Greystoke Rd *FERR* BN12 .... 53 E3
Greystone Av *SALV* BN13 .... 36 D5
Griffith's Av *LAN/SOMP* BN15 ...... 39 F2
Grinstead Av *LAN/SOMP* BN15 .... 39 G4
Grinstead La *LAN/SOMP* BN15 .... 39 G4
Grosvenor Rd *SEAF* BN25 .... 70 C4
   WTHG BN11 .... 4 E4
Grosvenor St *ROTT* BN2 .... 3 J5
Grove Hl *ROTT* BN2 .... 3 J3
The Grovelands
   LAN/SOMP BN15 .... 57 G1 🔲
Grover Av *LAN/SOMP* BN15 .... 39 F3
Grove Rd *FIN/BW* BN14 .... 37 G4
   SEAF BN25 .... 70 D5
Grove St *ROTT* BN2 .... 3 K2
The Grove *FERR* BN12 .... 53 E3 🔲
   NEWHV BN9 .... 65 E3
Guardswell Pl *SEAF* BN25 .... 70 C5
Guernsey Rd *FERR* BN12 .... 53 F5 🔲
Guildford Cl *FIN/BW* BN14 .... 55 E1 🔲
Guildford Rd *BRI* BN1 .... 3 F2
   FIN/BW BN14 .... 55 E2
Guildford St *BRI* BN1 .... 3 F2
Gundreda Rd *LEW* BN7 .... 16 D2

H

Haddington Cl *HOVE* BN3 .... 44 D4
Haddington St *HOVE* BN3 .... 44 D5 🔲
Hadley Av *FIN/BW* BN14 .... 37 H3
Hadlow Cl *ROTT* BN2 .... 46 D4
Hadlow Wy *LAN/SOMP* BN15 ...... 39 H4
Hadrian Av *STHW* BN42 .... 42 D2
Haig Av *BRI* BN1 .... 28 D1
Haigh Cl *LAN/SOMP* BN15 .... 40 B4
Hailsham Av *ROTT* BN2 .... 61 H2
Hailsham Cl *ANG/EP* BN16 .... 52 B2 🔲
Hailsham Rd *WTHG* BN11 .... 54 D4
Hairpin Cft *PEAHV* BN10 .... 63 E4
Halewick Cl *LAN/SOMP* BN15 .. 39 E2 🔲
Halewick La *LAN/SOMP* BN15 ... 39 E2
Half Moon La *SALV* BN13 .... 36 D2
Halifax Dr *SALV* BN13 .... 36 A4
Halland Rd *ROTT* BN2 .... 29 F3
Hall Av *FIN/BW* BN14 .... 37 E3
Hall Cl *FIN/BW* BN14 .... 37 E3
Hallett Rd *ROTT* BN2 .... 46 D5
Hallyburton Rd *HOVE* BN3 .... 43 H2
Halsbury Cl *WTHG* BN11 .... 5 H2
Halsbury Rd *WTHG* BN11 .... 5 J2
Hamble Gdns *SALV* BN13 .... 36 A3
Hamble Rd *LAN/SOMP* BN15 ...... 38 D4
Hamble Wy *SALV* BN13 .... 36 A3
Ham Cl *WTHG* BN11 .... 56 C1 🔲
Hamilton Cl *FIN/BW* BN14 .... 38 A5
   PTSD BN41 .... 25 E4
Hamilton Rd *BRI* BN1 .... 45 H2
   LAN/SOMP BN15 .... 39 F3
Ham La *LEW* BN7 .... 17 F4
Hammond Dr *SALV* BN13 .... 36 B2
Hammy Cl *SHOR* BN43 .... 41 H2
Hammy La *SHOR* BN43 .... 41 H2
Hammy Wy *SHOR* BN43 .... 41 H2
Hampden Rd *ROTT* BN2 .... 46 C3
Hampstead Rd *BRI* BN1 .... 45 F1
Hampton Pl *BRI* BN1 .... 2 D4
Hampton St *BRI* BN1 .... 2 D4 🔲
Ham Rd *SHOR* BN43 .... 41 F3
   WTHG BN11 .... 56 C2
Hamsey Cl *ROTT* BN2 .... 47 F5
Hamsey Crs *LEW* BN7 .... 16 C2
Hamsey La *SEAF* BN25 .... 73 C1
Hamsey Rd *ROTT* BN2 .... 61 H5
Ham Wy *WTHG* BN11 .... 56 C1
Hangleton Cl *HOVE* BN3 .... 25 H5
Hangleton Gdns *HOVE* BN3 .... 43 H1
Hangleton Gra *FERR* BN12 .... 53 E2 🔲
Hangleton La *FERR* BN12 .... 52 D1
   HOVE BN3 .... 25 G5
   PTSD BN41 .... 25 F5
Hangleton Manor Cl *HOVE* BN3 . 25 G5
Hangleton Rd *HOVE* BN3 .... 26 A5
Hangleton Valley Dr *HOVE* BN3 . 25 G4
Hangleton Wy *HOVE* BN3 .... 25 H5

Hanover Cl *SEAF* BN25 .... 69 H2
Hanover Cl *ROTT* BN2 .... 3 J1
Hanover Ms *ROTT* BN2 .... 3 K1
Hanover St *ROTT* BN2 .... 3 K1
Hanover Ter *ROTT* BN2 .... 3 K1
Hanson Rd *NEWHV* BN9 .... 68 B2
Harbour View Cl *SEAF* BN25 ...... 69 H2 🔲
Harbour View Rd *NEWHV* BN9 ... 68 B3
Harbour Wy *SHOR* BN43 .... 41 H4
Hardwick Rd *HOVE* BN3 .... 26 A4
Hardwick Wy *HOVE* BN3 .... 26 A3
Hardy Cl *SHOR* BN43 .... 41 F4 🔲
Harebell Dr *PTSD* BN41 .... 25 E4
Harefield Av *SALV* BN13 .... 54 D1
Harfield Cl *NEWHV* BN9 .... 65 F3
Harison Rd *SEAF* BN25 .... 71 E4
Harlech Cl *SALV* BN13 .... 35 H5
Harmsworth Crs *HOVE* BN3 .... 26 A4 🔲
Harpers Rd *NEWHV* BN9 .... 68 C1
Harrington Pl *BRI* BN1 .... 28 B5
Harrington Rd *BRI* BN1 .... 27 G5
Harrington Vls *BRI* BN1 .... 27 H5
Harrison Ct *FIN/BW* BN14 .... 38 A5
Harrison Rd *FIN/BW* BN14 .... 38 A5
Harrow Cl *SEAF* BN25 .... 71 E4
Harrow Rd *WTHG* BN11 .... 4 A2
Hartfield Av *ROTT* BN2 .... 28 A3
Hartfield Rd *ROTT* BN2 .... 61 H4
   SEAF BN25 .... 71 E5
Harting Cl *FERR* BN12 .... 53 H1
Hartington Pl *ROTT* BN2 .... 46 C2
Hartington Rd *ROTT* BN2 .... 46 C2
Hartington Ter *ROTT* BN2 .... 46 C2
Hartington Vls *HOVE* BN3 .... 44 D2
Harvard Cl *LEW* BN7 .... 17 E1
Harvest Cl *PEAHV* BN10 .... 62 D3 🔲
Harvey Rd *FERR* BN12 .... 54 C4
Harveys Wy *LEW* BN7 .... 17 G3
Harwood Av *FERR* BN12 .... 54 B1
Hastings Av *SEAF* BN25 .... 71 G3
Hastings Rd *ROTT* BN2 .... 46 C2
   WTHG BN11 .... 55 E4 🔲
Havelock Rd *BRI* BN1 .... 45 H1
Haven Brow *SEAF* BN25 .... 71 E4
Havenside *SHOR* BN43 .... 40 D5
Hawkenbury Wy *LEW* BN7 .... 16 C3
Hawkhurst Rd *BRI* BN1 .... 28 D1
Hawkins Cl *SHOR* BN43 .... 42 B1
Hawkins Crs *SHOR* BN43 .... 24 B5
Hawkins Rd *SHOR* BN43 .... 42 B1
Hawth Cl *SEAF* BN25 .... 70 A4
Hawth Crs *SEAF* BN25 .... 70 A4
Hawth Gv *SEAF* BN25 .... 70 A3 🔲
Hawth Hl *SEAF* BN25 .... 69 H3
Hawthorn Cl *ROTT* BN2 .... 61 G3
Hawthorn Crs *FIN/BW* BN14 ...... 37 H4
Hawthorn Gdns *FIN/BW* BN14 ... 37 H4
Hawthorn Ri *NEWHV* BN9 .... 68 B1 🔲
Hawthorn Rd *FIN/BW* BN14 .... 37 G4
Hawthorn Wy *PTSD* BN41 .... 25 E4
Hawth Park Rd *SEAF* BN25 .... 70 A3 🔲
Hawth Ri *SEAF* BN25 .... 70 A3 🔲
Hawth Wy *SEAF* BN25 .... 70 B4
Haybourne Cl *ROTT* BN2 .... 47 E3 🔲
Haybourne Rd *ROTT* BN2 .... 47 E3
Hayes Cl *PTSD* BN41 .... 43 G2
Hayley Rd *LAN/SOMP* BN15 ...... 39 H3
Hayling Gdns *SALV* BN13 .... 36 C1
Hayling Ri *SALV* BN13 .... 36 C1
Haynes Rd *FIN/BW* BN14 .... 55 E1
Haynes Wy *FIN/BW* BN14 .... 4 A1
Hayward Rd *LEW* BN7 .... 16 C1
Haywards Rd *BRI* BN1 .... 28 A1
Hazel Cl *NEWHV* BN9 .... 68 B1 🔲
   PTSD BN41 .... 25 F4
Hazeldene *SEAF* BN25 .... 71 E5
Hazeldene Meads *BRI* BN1 .... 27 F5
Hazelhurst Crs *FIN/BW* BN14 .... 18 D4
Hazelmead Dr *ANG/EP* BN16 .... 52 A4
Hazelwood Cl *FIN/BW* BN14 ...... 38 B5
Headland Av *SEAF* BN25 .... 71 E5
Headlands Cl *PEAHV* BN10 .... 67 G1 🔲
Heathdown Cl *PEAHV* BN10 .... 63 F3
Heather La *SALV* BN13 .... 18 C5
Heatherstone Rd *WTHG* BN11 .... 56 C2
Heathfield Av *ROTT* BN2 .... 61 H3
Heathfield Cl *SALV* BN13 .... 36 D5
Heathfield Crs *PTSD* BN41 .... 24 D3
Heathfield Dr *PTSD* BN41 .... 24 D4
Heathfield Rd *SEAF* BN25 .... 70 D5
Heath Hill Av *ROTT* BN2 .... 47 F1
Heathy Brow *PEAHV* BN10 .... 62 D4
Hebe Rd *SHOR* BN43 .... 41 E3
Heene Pl *WTHG* BN11 .... 4 B6
Heene Rd *WTHG* BN11 .... 4 B5
Heene Ter *WTHG* BN11 .... 4 B7
Heene Wy *WTHG* BN11 .... 4 A5
Heighton Crs *NEWHV* BN9 .... 64 D3

Heighton Rd *NEWHV* BN9 .... 65 E3
The Heights *BRI* BN1 .... 26 D2
   FIN/BW BN14 .... 37 E1
Helena Cl *PTSD* BN41 .... 43 C1
Helena Rd *ROTT* BN2 .... 48 B1 🔲
Hellingly Cl *ROTT* BN2 .... 47 E5
Hempstead Rd *ROTT* BN2 .... 61 H3
Hendon St *ROTT* BN2 .... 46 C5
Henfield Cl *FERR* BN12 .... 53 H1
   ROTT BN2 .... 59 F1
Henfield Rd *STEY/UB* BN44 .... 8 B3
Henfield Wy *HOVE* BN3 .... 26 B4
Henge Wy *PTSD* BN41 .... 25 F5
Henley Rd *ROTT* BN2 .... 59 F1
Henty Rd *FERR* BN12 .... 53 F5
   FIN/BW BN14 .... 4 C1
Herbert Rd *BRI* BN1 .... 27 H5
   LAN/SOMP BN15 .... 38 D1
Hereford St *ROTT* BN2 .... 3 K5
Hereward Wy *LEW* BN7 .... 17 F2
Hermione Cl *FERR* BN12 .... 52 D2
Herm Rd *FERR* BN12 .... 53 F5
Heronsdale Rd *ROTT* BN2 .... 48 D2
Hertford Rd *BRI* BN1 .... 28 B5
   WTHG BN11 .... 4 E3
Heston Av *BRI* BN1 .... 13 H5
Heyshott Cl *LAN/SOMP* BN15 .... 39 G2
Heyworth Cl *ROTT* BN2 .... 48 D2
Highbank *BRI* BN1 .... 27 E2
Highbrook Cl *ROTT* BN2 .... 26 D5
Highclere Wy *SALV* BN13 .... 35 H5 🔲
High Cl *PTSD* BN41 .... 43 E1 🔲
Highcroft Vls *BRI* BN1 .... 45 G1
Highdown *STHW* BN42 .... 42 D1
Highdown Av *SALV* BN13 .... 37 E5
Highdown Cl *FERR* BN12 .... 53 E2
   STHW BN42 .... 42 D1
Highdown Rd *HOVE* BN3 .... 45 G3
   LEW BN7 .... 16 C2
Highdown Wy *FERR* BN12 .... 53 E2
Highfield *ANG/EP* BN16 .... 34 A5 🔲
Highfield Crs *BRI* BN1 .... 28 A2
Highfield Rd *SALV* BN13 .... 37 E4
Highfields *BRI* BN1 .... 29 E2
Highgrove Gdns *WTHG* BN11 ...... 4 B5
Highlands *SALV* BN13 .... 36 C1
Highlands Rd *PTSD* BN41 .... 43 F1
   SEAF BN25 .... 70 D5
High Park Av *HOVE* BN3 .... 26 A4
Highsted Pk *PEAHV* BN10 .... 63 F3
High St *FIN/BW* BN14 .... 18 C2
   LEW BN7 .... 17 F3
   NEWHV BN9 .... 68 C1
   PTSD BN41 .... 43 E1
   ROTT BN2 .... 3 J5
   ROTT BN2 .... 60 D4
   SALV BN13 .... 37 E5
   SEAF BN25 .... 72 C1
   SHOR BN43 .... 41 E3
   STEY/UB BN44 .... 7 F1
   STEY/UB BN44 .... 8 A2
   WTHG BN11 .... 5 G3
Highview *LAN/SOMP* BN15 .... 39 F1
High Vw *SALV* BN13 .... 36 D1
Highview Av North *BRI* BN1 ...... 27 G1
Highview Av South *BRI* BN1 ...... 27 G1
Highview Rd *BRI* BN1 .... 27 G1 🔲
   PEAHV BN10 .... 62 B5
Highview Wy *BRI* BN1 .... 27 G1
Highway Cl *ROTT* BN2 .... 28 D5
Highways *PTSD* BN41 .... 25 F5 🔲
The Highway *PEAHV* BN10 .... 67 H2
   ROTT BN2 .... 28 D5
Hildon Cl *SALV* BN13 .... 36 B5
Hilgrove Rd *ROTT* BN2 .... 61 H2
Hillbank Cl *PTSD* BN41 .... 24 D4
Hillbarn Av *LAN/SOMP* BN15 .... 39 F1
Hill Brow *HOVE* BN3 .... 26 D3
Hillbrow Rd *BRI* BN1 .... 27 E3
Hillcrest *BRI* BN1 .... 27 E2
Hill Crest Rd *NEWHV* BN9 .... 68 C2
Hillcroft *PTSD* BN41 .... 24 D5
Hill Dr *HOVE* BN3 .... 26 D4
Hill Farm Wy *STHW* BN42 .... 24 B5
Hill Ri *NEWHV* BN9 .... 65 F4
   SEAF BN25 .... 70 A3
Hillrise Av *LAN/SOMP* BN15 ..... 39 E2
Hill Rd *LEW* BN7 .... 16 C2
   NEWHV BN9 .... 65 F4
   ROTT BN2 .... 61 F4
Hill Side *NEWHV* BN9 .... 68 D1 🔲
Hillside *PTSD* BN41 .... 43 G1
   ROTT BN2 .... 28 D5
   STHW BN42 .... 42 D1
Hillside Av *FIN/BW* BN14 .... 37 F3
   SEAF BN25 .... 71 F3 🔲
Hillside Crs *ANG/EP* BN16 .... 34 A5

Hillside Rd *LAN/SOMP* BN15 3
Hillside Wy *BRI* BN1 2
Hills Rd *STEY/UB* BN44 ....
Hill Top *BRI* BN1 2
Hill Top Cl *PTSD* BN41 2
Hillview Crs *ANG/EP* BN16 5
Hillview Ri *FIN/BW* BN14 3
Hillview Rd *FIN/BW* BN14 1
   ROTT BN2 4
Hillyfield *LEW* BN7 1
Hindover Crs *SEAF* BN25 .... 71 E
Hindover Rd *SEAF* BN25 7
Hinton Cl *BRI* BN1 3
Hobart Cl *SALV* BN13 3
Hobs Acre *STEY/UB* BN44 ....
Hoddern Av *PEAHV* BN10 6
Hodshrove Rd *ROTT* BN2 3
Hoe Ct *LAN/SOMP* BN15 4
Hogarth Rd *HOVE* BN3 4
The Holdings *LEW* BN7 ....
Holland Ms *HOVE* BN3 ....
Holland Rd *HOVE* BN3 ....
   STEY/UB BN44 ....
Holland St *ROTT* BN2 ....
Hollingbury Copse *BRI* BN1 2
Hollingbury Crs *BRI* BN1 4
Hollingbury Gdns *FIN/BW* BN14 . 19
Hollingbury Park Av *BRI* BN1 ... 2
Hollingbury Pl *BRI* BN1 2
Hollingbury Ri *BRI* BN1 2
Hollingbury Ri West *BRI* BN1 ... 2
Hollingbury Rd *BRI* BN1 4
Hollingbury Ter *BRI* BN1 .... 28 A
Hollingdean La *BRI* BN1 4
Hollingdean Rd *ROTT* BN2 4
Hollingdean St *BRI* BN1 4
Hollingdean Ter *BRI* BN1 4
Holly Cl *BRI* BN1 2
   SALV BN13 3
Holmbush Cl *SHOR* BN43 2
Holmbush Wy *STHW* BN42 4
Holmcroft Gdns *FIN/BW* BN14 .. 18
Holmdale Rd *NEWHV* BN9 65
Holmes Av *HOVE* BN3 2
Holmes Cl *SEAF* BN25 7
Holters Wy *SEAF* BN25 .... 7C
Holton Hl *ROTT* BN2 4
The Holt *SEAF* BN25 .... 7C
Holtview Rd *ROTT* BN2 47
Homebush Av *ROTT* BN2 2
   ROTT BN2 62
Home Farm Rd *BRI* BN1 28
Homefield Cl *SEAF* BN25 ...... 70 D
Homefield Rd *SEAF* BN25 70
   WTHG BN11 5
Homelands Av *ANG/EP* BN16 ... 52
Home Rd *BRI* BN1 2
Honey Cft *HOVE* BN3 25
Honey La *ANG/EP* BN16 34
Honeysuckle Cl *LAN/SOMP* BN15 .. 39
Honeysuckle La *SALV* BN13 18
Hoopers Cl *LEW* BN7 .... 17 E
Horley Pl *ROTT* BN2 47
Hornby Rd *ROTT* BN2 47
Horsfield Rd *LEW* BN7 16
Horsham Av *PEAHV* BN10 66
Horsham Av North *PEAHV* BN10 . 6
Horsham Cl *ROTT* BN2 .... 47 F
Horton Rd *BRI* BN1 46
Houndean Cl *LEW* BN7 16
Houndean Ri *LEW* BN7 16
Hova Vls *HOVE* BN3 44
Hove Park Gdns *HOVE* BN3 44
Hove Park Rd *HOVE* BN3 45
Hove Park Vls *HOVE* BN3 44
Hove Park Wy *HOVE* BN3 45
Hove Pl *HOVE* BN3 44
Hove St *HOVE* BN3 44
Howard Pl *BRI* BN1 2
Howard Rd *LAN/SOMP* BN15 39
   ROTT BN2 ....
Howard St *WTHG* BN11 4
Howard Ter *BRI* BN1 2
Howey Cl *NEWHV* BN9 67
Hoyle Rd *PEAHV* BN10 67
Hudson Cl *SALV* BN13 36
Hughes Rd *ROTT* BN2 46
Humber Av *SALV* BN13 36
Humber Cl *SALV* BN13 36
Humphrey's Gap *SHOR* BN43 ... 41
Humphrys Rd *WTHG* BN11 4
Hunston Cl *ROTT* BN2 48
Hurdis Rd *SEAF* BN25 69
Hurley Rd *SALV* BN13 36
Hurst Av *WTHG* BN11 54
Hurst Crs *PTSD* BN41 43
Hurstfield *LAN/SOMP* BN15 .. 39 F5
   LAN/SOMP BN15 .... 39 E

st Hl BRI BN1 .... 28 C2
...ston Cl FIN/BW BN14 .... 37 E2
...ton Rd BRI BN1 .... 28 B4
...e Cl LEW BN7 .... 32 A2
...e La STEY/UB BN44 .... 8 B3
...e Sq STEY/UB BN44 .... 8 B2
...e St STEY/UB BN44 .... 8 B2
...Hyde BRI BN2 .... 47 F1
...den Cl ROTT BN2 .... 47 H2
...BN25 .... 71 G3
...the Crs SEAF BN25 .... 55 E4
...WTHG BN11 .... 55 E4
...he Crs SEAF BN25 .... 71 G4
...he Rd BRI BN1 .... 28 A5
...WTHG BN11 .... 55 E4
...he Vw SEAF BN25 .... 71 G4

I

...n Cl ROTT BN2 .... 47 E5
...d Cl ROTT BN2 .... 62 A3
...d Cl NEWHV BN9 .... 64 D3
... Wy FERR BN12 .... 53 H3
...ham Dr BRI BN1 .... 28 D1
...e Green Cl FERR BN12 ..... 53 E5
...leside Crs LAN/SOMP BN15 .. 39 G5
...leside Crs LAN/SOMP BN15 .. 39 G5
...ram Cl HOVE BN3 .... 44 A3
...ram Crs East HOVE BN3 .... 44 A3
...ram Crs West HOVE BN3 .... 44 A3
...ram Rd STEY/UB BN44 ...... 7 E2
...erness Rd ROTT BN2 .... 46 C2
...wood Crs BRI BN1 .... 45 F1
...ands La LEW BN7 .... 16 D3
...e Av LAN/SOMP BN15 ...... 39 F3
...el Cl SEAF BN25 .... 70 C3
...el Crs HOVE BN3 .... 44 A2
...eld Rd BRI BN1 .... 28 C5
...gword Rd HOVE BN3 .... 44 C4
...gword Rd ROTT BN2 .... 3 K1
...gword St ROTT BN2 .... 3 K2
...agh Crs NEWHV BN9 .... 64 D4
...r Rd ROTT BN2 .... 48 A1
...ry Pl ROTT BN2 .... 3 J3
...Arch Cl FIN/BW BN14 ...... 18 D1
...Arch Rd FIN/BW BN14 ...... 5 F2
...dore Av SALV BN13 .... 36 B2
...dore Cl SALV BN13 .... 36 B3
...Pl HOVE BN3 .... 2 B4
...WTHG BN11 .... 4 B6

J

...kson Ms NEWHV BN9 .... 68 C1
...kson St ROTT BN2 .... 3 K1
...nes Cl SALV BN13 .... 36 D4
...onica Cl SHOR BN43 .... 41 H1
...vis La STEY/UB BN44 ...... 7 F1
...son Cl PEAHV BN10 .... 67 E1
...r PEAHV BN10 .... 67 G2
...feries La FERR BN12 ...... 54 A4
...sey Rd FERR BN12 .... 53 F4
...sey St ROTT BN2 .... 3 J2
...mond Rd HOVE BN3 .... 44 A3
...ington Cl SALV BN13 ...... 35 H5
...ington Dr ROTT BN2 .... 46 D1
...SEAF BN25 .... 70 A4
...w St BRI BN1 .... 3 G4
...nns Cl PEAHV BN10 .... 63 E3
...nn St ROTT BN2 .... 3 J4
...SHOR BN43 .... 41 E3
...bilee Gdns SEAF BN25 ..... 71 E3
...bilee Rd PTSD BN41 .... 43 E2
...bilee St BRI BN1 .... 3 G4
...ggs Cl LEW BN7 .... 16 D4
...ggs Rd LEW BN7 .... 16 C5
...LEW BN7 .... 16 D4
...lian Rd HOVE BN3 .... 2 D1
...nction Rd BRI BN1 .... 3 F2
...niper Cl PTSD BN41 .... 25 F4
...SALV BN13 .... 36 A5
...SEAF BN25 .... 71 G5
...pp's La FERR BN12 .... 53 H2

K

...mmond Av SEAF BN25 .... 71 F1
...atherine Wy SEAF BN25 .... 70 B3
...arsley Dr FIN/BW BN14 .... 37 E1
...dale Rd SEAF BN25 .... 70 C4
...ere St LEW BN7 .... 17 E4
...lly Rd HOVE BN3 .... 45 F1
...lso Cl SALV BN13 .... 54 C1

Kemp St BRI BN1 .... 3 G3
Kemp Town Pl ROTT BN2 .... 58 D1
Kendal Rd HOVE BN3 .... 44 B2
   LAN/SOMP BN15 .... 39 E4
Kenilworth Cl ROTT BN2 .... 29 C5
Kenmure Av BRI BN1 .... 14 A5
Kennedy Wy NEWHV BN9 .... 68 B1
Kennet Cl SALV BN13 ...... 36 B3
Kensington Gdns BRI BN1 ... 3 G3
Kensington Pl BRI BN1 ..... 3 G3
Kensington St BRI BN1 ..... 3 G3
Kent Cl SHOR BN43 .... 42 A3
Kent Flds LEW BN7 .... 32 A2
Kenton Rd HOVE BN3 .... 43 H3
Kenwards BRI BN1 .... 14 D5
Kestrel Cl HOVE BN3 ...... 45 F2
Keswick Cl FERR BN12 ..... 36 B5
Kevin Gdns ROTT BN2 ...... 48 C2
Kew St BRI BN1 .... 3 F3
Keymer Av PEAHV BN10 ..... 67 F2
Keymer Crs FERR BN12 ..... 54 A4
Keymer Rd BRI BN1 .... 28 B1
Keymer Wy FERR BN12 ...... 54 A4
Kilmore Cl FIN/BW BN14 .... 18 C1
Kimber Cl LAN/SOMP BN15 ... 39 F5
Kimberley Rd ROTT BN2 .... 46 D2
   SEAF BN25 .... 70 A4
Kinfauns Dr SALV BN13 .... 18 B5
King Alfred Cl STEY/UB BN44 .. 7 F1
King Edward Av FIN/BW BN14 .. 5 F1
King Edward Cl FIN/BW BN14 .. 5 F2
Kingfisher Cl SALV BN13 ... 36 A5
King George Rd SHOR BN43 .. 42 A2
King George Vi Av HOVE BN3 .. 26 B4
King George Vi Dr HOVE BN3 .. 26 C4
King Henry's Rd LEW BN7 ... 16 D2
King Pl BRI BN1 .... 3 F4
King's Av NEWHV BN9 ...... 65 E4
King's Barn Vls STEY/UB BN44 .. 7 G1
Kingsbridge Ms SALV BN13 .. 36 B3
Kingsbury Rd BRI BN1 ...... 46 A3
Kingsbury St BRI BN1 ...... 46 A3
Kings Cl LAN/SOMP BN15 .... 39 H5
   PEAHV BN10 .... 62 D4
Kings Crs SHOR BN43 ...... 40 D5
Kings Dr SHOR BN43 .... 40 D4
King's Esp HOVE BN3 ...... 44 C5
Kings Gap SHOR BN43 ...... 40 D5
King's Gdns HOVE BN3 ...... 44 D5
Kingsland Cl SHOR BN43 .... 41 H4
Kingsland Rd FIN/BW BN14 .. 37 H4
Kingsley Rd BRI BN1 .... 45 F1
   LEW BN7 .... 16 D2
Kingsmead SEAF BN25 ...... 70 B3
Kingsmead Cl SEAF BN25 ... 70 C4
   STEY/UB BN44 .... 7 F3
King's Mead La SEAF BN25 .. 70 B4
Kingsmead Wk SEAF BN25 ... 70 C4
Kingsmead Wy SEAF BN25 ... 70 C4
Kings Ms HOVE BN3 .... 44 D4
Kings Ride SEAF BN25 ...... 70 B4
Kings Rd BRI BN1 .... 2 C5
   LAN/SOMP BN15 .... 39 G5
   STHW BN42 .... 42 B1
King's Stone Av STEY/UB BN44 .. 7 H2
Kingsthorpe Rd HOVE BN3 .. 44 A2
Kingston Av SEAF BN25 ..... 71 F5
Kingston Bay Rd SHOR BN43.. 42 A4
Kingston Broadway SHOR BN43 .. 42 A1
Kingston Cl BRI BN1 .... 29 E1
   HOVE BN3 .... 26 A5
   SEAF BN25 .... 71 F5
   SHOR BN43 .... 42 A2
Kingston Gn SEAF BN25 .... 71 F5
Kingston La ANG/EP BN16 ... 52 B4
   SHOR BN43 .... 42 B3
Kingston Rdg LEW BN7 ...... 31 H1
Kingston Rd LEW BN7 ...... 16 D5
Kingston Wy SEAF BN25 .... 73 F1
   SHOR BN43 .... 42 A1
King St BRI BN1 .... 3 G4
   FIN/BW BN14 .... 55 H1
Kings Wk SHOR BN43 ...... 40 D5
Kingsway HOVE BN3 .... 44 B4
   SEAF BN25 .... 70 B4
Kingswood St ROTT BN2 .... 3 H5
Kipling Av FERR BN12 ...... 53 H2
   ROTT BN2 .... 48 C2
Kirby Dr PEAHV BN10 ...... 62 C4
Kithurst Cl FERR BN12 ..... 53 H1
Kithurst Crs FERR BN12 .... 53 H1
Knepp Cl ROTT BN2 .... 29 F5
Knole Rd ROTT BN2 .... 61 E4
Knoll Cl HOVE BN3 .... 43 H1
Knoyle Rd BRI BN1 .... 27 G5

L

Laburnum Av HOVE BN3 ..... 44 A1
Laburnum Cl FERR BN12 .... 53 F4
   LAN/SOMP BN15 .... 57 F1
Ladies Mile Cl BRI BN1 .... 27 H1
Ladies' Mile Rd BRI BN1 ... 27 G1
Ladycross Cl SEAF BN25 ... 71 G5
Ladydell Rd WTHG BN11 .... 5 J1
Ladysmith Rd ROTT BN2 .... 46 D2
Laine Cl BRI BN1 .... 27 G4
Laines Rd STEY/UB BN44 ... 7 E2
Lake Dr PEAHV BN10 .... 62 D5
Lambert Pl LEW BN7 .... 17 F1
Lambleys La FIN/BW BN14 ... 38 B3
Lambourne Cl BRI BN1 ..... 28 C5
Lambourne Rd BRI BN1 ..... 28 C5
Lamorna Gdns FERR BN12 ... 53 F5
Lamorna Gv FIN/BW BN14 ... 37 G4
Lancaster Rd BRI BN1 ...... 45 H3
   FERR BN12 .... 54 C4
Lancaster St LEW BN7 ..... 17 E3
Lancing Cl LAN/SOMP BN15 .. 39 F4
Lancing Pk LAN/SOMP BN15 .. 57 F1
Landport Rd LEW BN7 ...... 17 E2
Landsdown Rd SEAF BN25 ... 71 F3
Landseer Rd HOVE BN3 ..... 44 C2
Lanfranc Rd HOVE BN3 ..... 44 A1
Langbury Cl FERR BN12 .... 52 D2
Langbury La FERR BN12 .... 53 E2
Langdale Cl LAN/SOMP BN15 .. 39 E5
Langdale Gdns HOVE BN3 ... 44 B4
Langdale Rd HOVE BN3 ..... 44 B4
Langham Gdns WTHG BN11 .. 55 E3
Langley Crs ROTT BN2 ..... 48 B1
Langridge Dr PTSD BN41 ... 25 F5
Langton Rd FIN/BW BN14 ... 4 E1
Lansdowne Ct WTHG BN11 .. 55 E3
Lansdowne Ms HOVE BN3 ... 2 A3
Lansdowne Pl HOVE BN3 .... 2 A4
Lansdowne Rd HOVE BN3 .... 2 B3
   WTHG BN11 .... 55 E3
Lansdowne Sq HOVE BN3 ... 2 A4
Lansdowne St HOVE BN3 .... 2 A3
Lansdown Pl LEW BN7 ...... 17 F4
Lapierre Rd NEWHV BN9 .... 68 B1
Larch Rd ROTT BN2 .... 48 D3
Larke Cl SHOR BN43 .... 42 A3
Larkfield Cl LAN/SOMP BN15 .. 39 H5
Larkfield Wy BRI BN1 ...... 28 A3
Lark Hl HOVE BN3 .... 26 A4
Lashmar Rd ANG/EP BN16 ... 52 A4
Latimer Rd WTHG BN11 ..... 54 D4
Laughton Rd ROTT BN2 ..... 48 D2
Laurel Cl SALV BN13 ...... 54 A1
Lauriston Rd BRI BN1 ...... 27 G5
Lavant Cl FERR BN12 ...... 53 G1
Lavender Hl SHOR BN43 .... 41 H1
Lavender St ROTT BN2 ..... 3 K6
Lavington Rd FIN/BW BN14 .. 37 F4
Lavinia Ct FERR BN12 ..... 54 A2
Lavinia Wy ANG/EP BN16 ... 52 A4
Lawes Av NEWHV BN9 ...... 68 C1
The Lawns STEY/UB BN44 ... 7 H3
Lawrence Rd HOVE BN3 ..... 44 B3
Laylands Rd PTSD BN41 .... 43 E3
Leahurst Court Rd BRI BN1 .. 27 G4
Lea Rd PEAHV BN10 .... 62 D5
The Leas PEAHV BN10 ...... 67 H3
Leconfield Rd LAN/SOMP BN15.. 39 E5
Leeds Cl SALV BN13 .... 35 H5
Lee Rd LEW BN7 .... 16 D2
Leeward Cl SALV BN13 ..... 36 D5
Leeward Rd SALV BN13 ..... 36 D5
Lee Wy NEWHV BN9 .... 64 B5
Leicester Rd LEW BN7 ..... 16 D3
Leicester St ROTT BN2 ..... 3 K5
Leicester Vls FIN/BW BN14 .. 43 H3
Leigh Rd FIN/BW BN14 ..... 37 H4
Leighton Av FIN/BW BN14 .. 38 A4
Leighton Rd HOVE BN3 ..... 44 C2
Lenham Av ROTT BN2 ...... 61 F4
Lenham Rd East ROTT BN2 .. 61 F4
Lenham Rd West ROTT BN2.. 61 E4
Lenhurst Wy SALV BN13 .... 36 D5
Lennox Rd HOVE BN3 ...... 44 B2
   SHOR BN43 .... 41 H2
   WTHG BN11 .... 5 F3
Lennox St ROTT BN2 .... 3 K4
Leopold Rd BRI BN1 .... 2 E1
Lesser Foxholes SHOR BN43 .. 40 D2
Letchworth Cl FERR BN12 .. 53 E4
Lewes Cl ROTT BN2 .... 62 A4
Lewes Crs ROTT BN2 .... 59 E1
Lewes Rd BRI BN1 .... 29 G1
   NEWHV BN9 .... 64 B5

   ROTT BN2 .... 3 J2
   ROTT BN2 .... 46 B3
Lewes St ROTT BN2 .... 3 J2
Lewin Cl LAN/SOMP BN15 ... 39 H3
Lewis Cl NEWHV BN9 .... 65 F3
Lewis Ct SALV BN13 .... 35 H5
Lewis Rd LAN/SOMP BN15 ... 39 F2
Lewry Cl NEWHV BN9 .... 68 B1
Lexden Ct SEAF BN25 ...... 71 E4
Lexden Dr SEAF BN25 ...... 70 D3
Lexden Rd SEAF BN25 ...... 70 D2
Leybourne Cl ROTT BN2 .... 47 G1
Leybourne Rd ROTT BN2 .... 29 G5
Library Pl WTHG BN11 ..... 5 G5
Lilac Cl SALV BN13 .... 35 H5
Limbrick Cl FERR BN12 .... 54 A2
Limbrick La FERR BN12 .... 54 A2
Limbrick Wy FERR BN12 .... 53 H1
Lime Tree Av FIN/BW BN14 .. 19 E5
Limney Rd ROTT BN2 .... 47 E3
Lincett Av SALV BN13 ..... 54 D1
Lincett Dr SALV BN13 ..... 54 D2
Linchmere Av ROTT BN2 .... 61 G4
Lincoln Av PEAHV BN10 .... 66 C1
Lincoln Av South PEAHV BN10 .. 66 C1
Lincoln Cottages ROTT BN2 .. 3 K2
Lincoln Rd PTSD BN41 ..... 43 F3
   SALV BN13 .... 54 D1
Lincoln St ROTT BN2 ...... 3 K2
Lindfield Av SEAF BN25 ... 73 G5
Lindfield Cl ROTT BN2 .... 61 F3
Lindum Rd SALV BN13 ...... 36 D5
Lindum Wy SALV BN13 ...... 36 D5
Lingfield Cl SALV BN13 ... 36 D4
Links Av NEWHV BN9 .... 68 A1
Links Cl PTSD BN41 .... 43 G2
   SEAF BN25 .... 71 E5
Links Rd FIN/BW BN14 ..... 37 E2
   LAN/SOMP BN15 .... 39 H4
   PTSD BN41 .... 43 G2
   SEAF BN25 .... 73 E1
The Linkway BRI BN1 ...... 46 B1
Linthouse Cl PEAHV BN10 .. 63 F3
Linton Rd HOVE BN3 .... 44 B2
Lions Pl SEAF BN25 .... 72 D1
Liphook Cl BRI BN1 .... 46 C1
Lisher Rd LAN/SOMP BN15.. 39 H3
Little Crs ROTT BN2 ...... 61 F4
Little Dr FERR BN12 ...... 53 E4
Little Dro STEY/UB BN44 ... 7 F3
Little East St LEW BN7 .... 17 E3
Little Gables SALV BN13 .. 36 A4
Littlehampton Rd ANG/EP BN16.. 52 C2
   FERR BN12 .... 53 H1
   SALV BN13 .... 36 C5
Little High St SHOR BN43 .. 41 E3
   WTHG BN11 .... 5 F3
Little Pembrokes WTHG BN11 .. 55 E2
Little Preston St BRI BN1 .. 2 D5
Littlestone Rd SALV BN13 .. 36 C4
Little Western St BRI BN1 .. 2 B4
Littleworth Cl ROTT BN2 .. 48 D3
Liverpool Gdns WTHG BN11 .. 5 F5
Liverpool Rd WTHG BN11 .. 5 F5
Liverpool Ter WTHG BN11 .. 5 F5
Livesay Crs FIN/BW BN14 .. 55 H1
Livingstone Rd HOVE BN3 .. 44 D3
Livingstone St ROTT BN2 .. 46 D5
Lloyd Cl HOVE BN3 .... 45 E2
Lloyd Rd HOVE BN3 .... 45 E2
Lockitt Wy LEW BN7 .... 32 A2
Locks Crs PTSD BN41 ...... 43 F2
Locks Hl PTSD BN41 .... 43 F1
Lockwood Cl ROTT BN2 ..... 48 C3
Lockwood Crs ROTT BN2 .... 48 C3
Loddon Cl SALV BN13 ...... 36 A2
Loder Gdns FIN/BW BN14 ... 37 G5
Loder Pl BRI BN1 .... 27 H5
Loder Rd BRI BN1 .... 27 H5
Lodge Cl LEW BN7 .... 16 C4
   PTSD BN41 .... 24 D5
Lodge Ct SHOR BN43 ...... 41 E1
Lodsworth Cl ROTT BN2 .... 47 F5
Lomond Av ROTT BN2 ...... 14 A5
London Rd BRI BN1 .... 13 F5
   BRI BN1 .... 46 A3
London St WTHG BN11 ..... 4 C2
London Ter BRI BN1 .... 46 A3
Longfellow Rd WTHG BN11 .. 4 B3
Long Furlong SALV BN13 ... 35 E1
Longhill Cl ROTT BN2 ..... 60 C1
Longhill Rd ROTT BN2 ..... 60 B1
Longlands FIN/BW BN14 .... 37 G2
Longlands Gld FIN/BW BN14 .. 37 H2
Longlands Spinney FIN/BW BN14.. 37 H2
Long Meadow FIN/BW BN14 .. 18 D3
Longridge Av ROTT BN2 ... 61 G5
The Lookout PEAHV BN10 ... 63 E2

Loose La FIN/BW BN14 ..... 38 C5
LAN/SOMP BN15 ..... 38 D4
The Lords SEAF BN25 ..... 70 C2
Lorna Rd HOVE BN3 ..... 45 F3
Lorne Rd BRI BN1 ..... 46 A2
Lorraine Rd NEWHV BN9 ..... 68 D1 ▣
Lotts La LAN/SOMP BN15 ..... 39 E4
Lover's Wk BRI BN1 ..... 45 H2
Lower Beach Rd SHOR BN43 ..... 41 F4
Lower Bevendean Av ROTT BN2 ..... 47 E1
Lower Chalvington Pl
ROTT BN2 ..... 47 E5 ▣
STHW BN42 ..... 42 C1
Lower Dr SEAF BN25 ..... 70 D3
STHW BN42 ..... 42 C1
Lower Market St HOVE BN3 ..... 2 B4
Lower Pl NEWHV BN9 ..... 68 C1 ▣
Lower Rock Gdns ROTT BN2 ..... 3 K6
Lowther Rd BRI BN1 ..... 28 A5
SALV BN13 ..... 36 D3
Loxwood ANG/EP BN16 ..... 52 B2 ▣
Loxwood Av FIN/BW BN14 ..... 37 F5
Lucerne Cl PTSD BN41 ..... 43 F1
Lucerne Rd BRI BN1 ..... 45 H1
Lucinda Wy SEAF BN25 ..... 70 D3
Lucraft Rd ROTT BN2 ..... 29 F2
Ludlow Ri ROTT BN2 ..... 47 G1
Lulham Cl PEAHV BN10 ..... 62 D4 ▣
Lullington Av HOVE BN3 ..... 44 B2
Lullington Cl SEAF BN25 ..... 73 F1
Lustrells Cl ROTT BN2 ..... 61 F3
Lustrells Crs ROTT BN2 ..... 61 F3
Lustrells V ROTT BN2 ..... 61 F3
Luther St ROTT BN2 ..... 46 C3
Lyminster Av BRI BN1 ..... 28 A2
Lynchet Cl BRI BN1 ..... 28 C5
Lynchet Down BRI BN1 ..... 28 C5
Lynchets Crs HOVE BN3 ..... 25 H4
Lynchmere Av LAN/SOMP BN15 ..... 39 F2
Lyndhurst Rd HOVE BN3 ..... 45 F3
WTHG BN11 ..... 5 G4
Lyn Rd SALV BN13 ..... 36 A4
Lynton St ROTT BN2 ..... 46 C3
Lynwood Rd ROTT BN2 ..... 61 G5
Lyon Cl HOVE BN3 ..... 2 B1
Lyons Wy FIN/BW BN14 ..... 38 A2

M

Mackie Av BRI BN1 ..... 27 H1
Madehurst Cl ROTT BN2 ..... 46 D5
Madeira Av WTHG BN11 ..... 5 H4
Madeira Dr ROTT BN2 ..... 3 J6
Madeira Pl ROTT BN2 ..... 3 J6
Mafeking Rd ROTT BN2 ..... 46 C2
Magnolia Cl SALV BN13 ..... 35 H5 ▣
Mainstone Rd HOVE BN3 ..... 44 B3 ▣
Major Cl BRI BN1 ..... 46 B1
Malcolm Cl BRI BN12 ..... 53 E4
Maldon Rd BRI BN1 ..... 27 F5
Malines Av PEAHV BN10 ..... 66 D1
Malines Av South PEAHV BN10 ..... 66 C1
Mallett Cl SEAF BN25 ..... 72 C1 ▣
Malling Cl LEW BN7 ..... 17 F1 ▣
Malling Down LEW BN7 ..... 17 G1
Malling Hl LEW BN7 ..... 17 G1
Malling St LEW BN7 ..... 17 G3
Mallory Rd HOVE BN3 ..... 27 E5
Malthouse Cl LAN/SOMP BN15 ..... 38 D3
Malthouse La ROTT BN2 ..... 3 J2 ▣
Malvern St HOVE BN3 ..... 44 D3 ▣
Manchester St ROTT BN2 ..... 3 H6
Manitoba Wy SALV BN13 ..... 36 A4
Manor Cl LAN/SOMP BN15 ..... 39 H3
LAN/SOMP BN15 ..... 40 B4
ROTT BN2 ..... 47 E5
SEAF BN25 ..... 71 F5
STHW BN42 ..... 43 E2
WTHG BN11 ..... 4 A5
Manor Dr PEAHV BN10 ..... 62 D4
Manor Gdns ROTT BN2 ..... 47 E5
Manor Gn ROTT BN2 ..... 47 E5
Manor Hall Rd STHW BN42 ..... 42 C2
Manor Hl ROTT BN2 ..... 47 E5
Manor Paddock ROTT BN2 ..... 59 E1
Manor Pl ROTT BN2 ..... 47 E5
Manor Rd ANG/EP BN16 ..... 52 A5
LAN/SOMP BN15 ..... 39 F2
PTSD BN41 ..... 43 F1
ROTT BN2 ..... 59 E1
SEAF BN25 ..... 71 F5
STEY/UB BN44 ..... 8 C2
WTHG BN11 ..... 4 A5

Manor Rd North SEAF BN25 ..... 71 F5
Manor Wy LAN/SOMP BN15 ..... 39 H3
ROTT BN2 ..... 47 E5
Mansell Rd SHOR BN43 ..... 41 H2
Mansfield Cl WTHG BN11 ..... 56 C1
Mansfield Rd HOVE BN3 ..... 44 A3
WTHG BN11 ..... 56 C1
Manton Rd ROTT BN2 ..... 47 E1
Maple Cl ROTT BN2 ..... 48 C3
SALV BN13 ..... 36 C1
Maple Gdns HOVE BN3 ..... 44 A1
Maplehurst Rd PTSD BN41 ..... 43 E1
Maple Leaf Cl NEWHV BN9 ..... 68 B1
The Maples FERR BN12 ..... 53 F5
Maple Wk LAN/SOMP BN15 ..... 38 D3
Mardale Rd SALV BN13 ..... 36 D4
Mardyke SHOR BN43 ..... 40 D4
Maresfield Rd ROTT BN2 ..... 47 E5
Margaret St ROTT BN2 ..... 3 J6
Margery Rd HOVE BN3 ..... 43 H2
Marina Wy ROTT BN2 ..... 59 E2
Marine Av HOVE BN3 ..... 43 H4
Marine Cl ROTT BN2 ..... 61 F4
WTHG BN11 ..... 55 E4
Marine Crs FERR BN12 ..... 54 B4
SEAF BN25 ..... 72 C1
Marine Dr FERR BN12 ..... 53 G5
ROTT BN2 ..... 59 E2
SEAF BN25 ..... 69 G2
Marine Gdns ROTT BN2 ..... 3 K6
Marine Pde ROTT BN2 ..... 3 J6
SEAF BN25 ..... 69 H4
WTHG BN11 ..... 4 C7
Marine Pl WTHG BN11 ..... 5 G6
Mariners Cl SHOR BN43 ..... 40 D5 ▣
Marine Sq ROTT BN2 ..... 58 C1
Marine Terrace Ms ROTT BN2 ..... 58 C1 ▣
Marine Vw ROTT BN2 ..... 3 K4
Marjoram Pl SHOR BN43 ..... 41 H1 ▣
Mark Cl SEAF BN25 ..... 73 G1 ▣
Market Fld STEY/UB BN44 ..... 7 F1
Market La LEW BN7 ..... 17 F3 ▣
Market St BRI BN1 ..... 3 G5
LEW BN7 ..... 17 F3
WTHG BN11 ..... 5 F5
Markwick Ms WTHG BN11 ..... 5 G3
Marlborough Ms BRI BN1 ..... 2 E4 ▣
Marlborough Pl BRI BN1 ..... 3 H4 ▣
Marlborough Rd FERR BN12 ..... 54 B3
LAN/SOMP BN15 ..... 57 E1
Marlborough St BRI BN1 ..... 2 E4
Marlborough Wy FERR BN12 ..... 54 B3 ▣
The Marlinspike SHOR BN43 ..... 41 G4
Marlowe Rd FIN/BW BN14 ..... 38 A5
Marlow Rd ROTT BN2 ..... 59 F1
Marmion Rd HOVE BN3 ..... 44 B3
Marshall Av FIN/BW BN14 ..... 18 D4
Marshalls Rw BRI BN1 ..... 3 H1
Marshall Wy HOVE BN3 ..... 44 B3
Marston Rd FIN/BW BN14 ..... 56 A1 ▣
Martello Rd SEAF BN25 ..... 72 C1
Martha Gunn Rd ROTT BN2 ..... 46 D1
Martin Rd HOVE BN3 ..... 43 H1
The Martins PEAHV BN10 ..... 62 D4 ▣
The Martlets LAN/SOMP BN15 ..... 39 E4
LEW BN7 ..... 17 F1 ▣
SHOR BN43 ..... 41 F2
Martlets Wy FERR BN12 ..... 54 A2
The Martlet HOVE BN3 ..... 45 F2
Martyn's Cl ROTT BN2 ..... 60 C1
Mash Barn La LAN/SOMP BN15 ..... 40 A3
Mason Rd SEAF BN25 ..... 70 D4
Matlock Rd BRI BN1 ..... 45 F1
Maudlin La STEY/UB BN44 ..... 7 F3
Maudlyn Cl STEY/UB BN44 ..... 7 G3
Maudlyn Pk STEY/UB BN44 ..... 7 F3
Maudlyn Pkwy STEY/UB BN44 ..... 7 F3
Maurice Rd SEAF BN25 ..... 72 D2
May Av SEAF BN25 ..... 71 F5
Maybridge Crs FERR BN12 ..... 54 A2
Maybridge Sq FERR BN12 ..... 54 A1
May Cl FERR BN12 ..... 54 A1
Mayfield ANG/EP BN16 ..... 52 A2
Mayfield Av PEAHV BN10 ..... 67 F2
Mayfield Cl BRI BN1 ..... 27 H2
FIN/BW BN14 ..... 37 E1
Mayfield Crs BRI BN1 ..... 27 H2
Mayflower Wy ANG/EP BN16 ..... 52 A2
Mayhew Wy LEW BN7 ..... 17 F1
Mayo Rd ROTT BN2 ..... 46 B2
May Rd ROTT BN2 ..... 46 D3
May Tree Av FIN/BW BN14 ..... 18 D4
Maytree Cl LAN/SOMP BN15 ..... 38 D4
Maytree Wk HOVE BN3 ..... 44 A1
Mckerchar Cl LAN/SOMP BN15 ..... 39 H3 ▣
Mcwilliam Rd ROTT BN2 ..... 48 A1
Meadow Cl HOVE BN3 ..... 26 D4
PTSD BN41 ..... 25 F5 ▣

ROTT BN2 ..... 60 C2
STHW BN42 ..... 43 E2
WTHG BN11 ..... 56 D2
Meadow Crs WTHG BN11 ..... 56 C2
Meadow La LAN/SOMP BN15 ..... 39 C5 ▣
Meadow Pde ROTT BN2 ..... 60 D2
Meadow Pk ANG/EP BN16 ..... 52 B4
Meadow Rd WTHG BN11 ..... 56 C2
Meadowside ANG/EP BN16 ..... 34 A4
The Meadows HOVE BN3 ..... 25 G4
LEW BN7 ..... 17 G1
Meadow Sweet Cl SALV BN13 ..... 35 G5 ▣
Meadowview ROTT BN2 ..... 47 E1
Meadowview Rd
LAN/SOMP BN15 ..... 39 F2
Meadow Wy FERR BN12 ..... 53 E3
SEAF BN25 ..... 71 E5
Meads Av HOVE BN3 ..... 25 G4
Meads Cl HOVE BN3 ..... 25 G4 ▣
Meads Rd SEAF BN25 ..... 70 D5
The Meads BRI BN1 ..... 28 D2
Meadway Ct STHW BN42 ..... 42 B2
Meadway Crs HOVE BN3 ..... 26 B5
The Meadway ROTT BN2 ..... 47 F5
SHOR BN43 ..... 41 F4
Mealla Cl LEW BN7 ..... 17 E1 ▣
Measham Cl FERR BN12 ..... 53 F4
Medina Pl HOVE BN3 ..... 44 D5
Medina Ter HOVE BN3 ..... 44 D5 ▣
Medina Vls HOVE BN3 ..... 44 D5
Medmerry Hl ROTT BN2 ..... 29 F5
Medway Cl SALV BN13 ..... 36 B3 ▣
Meeching Ri NEWHV BN9 ..... 68 C1
Meeching Rd NEWHV BN9 ..... 68 D1
Meeting House La BRI BN1 ..... 3 G5 ▣
Melbourne Av FERR BN12 ..... 54 A3
Melbourne Rd FERR BN12 ..... 54 A3
Melbourne St ROTT BN2 ..... 46 C2
Melrose Av PTSD BN41 ..... 43 E1
SALV BN13 ..... 54 C1
Melrose Cl BRI BN1 ..... 28 C5
SALV BN13 ..... 54 C1
Melville Rd HOVE BN3 ..... 2 D1
Melville Wy FERR BN12 ..... 54 A1
Mendip Cl ANG/EP BN16 ..... 52 A3 ▣
Mendip Crs SALV BN13 ..... 36 C3
Mendip Rd SALV BN13 ..... 36 C3
Mercread Rd SEAF BN25 ..... 70 D5
Meredith Rd FIN/BW BN14 ..... 5 J1
Merevale BRI BN1 ..... 28 B5
Meridian Rd LEW BN7 ..... 16 D2
Merlin Cl HOVE BN3 ..... 45 F2
Merryfield Crs ANG/EP BN16 ..... 34 A4
Mersey Cl SALV BN13 ..... 36 A4
Mersey Rd SALV BN13 ..... 36 A4
Mersham Gdns FERR BN12 ..... 54 A3 ▣
Merston Cl ROTT BN2 ..... 48 C4
Merton Rd WTHG BN11 ..... 5 J5
Metcalfe Av NEWHV BN9 ..... 64 B5
Meyners Cl HOVE BN3 ..... 25 G4 ▣
Middle Furlong SEAF BN25 ..... 70 D5
Middle Onslow Cl FERR BN12 ..... 53 E2 ▣
Middle Rd BRI BN1 ..... 45 G1
LAN/SOMP BN15 ..... 39 F5
SHOR BN43 ..... 41 H3
Middle St BRI BN1 ..... 3 F6
BRI BN1 ..... 30 A1
PTSD BN41 ..... 43 F4
SHOR BN43 ..... 41 F3
Middleton Av HOVE BN3 ..... 43 H4
Middleton Ri BRI BN1 ..... 29 E2
Middle Tyne SALV BN13 ..... 36 B5
Middle Wy ANG/EP BN16 ..... 52 D5
LEW BN7 ..... 16 C3
Midhurst Cl FERR BN12 ..... 53 F3
Midhurst Dr FERR BN12 ..... 53 F3
Midhurst Ri BRI BN1 ..... 28 B1
Midhurst Wk HOVE BN3 ..... 26 B4 ▣
Midway Rd ROTT BN2 ..... 48 A2
Mighell St ROTT BN2 ..... 3 J4
Milbury Cl FERR BN12 ..... 53 F5 ▣
Milcote Av HOVE BN3 ..... 44 B2
Mildmay Rd LEW BN7 ..... 16 C3
Mile Oak Crs STHW BN42 ..... 42 D1
Mile Oak Gdns PTSD BN41 ..... 43 E1
Mile Oak Rd PTSD BN41 ..... 24 D4
Mill Av SHOR BN43 ..... 41 F1 ▣
Millberg Rd SEAF BN25 ..... 71 F4
Mill Cl PTSD BN41 ..... 43 G1
Millcroft BRI BN1 ..... 27 E2
Millcroft Av STHW BN42 ..... 42 C1
Millcroft Gdns STHW BN42 ..... 42 C1
Millcross Rd PTSD BN41 ..... 43 F1
Mildown Rd SEAF BN25 ..... 70 D4
Mill Dr HOVE BN3 ..... 26 C4
SEAF BN25 ..... 71 E5
Mill Dro SEAF BN25 ..... 69 F3
Millennium Cl LAN/SOMP BN15 ..... 40 B4

Miller Rd BRI BN1 4
Miller's Rd BRI BN1 45
Millfield LAN/SOMP BN15 3
Millfield Cl SEAF BN25 7
Millfield Cottages ROTT BN2 58
Mill Hl SHOR BN43 2
Mill Hill Cl SHOR BN43 4
Mill Hill Dr SHOR BN43 4
Mill Hill Gdns SHOR BN43 4
Mill House Gdns WTHG BN11 5
Mill La LEW BN7 5
PTSD BN41 1
SALV BN13 1
SHOR BN43 4
Mill Ri BRI BN1 2
LAN/SOMP BN15 3
LEW BN7 1
PTSD BN41 4
STEY/UB BN44 4
WTHG BN11 4
Millyard Crs ROTT BN2 48
Milner Rd ROTT BN2 4
Milnthorpe Rd HOVE BN3 44
Milton Cl LAN/SOMP BN15 39
Milton Dr STHW BN42 42
Milton Rd ROTT BN2 3
WTHG BN11 4
Milton St WTHG BN11 4
Mitchelldean PEAHV BN10 62
Moat Wy FERR BN12 54
Modena Rd HOVE BN3 44
Molesworth St HOVE BN3 44
Monarch Gdns SEAF BN25 71
Monarchs Wy HOVE BN3 45
PTSD BN41 25
SHOR BN43 9
STEY/UB BN44 6
STEY/UB BN44 9
STHW BN42 24
Monckton Wy LEW BN7 32
Monk Cl BRI BN1 29
Monks Av LAN/SOMP BN15 39
Monks Cl LAN/SOMP BN15 39
Monks Wk STEY/UB BN44 8
Monmouth St HOVE BN3 ..... 44 D
Montacute Rd LEW BN7 16
Montague Cl SHOR BN43 ..... 42 B
Montague Pl ROTT BN2 3
WTHG BN11 5
Montague St ROTT BN2 58
WTHG BN11 4
Montefiore Rd HOVE BN3 2
Montford Cl SHOR BN43 42
Montgomery St HOVE BN3 44
Montpelier Crs HOVE BN3 2
Montpelier Pl BRI BN1 2
Montpelier Rd ANG/EP BN16 52
BRI BN1 2
Montpelier St BRI BN1 2
Montpelier Ter BRI BN1 2
Montpelier Vls BRI BN1 2
Montreal Rd ROTT BN2 3
Montreal Wy SALV BN13 36
Montrose Cl FERR BN12 54
Monument Vw ROTT BN2 46
Moore Cl SALV BN13 35
Moorfoot Rd SALV BN13 36
The Moorings LAN/SOMP BN15 39
SHOR BN43 42
Morecambe Rd BRI BN1 28
Morestead PEAHV BN10 63
Morland Av FIN/BW BN14 38
Morley Cl LEW BN7 16
Morley St ROTT BN2 3
Morningside Cl SEAF BN25 70
Mornington Crs HOVE BN3 ..... 43 H
Morris Rd LEW BN7 ..... 17 G
Mortimer Rd HOVE BN3 44
Moulsecoomb Wy ROTT BN2 29
Mount Caburn Crs
PEAHV BN10 ..... 63 E
Mount Cl NEWHV BN9 65
Mount Dr ROTT BN2 61
Mountfield Rd LEW BN7 17
Mountfields BRI BN1 28
Mount Harry Rd LEW BN7 16
Mount Pl LEW BN7 17
Mount Pleasant ROTT BN2 ..... 3 K5
Mount Rd NEWHV BN9 65
Mount St LEW BN7 17
Mountview Rd LAN/SOMP BN15 39
Mountway LAN/SOMP BN15 39
Mount Zion Pl BRI BN1 ..... 3 F
Moyne Cl HOVE BN3 44
Muirfield Cl SALV BN13 ..... 36 C4
Muirfield Rd SALV BN13 36
Mulberry Cl BRI BN1 ..... 27 H4

FERR BN12 .... 53 E3
FERR BN12 .... 54 A2
/SOMP BN15 .... 39 G4
HOR BN43 .... 42 B1
berry Gdns *FERR* BN12 .... 54 A3
berry La *FERR* BN12 .... 54 A2
ray Av *NEWHV* BN9 .... 68 C1
shroom Fld *LEW* BN7 .... 32 A2
tle Crs *LAN/SOMP* BN15 .... 39 E5
tle Rd *LAN/SOMP* BN15 .... 39 F5

N

nrik Ms *HOVE* BN3 .... 44 C4
son Rd *BRI* BN1 .... 28 D1
al Rd *ROTT* BN2 .... 28 C5
arino La *WTHG* BN11 .... 56 C2
I's Cl *NEWHV* BN9 .... 68 C1
son Cl *LAN/SOMP* BN15 .... 39 F2
son Cl *FERR* BN12 .... 54 B1
son Rw *ROTT* BN2 .... 3 J4
cote La *FIN/BW* BN14 .... 18 C1
field Cl *FIN/BW* BN14 .... 18 C2
bitt Rd *ROTT* BN2 .... 46 D1
herfield Gn *ROTT* BN2 .... 48 D2
vill Av *HOVE* BN3 .... 44 B1
vill Cl *HOVE* BN3 .... 26 C5
vill Crs *LEW* BN7 .... 16 C3
ville Rd *PEAHV* BN10 .... 67 F2
vill Gdns *HOVE* BN3 .... 26 C5
vill Pl *HOVE* BN3 .... 26 C5
vill Rd *HOVE* BN3 .... 26 C5
LEW BN7 .... 16 C2
OTT BN2 .... 60 D4
vill Wy *HOVE* BN3 .... 26 C5
wark Pl *ROTT* BN2 .... 3 J2
v Barn Cl *PTSD* BN41 .... 25 F5
HOR BN43 .... 41 H1
v Barn Rd *ROTT* BN2 .... 60 C2
HOR BN43 .... 41 H1
v Church Rd *HOVE* BN3 .... 43 H3
v Dorset St *BRI* BN1 .... 3 F3
wells Rd *ROTT* BN2 .... 48 C1
v England Ri *PTSD* BN41 .... 25 E3
v England Rd *BRI* BN1 .... 2 E1
wfield La *NEWHV* BN9 .... 68 C1
wfield Rd *NEWHV* BN9 .... 68 C1
wham Cl *STEY/UB* BN44 .... 7 E1
wham La *STEY/UB* BN44 .... 6 D2
whaven Rd *SEAF* BN25 .... 69 G3
whaven St *ROTT* BN2 .... 3 J2
wick Cl *SEAF* BN25 .... 73 G1
wick Rd *BRI* BN1 .... 29 E3
wland St *STEY/UB* BN44 .... 8 B2
VTHG BN11 .... 5 F2
wlands Rd *ROTT* BN2 .... 61 E4
wland St *WTHG* BN11 .... 5 F2
wling Wy *SALV* BN13 .... 36 C1
wman's Gdns
/SOMP BN15 .... 38 D3
wmarket Rd *ROTT* BN2 .... 46 C2
v Pde *WTHG* BN11 .... 5 J5
wport Ms *WTHG* BN11 .... 56 D2
wport St *ROTT* BN2 .... 46 B3
w Rd *BRI* BN1 .... 3 H1
LEW BN7 .... 17 E3
NEWHV BN9 .... 64 D4
SALV BN13 .... 36 A3
SHOR BN43 .... 41 F3
STEY/UB BN44 .... 8 B3
w Steine *ROTT* BN2 .... 3 J6
w Steine Ms *ROTT* BN2 .... 3 J6
w St *WTHG* BN11 .... 4 E6
wtimber Av *FERR* BN12 .... 53 H2
wtimber Dr *PTSD* BN41 .... 43 E1
wtimber Gdns *SHOR* BN43 .... 41 F1
wton Rd *LEW* BN7 .... 16 D2
PEAHV BN10 .... 67 E1
wtown Rd *HOVE* BN3 .... 44 D2
colson Dr *SHOR* BN43 .... 41 F2
e St *BRI* BN1 .... 3 G5
nfield Pl *ROTT* BN2 .... 47 E3
zells Av *HOVE* BN3 .... 2 B1
lan Rd *ROTT* BN2 .... 48 C3
e Nookery *ANG/EP* BN16 .... 52 A4
rbury Cl *LAN/SOMP* BN15 .... 39 H2
rbury Dr *LAN/SOMP* BN15 .... 39 G2
re Rd *NEWHV* BN9 .... 68 B2
folk Buildings *BRI* BN1 .... 2 C4
folk Ms *BRI* BN1 .... 2 C4
folk Rd *BRI* BN1 .... 2 C4
folk Sq *BRI* BN1 .... 2 C4
folk St *BRI* BN1 .... 2 C5
folk Ter *BRI* BN1 .... 2 C5
WTHG BN11 .... 4 C3
rman Cl *SEAF* BN25 .... 69 H2

Norman Crs *SHOR* BN43 .... 41 F1
Normandy La *ANG/EP* BN16 .... 52 A5
Normandy Rd *FIN/BW* BN14 .... 55 G1
Norman Rd *HOVE* BN3 .... 44 A4
NEWHV BN9 .... 68 C1
Normansal Cl *SEAF* BN25 .... 71 E2
Normansal Park Av *SEAF* BN25 ...... 70 D3
Normanton St *ROTT* BN2 .... 46 C3
North Av *FERR* BN12 .... 54 C4
Northbourne Cl *SHOR* BN43 .... 41 F2
Northbrook Cl *FIN/BW* BN14 .... 38 A4
Northbrook Rd *FIN/BW* BN14 .... 38 A4
North Camp La *SEAF* BN25 .... 70 D3
Northcliffe Cl *SEAF* BN25 .... 70 D4
North Cl *PTSD* BN41 .... 25 E5
Northcote La *PEAHV* BN10 .... 62 C4
North Ct *LEW* BN7 .... 17 G3
Northcourt Rd *FIN/BW* BN14 .... 4 D1
Northcourt Cl *NEWHV* BN9 .... 68 C2
Northdown Rd *NEWHV* BN9 .... 68 B2
North Dr *ROTT* BN2 .... 46 C4
Northease Cl *HOVE* BN3 .... 25 H5
Northease Dr *HOVE* BN3 .... 25 H5
Northease Gdns *HOVE* BN3 .... 26 A4
North Farm Rd
LAN/SOMP BN15 .... 39 G4
Northfield Cl *SEAF* BN25 .... 70 D3
Northfield Ri *HOVE* BN3 .... 25 H3
ROTT BN2 .... 61 E3
Northfield Rd *SALV* BN13 .... 37 E4
Northfield Wy *BRI* BN1 .... 28 A3
North Gdns *BRI* BN1 .... 3 F3
Northgate Cl *LAN/SOMP* BN15 .... 39 G4
ROTT BN2 .... 60 D3
North La *ANG/EP* BN16 .... 52 A4
PTSD BN41 .... 25 E5
North Pl *BRI* BN1 .... 3 H4
North Quay Rd *NEWHV* BN9 .... 64 D4
North Rd *BRI* BN1 .... 3 H4
BRI BN1 .... 45 G1
LAN/SOMP BN15 .... 39 G5
PTSD BN41 .... 25 E5
North St *BRI* BN1 .... 3 F4
LEW BN7 .... 17 E2
PTSD BN41 .... 43 F3
SHOR BN43 .... 41 F3
WTHG BN11 .... 5 F3
North Wy *LEW* BN7 .... 16 C2
NEWHV BN9 .... 68 C1
SEAF BN25 .... 70 D3
Northwood Av *ROTT* BN2 .... 62 A4
Norton Cl *HOVE* BN3 .... 44 D4
Norton Dr *ROTT* BN2 .... 48 B1
Norton Rd *HOVE* BN3 .... 44 D4
LAN/SOMP BN15 .... 39 F5
NEWHV BN9 .... 69 E1
Norton Ter *NEWHV* BN9 .... 69 E1
Norway St *PTSD* BN41 .... 43 G3
Norwich Cl *ROTT* BN2 .... 29 G5
Norwich Dr *ROTT* BN2 .... 29 G5
Nunnery Stable *LEW* BN7 .... 16 D3
Nursery Av *ANG/EP* BN16 .... 52 A5
LAN/SOMP BN15 .... 39 F2
PTSD BN41 .... 24 C3
SHOR BN43 .... 41 H2
Nursery La *WTHG* BN11 .... 4 C6
Nutbourne Ri *FIN/BW* BN14 .... 55 F1
Nuthurst Cl *ROTT* BN2 .... 47 F4
Nuthurst Pl *ROTT* BN2 .... 47 F5
Nutley Av *FERR* BN12 .... 54 A4
ROTT BN2 .... 61 H5
Nutley Cl *FERR* BN12 .... 54 A4
HOVE BN3 .... 26 B4
Nutley Crs *FERR* BN12 .... 54 A4
Nutley Dr *FERR* BN12 .... 54 A4
Nyetimber Hl *ROTT* BN2 .... 29 E5

O

Oakapple Rd *STHW* BN42 .... 24 B5
Oak Cl *BRI* BN1 .... 27 G4
SALV BN13 .... 36 C1
Oakdene Av *PTSD* BN41 .... 24 C4
Oakdene Cl *PTSD* BN41 .... 24 C4
Oakdene Crs *PTSD* BN41 .... 24 C4
Oakdene Gdns *PTSD* BN41 .... 24 C4
Oakdene Ri *PTSD* BN41 .... 24 C3
Oakdene Wy *PTSD* BN41 .... 24 C4
Oaklands Av *ROTT* BN2 .... 61 G4
Oakleigh Cl *WTHG* BN11 .... 56 C1
Oakleigh Rd *FIN/BW* BN14 .... 56 C1
Oakley Gdns *ANG/EP* BN16 .... 52 A5
Ocean Cl *FERR* BN12 .... 53 E5
Ocean Dr *FERR* BN12 .... 53 E5
Offham Cl *SEAF* BN25 .... 70 D3
Offham Rd *LEW* BN7 .... 16 C2

Offington Av *FIN/BW* BN14 .... 37 F3
Offington Ct *FIN/BW* BN14 .... 37 G4
Offington Dr *FIN/BW* BN14 .... 37 F3
Offington Gdns *FIN/BW* BN14 .... 37 E3
Offington La *FIN/BW* BN14 .... 37 E4
Old Barn Wy *STHW* BN42 .... 43 E3
Old Boat Wk *BRI* BN1 .... 14 B5
Old Court Ms *ROTT* BN2 .... 60 D4
Olde Place Ms *ROTT* BN2 .... 60 D4
Old Farm Rd *BRI* BN1 .... 27 H2
Oldfield Crs *STHW* BN42 .... 42 B3
Old Fort Rd *SHOR* BN43 .... 41 G4
Old London Rd *BRI* BN1 .... 27 G2
Old Malling Wy *LEW* BN7 .... 17 E1
Old Mill Cl *BRI* BN1 .... 27 G2
Old Parish La *ROTT* BN2 .... 48 B2
Old Patcham Ms *BRI* BN1 .... 27 G1
Old Rectory Gdns *STHW* BN42 .... 42 B2
Old Salts Farm Rd
LAN/SOMP BN15 .... 39 H5
Old Shoreham Rd *BRI* BN1 .... 45 G3
HOVE BN3 .... 45 E3
LAN/SOMP BN15 .... 39 H3
LAN/SOMP BN15 .... 40 A2
STHW BN42 .... 42 D2
Old Steine *BRI* BN1 .... 3 H5
BRI BN1 .... 3 H4
Old Worthing Rd *ANG/EP* BN16 ...... 52 B3
Oliver Cl *ROTT* BN2 .... 46 C5
Olive Rd *HOVE* BN3 .... 44 A2
Onslow Dr *FERR* BN12 .... 53 E3
Onslow Rd *HOVE* BN3 .... 45 E1
Ontario Cl *SALV* BN13 .... 36 A4
Ontario Gdns *SALV* BN13 .... 36 A4
Ophir Rd *WTHG* BN11 .... 56 C2
Orchard Av *FIN/BW* BN14 .... 37 F5
HOVE BN3 .... 44 C1
LAN/SOMP BN15 .... 39 G3
Orchard Cl *FERR* BN12 .... 53 F2
FIN/BW BN14 .... 37 F5
SHOR BN43 .... 41 E2
STHW BN42 .... 42 D2
Orchard Gdns *HOVE* BN3 .... 44 D1
Orchard Ms *NEWHV* BN9 .... 65 F3
Orchard Rd *ANG/EP* BN16 .... 52 A3
HOVE BN3 .... 44 C1
LEW BN7 .... 17 G2
Orchard Wy *LAN/SOMP* BN15 .... 39 G3
Orchid Vw *BRI* BN1 .... 28 C1
Oriental Pl *BRI* BN1 .... 2 C5
Orient Rd *LAN/SOMP* BN15 .... 40 C5
Orkney Ct *SALV* BN13 .... 35 H5
Orme Rd *WTHG* BN11 .... 4 C2
Ormonde Wy *SHOR* BN43 .... 40 D4
Orpen Rd *HOVE* BN3 .... 45 F1
Osborne Av *LAN/SOMP* BN15 .... 39 E4
Osborne Dr *LAN/SOMP* BN15 .... 39 E4
Osborne Rd *BRI* BN1 .... 27 H5
Osborne Vls *ROTT* BN2 .... 44 D5
Osmonde Cl *FIN/BW* BN14 .... 4 D1
Osmond Rd *HOVE* BN3 .... 2 C1
Ousedale Cl *LEW* BN7 .... 16 D3
Outlook Av *PEAHV* BN10 .... 67 H2
Oval Cl *PEAHV* BN10 .... 63 E3
The Oval *SALV* BN13 .... 36 D5
Oval Waye *FERR* BN12 .... 53 E5
Overdown Ri *PTSD* BN41 .... 24 D3
Overhill *STHW* BN42 .... 42 C1
Overhill Dr *BRI* BN1 .... 27 G2
Overhill Gdns *BRI* BN1 .... 27 G2
Overhill Wy *BRI* BN1 .... 27 G1
Overmead *SHOR* BN43 .... 41 E2
Over St *BRI* BN1 .... 3 G3
Ovingdean Cl *ROTT* BN2 .... 48 B5
Ovingdean Rd *ROTT* BN2 .... 60 D1
Oxen Av *SHOR* BN43 .... 41 F2
Oxford Ct *BRI* BN1 .... 3 H1
Oxford Ms *HOVE* BN3 .... 45 E3
Oxford Pl *BRI* BN1 .... 3 H1
Oxford Rd *WTHG* BN11 .... 4 D3
Oxford St *BRI* BN1 .... 3 H1

P

Paddock La *LEW* BN7 .... 17 E3
Paddock Rd *LEW* BN7 .... 17 E3
The Paddocks *LAN/SOMP* BN15 .... 39 H5
LEW BN7 .... 51 F2
STEY/UB BN44 .... 8 B1
The Paddock *HOVE* BN3 .... 45 E1
SHOR BN43 .... 40 D1
Paddock Wy *FIN/BW* BN14 .... 18 C1
Pages La *WTHG* BN11 .... 56 C2
Palace Pl *BRI* BN1 .... 3 H5
Palatine Rd *FERR* BN12 .... 54 A1
The Pallant *FERR* BN12 .... 53 H1

Palm Ct *SALV* BN13 .... 36 C3
Palmeira Av *HOVE* BN3 .... 45 E4
Palmeira Sq *HOVE* BN3 .... 45 E5
Palmerston Av *FERR* BN12 .... 54 A3
Palmerston Rd *NEWHV* BN9 .... 65 G4
Palmers Wy *SALV* BN13 .... 36 B1
Pankhurst Av *ROTT* BN2 .... 46 C4
Parham Cl *FIN/BW* BN14 .... 36 D1
ROTT BN2 .... 46 D5
Parham Rd *FIN/BW* BN14 .... 36 D1
Park Av *HOVE* BN3 .... 44 A3
PEAHV BN10 .... 62 C5
SHOR BN43 .... 41 G2
WTHG BN11 .... 5 H2
Park Cl *BRI* BN1 .... 29 E2
FIN/BW BN14 .... 38 A4
HOVE BN3 .... 26 A4
PTSD BN41 .... 43 F1
Park Crs *PTSD* BN41 .... 43 E2
ROTT BN2 .... 60 D4
WTHG BN11 .... 4 C4
Park Crescent Pl *ROTT* BN2 .... 46 B3
Park Crescent Rd *ROTT* BN2 .... 46 B3
Park Crescent Ter *ROTT* BN2 .... 46 B3
Park Dr *FERR* BN12 .... 53 F3
Park Drive Cl *NEWHV* BN9 .... 65 F3
Parkfield Ct *SALV* BN13 .... 55 E1
Parkfield Rd *SALV* BN13 .... 55 E1
Park Hl *ROTT* BN2 .... 3 K4
Parklands *SHOR* BN43 .... 42 A2
Parklands Av *FERR* BN12 .... 54 B4
Park La *STHW* BN42 .... 42 B3
Parkmore Ter *BRI* BN1 .... 45 H2
Park Ri *HOVE* BN3 .... 26 A4
Park Rd *BRI* BN1 .... 29 E2
LEW BN7 .... 17 E3
PEAHV BN10 .... 67 H3
ROTT BN2 .... 60 D4
SEAF BN25 .... 70 B5
SHOR BN43 .... 41 G2
WTHG BN11 .... 5 G2
Park Road Ter *ROTT* BN2 .... 3 K4
Parkside *SHOR* BN43 .... 41 G1
Parkside Rd *SEAF* BN25 .... 70 D4
The Parks *PTSD* BN41 .... 25 F4
Park St *BRI* BN1 .... 30 A1
ROTT BN2 .... 3 K5
The Park *ROTT* BN2 .... 61 E4
Park View Cl *PEAHV* BN10 .... 62 C4
Park View Ri *PEAHV* BN10 .... 62 C5
Park View Rd *HOVE* BN3 .... 44 D1
Park Wy *STHW* BN42 .... 42 D2
Park Way *STHW* BN42 .... 42 D2
Paston Pl *ROTT* BN2 .... 58 D1
Patcham By-pass *BRI* BN1 .... 27 G1
Patcham Gra *BRI* BN1 .... 27 G2
Patchdean *BRI* BN1 .... 27 H2
Patching Cl *ROTT* BN2 .... 53 H1
Patricia Av *FERR* BN12 .... 54 B4
Patricia Cl *FERR* BN12 .... 54 B4
Pavilion Buildings *BRI* BN1 .... 3 G5
Pavilion Pde *ROTT* BN2 .... 3 H4
Pavilion Rd *FIN/BW* BN14 .... 4 B2
Pavilion St *ROTT* BN2 .... 3 H5
Paxmead Crs *FIN/BW* BN14 .... 38 B4
Payne Av *HOVE* BN3 .... 44 B2
Paythorne Cl *STHW* BN42 .... 42 B1
Peace Cl *BRI* BN1 .... 46 C1
Peacock La *BRI* BN1 .... 27 G3
Peak La *ANG/EP* BN16 .... 52 C5
Peckham Cl *LEW* BN7 .... 17 E1
Peel Rd *ROTT* BN2 .... 59 F1
Pegler Av *NEWHV* BN9 .... 68 B2
Pelham Cl *PEAHV* BN10 .... 63 F4
Pelham Rd *PEAHV* BN10 .... 63 E4
Pelham Rd *SALV* BN13 .... 36 D5
SEAF BN25 .... 72 C1
Pelham Sq *BRI* BN1 .... 3 H2
Pelham St *BRI* BN1 .... 3 H2
Pelham Ter *LEW* BN7 .... 17 E2
Pelham Yd *SEAF* BN25 .... 72 C1
Pellbrook Rd *LEW* BN7 .... 16 C1
Pemberton Cl
LAN/SOMP BN15 .... 39 G3
Pembroke Av *HOVE* BN3 .... 44 C4
WTHG BN11 .... 54 D3
Pembroke Crs *HOVE* BN3 .... 44 C3
Pembroke Gdns *HOVE* BN3 .... 44 C4
Pembury Cl *FIN/BW* BN14 .... 4 E1
Pende Cl *LAN/SOMP* BN15 .... 39 F2
Pendine Av *WTHG* BN11 .... 56 C2
Penfold Rd *FIN/BW* BN14 .... 38 A5
Penfold Wy *STEY/UB* BN44 .... 7 F2
Penhill Rd *LAN/SOMP* BN15 .... 39 H5
Penhurst Pl *ROTT* BN2 .... 47 F4
Penland's Cl *STEY/UB* BN44 .... 7 F2
Penlands Ri *STEY/UB* BN44 .... 7 E2
Penlands Rd *STEY/UB* BN44 .... 7 E2
Penlands V *STEY/UB* BN44 .... 7 E2

Penlands Wy STEY/UB BN44 7 F2
Penleigh Cl LAN/SOMP BN15 39 H5
Pennycress Av FERR BN12 35 G5
Penstone Pk LAN/SOMP BN15 39 F4
Pentland Rd SALV BN13 36 C2 1
Pepperscoombe La
STEY/UB BN44 8 A1
Percival Ter ROTT BN2 58 D1 10
Perrots La STEY/UB BN44 7 E2
Perry Hl ROTT BN2 61 G3
Perth Cl SEAF BN25 71 G5
Peter Rd LAN/SOMP BN15 57 E1
Pett Cl ROTT BN2 47 F4 2
Petworth Av FERR BN12 54 A5
Petworth Rd BRI BN1 28 B1
Pevensey Cl SEAF BN25 71 F4
Pevensey Gdn WTHG BN11 55 E4
Pevensey Rd NEWHV BN9 68 A3
ROTT BN2 46 C2 5
WTHG BN11 54 D4
The Peverells SEAF BN25 71 E3 5
Peverel Rd SALV BN13 55 E1
Peveril Cl LAN/SOMP BN15 38 C4
Peveril Dr LAN/SOMP BN15 38 C4
Phoenix Cswy LEW BN7 17 F3
Phoenix Crs STHW BN42 42 B2
Phoenix Pl LEW BN7 17 F3 6
ROTT BN2 3 J2 3
Phoenix Ri ROTT BN2 3 J2
Phoenix Wy STHW BN42 42 B2
Phrosso Rd WTHG BN11 54 D4
Phyllis Av PEAHV BN10 66 D1
Picton St ROTT BN2 46 C3
Piddinghoe Av PEAHV BN10 67 F2
Piddinghoe Cl PEAHV BN10 67 F1
Piddinghoe Md NEWHV BN9 64 B5 1
Pilgrims Wk SALV BN13 55 E2
Piltdown Rd ROTT BN2 47 F4
Pines Av FIN/BW BN14 37 H3
Pinewood Cl ANG/EP BN16 52 A3
SEAF BN25 70 D4 5
Pinfold Cl ROTT BN2 48 C4
Pinwell Rd LEW BN7 17 F4
Pipers Cl HOVE BN3 25 G4
Pitt Dr SEAF BN25 71 E3
Pitt Gdns ROTT BN2 48 B2
Place La SEAF BN25 70 C5
Plainfields Av BRI BN1 14 A5
Plaistow Cl ROTT BN2 47 F4
Plantation Cl SALV BN13 36 D3 2
Plantation Ri SALV BN13 37 E3
The Plantation ANG/EP BN16 52 A4
SALV BN13 36 D3
Plantation Wy SALV BN13 36 D3
Playden Cl ROTT BN2 59 E1
Plumpton Rd ROTT BN2 46 D4
Plymouth Av ROTT BN2 47 F1
Poling Cl FERR BN12 53 H1
Polperro Cl FERR BN12 52 D4
Pond La SALV BN13 36 B3
Pond Ms SALV BN13 36 B4 1
Pond Rd SHOR BN43 41 F3
Pony Farm FIN/BW BN14 18 D1
Pool Va BRI BN1 3 G6
Poplar Av HOVE BN3 26 A4
Poplar Cl BRI BN1 27 H5
HOVE BN3 26 A4
Poplar Rd SALV BN13 36 A5
Portfield Av BRI BN1 28 A1
Port Hall Av BRI BN1 45 G2 1
Port Hall Ms BRI BN1 45 G2 2
Port Hall Pl BRI BN1 45 G2
Port Hall Rd HOVE BN3 45 G2
Port Hall St BRI BN1 45 G2
Portland Av HOVE BN3 44 A3
Portland Pl ROTT BN2 58 C1
Portland Rd HOVE BN3 43 H3
WTHG BN11 4 E5
Portland St BRI BN1 3 F4
Portland Vls HOVE BN3 43 H3
Port Vw NEWHV BN9 65 E3
Portway STEY/UB BN44 7 E2
Potter's La LEW BN7 17 E4 2
Poulter's La FIN/BW BN14 37 F4
Pound La STEY/UB BN44 8 B2
Powell Gdns NEWHV BN9 65 E4 1
Powis Gv BRI BN1 2 E3
Powis Rd BRI BN1 2 D3
Powis Sq BRI BN1 2 D2
Powis Vls BRI BN1 2 E3 1
Poynings Cl SEAF BN25 73 G1 4
Poynings Dr HOVE BN3 26 B4
Poynter Rd HOVE BN3 44 C2
Pratton Av LAN/SOMP BN15 39 F3
Precincts Castle LEW BN7 17 E3 4
Preston Dro BRI BN1 27 H5
Preston Park Av BRI BN1 45 H1
Preston Rd BRI BN1 27 G5
Preston St BRI BN1 2 D5
Prestonville Rd BRI BN1 2 E1
Prince Albert St BRI BN1 3 G5 4
Prince Av LAN/SOMP BN15 40 B5
Prince Charles Cl STHW BN42 42 D1
Prince Charles Rd LEW BN7 17 G1
Prince Edward's Rd LEW BN7 16 D3
Prince Regent's Cl ROTT BN2 59 E1
Princes Av HOVE BN3 44 C4
Princes Cl SEAF BN25 70 C4
Princes Crs HOVE BN3 44 C4
ROTT BN2 46 B2
Prince's Pl BRI BN1 3 G5
Prince's Rd ROTT BN2 46 B2
Princess Av SALV BN13 54 D2
Princess Dr SEAF BN25 70 B3 5
Princes Sq HOVE BN3 44 C4
Prince's St ROTT BN2 3 H5
Prince's Ter ROTT BN2 59 E1
Prince William Cl FIN/BW BN14 37 E2
Prinsep Rd HOVE BN3 44 C2
Priory Cl LAN/SOMP BN15 38 D3
SALV BN13 55 E1
Priory Crs LEW BN7 17 E4
Priory Fld STEY/UB BN44 8 A2
Priory St LEW BN7 17 F4
Promenade PEAHV BN10 66 C2
Prospect Pl WTHG BN11 4 E6
Providence Pl BRI BN1 3 G1
Providence Ter WTHG BN11 5 G4
Pulborough Cl ROTT BN2 47 F3 1

Q

The Quadrangle FIN/BW BN14 18 C2
The Quadrant FERR BN12 54 A2
Quantock Cl SALV BN13 36 D2
Quantock Rd SALV BN13 36 D2
Quarry Bank Rd BRI BN1 28 B5 2
Quarry La SEAF BN25 71 E3
Quarry Rd NEWHV BN9 68 C3
The Quashetts FIN/BW BN14 5 F1
FIN/BW BN14 37 H5 2
Quebec St ROTT BN2 3 K3
Queen Alexandra Av HOVE BN3 26 C4
Queen Anne's Cl LEW BN7 17 E3 5
Queen Caroline Cl HOVE BN3 26 C4 2
Queen Mary Av HOVE BN3 26 C4
Queensbury Ms BRI BN1 2 D5 1
Queensdown School Rd BRI BN1 28 C4
Queen's Gdns BRI BN1 3 G3
HOVE BN3 45 E5
Queens Park Gdns SEAF BN25 70 A4
Queen's Park Ri ROTT BN2 46 C4
Queen's Park Rd ROTT BN2 3 K4
Queen's Park Ter ROTT BN2 46 C4
Queen's Pl BRI BN1 3 H1 4
HOVE BN3 45 E4
SHOR BN43 41 F3
Queen Sq BRI BN1 3 F4
Queen's Rd BRI BN1 3 G2 1
LAN/SOMP BN15 57 H1
LEW BN7 17 F1
STHW BN42 42 C1
WTHG BN11 4 C6
Queen St FIN/BW BN14 55 G1
Queensway LAN/SOMP BN15 39 G4 5
ROTT BN2 46 D4
SEAF BN25 71 E3
Queen Victoria Av HOVE BN3 26 C4
Querneby Cl SHOR BN43 42 B3 2

R

Rackham Cl SALV BN13 36 D5
Rackham Rd SALV BN13 36 D5
Radinden Dr HOVE BN3 45 F1
Radinden Manor Rd HOVE BN3 45 E2
Radnor Cl SALV BN13 54 D1 2
Radnor Rd SALV BN13 54 D1
Raglan Av SALV BN13 36 C5 2
Railway Ap NEWHV BN9 68 D1
WTHG BN11 4 D2
Railway La LEW BN7 17 F3
Railway Rd NEWHV BN9 68 D1
Railway St BRI BN1 3 F2
Raleigh Cl SHOR BN43 41 E4
Raleigh Crs FERR BN12 54 B2
Raleigh Wy FERR BN12 54 A1
Ranelagh Vls HOVE BN3 44 D2
Raphael Rd HOVE BN3 44 B3
Ravensbourne Av SHOR BN43 41 F1
Ravensbourne Cl SHOR BN43 41 F1 6
Raven's Rd SHOR BN43 41 F3
Ravenswood Dr ROTT BN2 48 D4
Rayford Cl PEAHV BN10 67 E1 2
Raymond Cl SEAF BN25 71 E3
Reading Rd ROTT BN2 59 F1
Rectory Cl NEWHV BN9 68 C2
SHOR BN43 42 B3
Rectory Farm Rd
LAN/SOMP BN15 38 D3
Rectory Gdns FIN/BW BN14 37 G5
Rectory Rd FIN/BW BN14 55 E1
NEWHV BN9 65 E3
SHOR BN43 42 A3
Rectory Wk LAN/SOMP BN15 38 D3
Redcross St BRI BN1 3 H2
Redhill Cl BRI BN1 27 E2
Redhill Dr BRI BN1 27 E3
Redvers Rd ROTT BN2 46 D1
Redwood Cl SALV BN13 36 A5 3
Reeves Hl BRI BN1 28 D2
Regency Ms BRI BN1 2 D4
Regency Rd BRI BN1 2 E5
Regency Sq BRI BN1 2 D5
Regent Cl LAN/SOMP BN15 40 B4
Regent Hl BRI BN1 2 E4
Regent Rw BRI BN1 2 E4 2
Regents Cl SEAF BN25 70 C3
Regent St BRI BN1 3 G4
Reigate Rd BRI BN1 45 F1
WTHG BN11 54 D3
Reynolds Rd HOVE BN3 44 B3
Richardson Rd HOVE BN3 44 B3
Richington Wy SEAF BN25 71 F3
Richmond Ct WTHG BN11 4 C4
Richmond Pde ROTT BN2 3 H3
Richmond Pl ROTT BN2 3 H2
Richmond Rd ROTT BN2 46 B2
SEAF BN25 70 B5
WTHG BN11 4 B5
Richmond St ROTT BN2 3 K3
Richmond Ter SEAF BN25 70 C5 2
The Ride BRI BN1 45 H1
Ridge Cl PTSD BN41 25 E3 1
Ridge Rd BRI BN1 15 H3
Ridgeside Av BRI BN1 27 G2
Ridge Vw BRI BN1 29 E2
Ridgeway PTSD BN41 42 D1 1
Ridgeway Cl STHW BN42 42 D1
Ridgeway Gdns ROTT BN2 48 C3 1
The Ridgeway SEAF BN25 70 D4
Ridgewood Av ROTT BN2 61 G2
Ridgway Cl ROTT BN2 48 B2
Ridgway Paddock LEW BN7 31 H1
The Ridgway ROTT BN2 48 B2
The Ridings PEAHV BN10 62 D4
SEAF BN25 70 D3
STEY/UB BN44 7 F3
Rifeside Gdns FERR BN12 53 E2 4
Rife Wy FERR BN12 53 E3
Rigden Rd HOVE BN3 45 E2
Riley Rd ROTT BN2 46 C1
Ringmer Cl BRI BN1 29 E3
Ringmer Rd BRI BN1 29 F3
NEWHV BN9 68 B2
SALV BN13 36 C5
SEAF BN25 72 C1
Ring Rd LAN/SOMP BN15 39 G1
Ripley Rd WTHG BN11 54 D2
The Rise PTSD BN41 24 D5
River Cl SHOR BN43 41 E4
Riverdale LEW BN7 17 E2
Riverside NEWHV BN9 68 D1
PTSD BN41 42 C4
SHOR BN43 41 F4
STEY/UB BN44 8 A2
Riverside Rd SHOR BN43 41 F4
Roadean Cl SEAF BN25 71 E4 4
Robertson Rd BRI BN1 27 F5
Roberts Rd LAN/SOMP BN15 57 G1
Robert St BRI BN1 3 G3
Robin Davis Cl ROTT BN2 47 E2
Robin Dene ROTT BN2 59 E1
Robinson Cl LAN/SOMP BN15 39 G4 6
Robinson Rd NEWHV BN9 64 C5
Robson Rd WTHG BN11 54 C3
Rochester Cl SALV BN13 35 H5 10
Rochester Gdns HOVE BN3 2 A3
Rochester St ROTT BN2 46 D5
Rochford Wy SEAF BN25 69 H2
Rock Gv ROTT BN2 58 D1
Rockingham Cl SALV BN13 36 C4
Rock Pl ROTT BN2 3 K6
Rock St ROTT BN2 59 E1
Roderick Av PEAHV BN10 63 E4
PEAHV BN10 66 D1
Roderick Av North PEAHV BN10 63 E3
Rodmell Av ROTT BN2 61 H4
Rodmell Rd SALV BN13 36 C5
SEAF BN25 73 F1
Roedale Rd BRI BN1 4
Roedean Crs ROTT BN2 5
Roedean Hts ROTT BN2 5
Roedean Pth ROTT BN2 5
Roedean Rd ROTT BN2 5
SALV BN13 3
Roedean V ROTT BN2 5
Rogate Cl LAN/SOMP BN15 3
SALV BN13 3
Rogate Rd SALV BN13 3
Roger's La FIN/BW BN14 1
Roman Cl SEAF BN25 69
Roman Crs STHW BN42 4
Roman Rd HOVE BN3 4
STEY/UB BN44
STHW BN42 4
Roman Wk LAN/SOMP BN15 3
Roman Wy STHW BN42 4
Romany Cl PTSD BN41 4
Romany Rd SALV BN13 3
Romney Cl SEAF BN25 71
Romney Rd ROTT BN2 6
WTHG BN11 5
Romsey Cl BRI BN1 2
Rookery Cl BRI BN1 4
NEWHV BN9 65
Rookery Wy NEWHV BN9 6
SEAF BN25 6
Ropetackle SHOR BN43 4
Rope Wk SHOR BN43 4
Rosebery Av FERR BN12 5
ROTT BN2 4
Rosecroft Cl LAN/SOMP BN15 39
Rosedene Cl ROTT BN2 4
Rose Hill Cl BRI BN1 4
Rose Hill Ter BRI BN1 4
Rosemary Av STEY/UB BN44
Rosemary Cl PEAHV BN10 6
STEY/UB BN44
Rosemary Dr SHOR BN43 4
Rosemount Cl SEAF BN25 6
Rose Wk FERR BN12 5
SEAF BN25 7
Rose Walk Cl NEWHV BN9 6
The Rose Wk NEWHV BN9 6
Rossiter Rd LAN/SOMP BN15 3
Rosslyn Av SHOR BN43 4
Rosslyn Ct SHOR BN43 4
Rosslyn Rd SHOR BN43 4
Rothbury Rd HOVE BN3 4
Rotherfield Cl BRI BN1 2
Rotherfield Crs BRI BN1 2
Rother Rd SEAF BN25 7
Rothesay Cl SALV BN13 5
Rothwell Ct NEWHV BN9 6
Rotten Rw LEW BN7 1
The Rotyngs ROTT BN2 6
Rough Brow SEAF BN25 7
Roundhay Av PEAHV BN10 67
Roundhill Crs ROTT BN2 4
Round Hill Rd ROTT BN2 46
Round Hill St ROTT BN2 46
Roundstone Dr ANG/EP BN16 5
Roundstone La ANG/EP BN16 5
Roundway BRI BN1 2
Rowan Av HOVE BN3 4
Rowan Cl PTSD BN41 4
SEAF BN25 71
The Rowans WTHG BN11 55
Rowan Wy ROTT BN2 6
Rowe Av PEAHV BN10 6
PEAHV BN10 6
Rowlands Rd WTHG BN11 4
Roxburgh Cl SALV BN13 36
Royal Crs ROTT BN2 58
Royal Crescent Ms ROTT BN2 58
Royal Dr SEAF BN25 70
Royal George Pde SHOR BN43 41
Royles Cl ROTT BN2 61
Rudgwick Av FERR BN12 53
Rudyard Cl ROTT BN2 48
Rudyard Rd ROTT BN2 48
Rufus Cl LEW BN7 17
Rugby Cl SEAF BN25 71
Rugby Pl ROTT BN2 59
Rugby Rd BRI BN1 46
WTHG BN11 55
Rusbridge La LEW BN7 17
Rushlake Cl BRI BN1 29
Rushlake Rd BRI BN1 29
Ruskin Rd FIN/BW BN14 56
HOVE BN3 44
Rusper Rd BRI BN1 28
SALV BN13 36
Rusper Rd South SALV BN13 36
Russell Cl FIN/BW BN14 38
Russell Crs BRI BN1 45
Russell Pl BRI BN1 2

sell Rd *BRI* BN1 .... 2 E5
sell's Cl *ANG/EP* BN16 ...... 52 B3
sell's Dr *LAN/SOMP* BN15 .... 39 G5
sell Sq *BRI* BN1 .... 2 D4
tic Cl *PEAHV* BN10 .... 62 D4
tic Rd *PEAHV* BN10 .... 62 D5
tington Rd *BRI* BN1 .... 28 A2
land Gdns *HOVE* BN3 .... 44 B3
land Rd *HOVE* BN3 .... 44 C3
roft Cl *FERR* BN12 .... 54 A4
le Rd *ROTT* BN2 .... 46 D3
ROTT BN2 .... 62 A3
SEAF BN25 .... 71 G4
THG BN11 .... 55 E4
croft Gdns *FERR* BN12 ...... 54 A3
lands Dr *ROTT* BN2 .... 28 D4

S

kville Cl *LEW* BN7 .... 17 E3
kville Rd *FIN/BW* BN14 ..... 56 A1
kville Gdns *HOVE* BN3 ...... 44 B4
kville Rd *FIN/BW* BN14 ..... 5 G1
OVE BN3 .... 44 C4
kville Wy *FIN/BW* BN14 ..... 5 H1
ler Wy *ROTT* BN2 .... 47 F4
ron Cl *SHOR* BN43 .... 42 A1
andrew's Cl *FERR* BN12 ..... 53 E3
andrew's Dr *SEAF* BN25 ..... 69 G2
andrew's La *LEW* BN7 .... 17 E4
EW BN7 .... 17 E3
andrew's Rd *BRI* BN1 .... 46 A1
TSD BN41 .... 43 F3
ALV BN13 .... 54 D1
anne's Crs *LEW* BN7 .... 16 D3
anselm's Rd *FIN/BW* BN14 ... 4 A1
aubins Rd *FERR* BN12 .... 53 F5
aubyns *HOVE* BN3 .... 44 C4
aubyn's Crs *PTSD* BN41 ..... 43 F3
aubyn's Md *ROTT* BN2 .... 61 E4
aubyn's Rd *PTSD* BN41 ...... 43 F3
aubyns South *HOVE* BN3 ..... 44 C5
Bernards Ct
AN/SOMP BN15 .... 39 C5
Botolph's Rd *WTHG* BN11 .... 4 A2
Crispians *SEAF* BN25 .... 70 B5
Cuthmans Cl *ROTT* BN2 ...... 47 E4
Dunstan's Rd *SALV* BN13 .... 55 E2
Elmo Rd *FIN/BW* BN14 .... 4 B1
George's Ms *BRI* BN1 .... 3 H3
George's Pl *BRI* BN1 .... 3 H2
George's Rd *ROTT* BN2 ...... 58 C1
WTHG BN11 .... 5 J3
George's Ter *ROTT* BN2 ..... 58 C1
Giles Cl *ROTT* BN2 .... 41 H2
Helen's Crs *HOVE* BN3 ...... 25 H4
Helen's Dr *HOVE* BN3 .... 25 H4
Helen's Rd *ROTT* BN2 .... 46 D3
Helier Rd *FERR* BN12 .... 53 F5
Heliers Av *HOVE* BN3 .... 44 A3
James Av *LAN/SOMP* BN15 .... 39 C2
James's Av *ROTT* BN2 .... 3 K6
James's St *ROTT* BN2 .... 3 H5
James's Street Ms *ROTT* BN2 . 3 J5
James St *LEW* BN7 .... 17 E4
John's Cl *FERR* BN12 .... 54 B4
John's Cl *FERR* BN12 .... 54 A4
John's Hl *LEW* BN7 .... 17 E3
John's Pl *HOVE* BN3 .... 45 E4
OTT BN2 .... 3 J4
John's Rd *HOVE* BN3 .... 45 E5
SEAF BN25 .... 72 C1
John's Ter *LEW* BN7 .... 17 E3
John St *LEW* BN7 .... 17 F3
Joseph's Cl *HOVE* BN3 ...... 44 C2
Julians Cl *SHOR* BN43 ...... 42 A3
Julian's La *SHOR* BN43 ..... 42 A3
Keyna Av *HOVE* BN3 .... 43 H4
Laurence Cl *PEAHV* BN10 .... 62 C4
Lawrence Av *FIN/BW* BN14 ... 55 F1
Leonards Cl *NEWHV* BN9 ..... 65 F3
Leonard's Av *HOVE* BN3 ..... 43 G4
Leonard's Gdns *HOVE* BN3 ... 43 G4
Leonard's Rd *HOVE* BN3 ..... 43 G4
JEWHV BN9 .... 46 C2
ROTT BN2 .... 46 C2
Louie Cl *STHW* BN42 .... 43 E2
Luke's Cl *WTHG* BN11 .... 56 D1
Luke's Rd *ROTT* BN2 .... 46 C4
Luke's Ter *ROTT* BN2 .... 46 C4
Malo Cl *FERR* BN12 .... 53 F5
Margaret's Pl *BRI* BN1 ..... 2 D5
Margaret's Rd *SEAF* BN25 ... 69 G2
Mark's Crs *WTHG* BN11 ...... 56 D1
Mark's St *ROTT* BN2 .... 59 E1
Martins Crs *NEWHV* BN9 ..... 64 D4

St Martin's Pl *ROTT* BN2 ... 46 B3
St Martin's St *ROTT* BN2 ... 46 B3
St Mary Magdalene St
  ROTT BN2 .... 46 B2
St Marys Cl *LAN/SOMP* BN15 . 38 C3
  SHOR BN43 .... 41 F3
St Mary's Pl *ROTT* BN2 ..... 3 K6
St Mary's Rd *SHOR* BN43 .... 41 F3
St Mary's Sq *ROTT* BN2 ..... 58 D1
St Matthew's Rd *WTHG* BN11 . 4 C3
St Maur's Rd *FERR* BN12 .... 53 E3
St Michael's Ct *WTHG* BN11 . 4 A5
St Michael's Pl *BRI* BN1 ... 2 D3
St Michael's Rd *PTSD* BN41 . 43 F3
  WTHG BN11 .... 4 A5
St Michael's Ter *LEW* BN7 .. 17 F2
St Nicholas La *LEW* BN7 .... 17 F3
St Nicholas Rd *BRI* BN1 .... 3 F3
  PTSD BN41 .... 43 F3
St Nicolas La *SHOR* BN43 ... 40 D2
St Osmund Rd *FERR* BN12 .... 52 D3
St Pancras Gdns *LEW* BN7 ... 16 D4
St Pancras Gn *LEW* BN7 ..... 31 H2
St Pancras Rd *LEW* BN7 ..... 16 D4
St Patrick's Rd *HOVE* BN3 .. 44 C3
St Paul's Av *WTHG* BN11 .... 56 D1
St Paul's St *BRI* BN1 ...... 2 E3
St Peter's Av *PEAHV* BN10 .. 62 C5
St Peter's Cl *HOVE* BN3 .... 26 B5
  SEAF BN25 .... 70 C3
St Peter's Pl *BRI* BN1 ..... 3 H2
  LEW BN7 .... 17 E4
  LEW BN7 .... 17 E3
St Peter's Rd *PTSD* BN41 ... 43 F3
  SEAF BN25 .... 70 C3
St Peter's St *BRI* BN1 ..... 3 H1
St Philips Ms *HOVE* BN3 .... 44 D4
St Raphael's Rd *WTHG* BN11 . 54 D3
St Richard's Rd *PTSD* BN41 . 43 F3
St Swithun's Ter *LEW* BN7 .. 17 E4
St Thomas's Rd *FIN/BW* BN14 . 55 F1
St Valerie Rd *HOVE* BN3 .... 44 B4
St Wilfred's Pl *SEAF* BN25 . 73 F1
St Wilfred's Rd *FIN/BW* BN14 . 55 H1
Salisbury Rd *HOVE* BN3 ..... 44 B5
  SEAF BN25 .... 70 C5
  WTHG BN11 .... 4 E4
Saltdean Dr *ROTT* BN2 ...... 61 F4
Saltdean Park Rd *ROTT* BN2 . 61 G4
Saltdean V *ROTT* BN2 .... 61 F4
The Saltings *LAN/SOMP* BN15 . 39 H5
  SHOR BN43 .... 40 D4
Saltings Wy *STEY/UB* BN44 .. 8 A2
Saltwood Rd *SEAF* BN25 ..... 71 G4
Salvington Cl *SALV* BN13 ... 36 B3
Salvington Gdns *SALV* BN13 . 36 D4
Salvington Hl *SALV* BN13 ... 36 C1
Salvington Rd *SALV* BN13 ... 36 C3
Samphire Dr *SALV* BN13 ..... 35 H5
Sandgate Cl *SEAF* BN25 ..... 71 G3
Sandgate Rd *BRI* BN1 .... 28 A5
Sandhurst Av *ROTT* BN2 ..... 48 B1
Sandore Cl *SEAF* BN25 ...... 71 F4
Sandore Rd *SEAF* BN25 ...... 71 E4
Sandown Av *FERR* BN12 ...... 54 A4
Sandown Cl *FERR* BN12 ...... 54 A4
Sandown Rd *ROTT* BN2 .... 46 D3
  STHW BN42 .... 42 B2
Sandringham Cl *HOVE* BN3 ... 26 C4
  SEAF BN25 .... 71 E2
Sandringham Dr *HOVE* BN3 ... 26 C4
Sandringham Ms *SALV* BN13 .. 36 B3
Sandwich Rd *WTHG* BN11 ..... 54 D4
Sanyhils Av *BRI* BN1 .... 13 H5
Sark Gdns *FERR* BN12 .... 53 F4
Saunders Hl *BRI* BN1 .... 14 D5
Saunders Park Vw *ROTT* BN2 . 46 C1
Saxifrage Wy *SALV* BN13 .... 35 G5
Saxon Cl *ANG/EP* BN16 ...... 52 B2
  ROTT BN2 .... 61 C3
Saxon La *SEAF* BN25 .... 72 C1
Saxon Rd *HOVE* BN3 .... 43 H4
  NEWHV BN9 .... 68 C1
  STEY/UB BN44 .... 7 H1
Saxons *SHOR* BN43 .... 41 F1
Saxony Rd *FIN/BW* BN14 ..... 55 G1
Scarborough Rd *BRI* BN1 .... 45 F1
School St *STHW* BN42 .... 42 C3
School Hl *FIN/BW* BN14 ..... 18 C1
School La *STEY/UB* BN44 .... 7 F1
School Ri *ROTT* BN2 .... 47 E4
School Rd *HOVE* BN3 .... 44 B3
  STEY/UB BN44 .... 8 A2
Scotland St *ROTT* BN2 ...... 3 K3
Scotney Cl *SALV* BN13 ...... 35 H5
Scott Rd *HOVE* BN3 .... 44 B3
Sea Cl *FERR* BN12 .... 54 C3
Sea Dr *FERR* BN12 .... 53 F5

Seafield Av *FERR* BN12 ..... 54 B5
Seafield Cl *SEAF* BN25 ..... 71 F3
Seafield Rd *HOVE* BN3 ...... 44 D5
Seaford Rd *HOVE* BN3 .... 43 G4
  NEWHV BN9 .... 69 F1
Seagrave Cl *SEAF* BN25 ..... 69 G2
Seagrove Wy *SEAF* BN25 ..... 70 D2
Seahaven Gdns *SHOR* BN43 ... 40 D5
Sea La *ANG/EP* BN16 .... 52 D5
  FERR BN12 .... 53 F3
  FERR BN12 .... 53 F3
Sea Lane Gdns *FERR* BN12 ... 53 F4
Seamill Park Av *WTHG* BN11 . 57 E2
Seamill Park Crs *WTHG* BN11 . 56 D2
Seamill Wy *WTHG* BN11 ...... 56 D2
Sea Pl *FERR* BN12 .... 54 C4
Searle Av *PEAHV* BN10 ...... 67 G2
Sea Rd *ANG/EP* BN16 .... 52 A4
Seasaw Wy *FERR* BN12 .... 47 F3
Seaside Av *LAN/SOMP* BN15 .. 39 H5
Seaside Cl *LAN/SOMP* BN15 .. 39 H5
Seaside Rd *LAN/SOMP* BN15 .. 39 H5
Seaview Av *ANG/EP* BN16 .... 52 A5
  ANG/EP BN16 .... 52 D5
  PEAHV BN10 .... 67 G2
Seaview Ct *LAN/SOMP* BN15 .. 57 F1
Seaview Rd *NEWHV* BN9 ...... 65 F4
  PEAHV BN10 .... 67 G3
  ROTT BN2 .... 47 H2
Sea View Rd *WTHG* BN11 ..... 4 A7
Seawares Cl *ANG/EP* BN16 ... 52 A4
Second Av *FIN/BW* BN14 ..... 37 H3
  HOVE BN3 .... 45 E5
  LAN/SOMP BN15 .... 39 G3
  NEWHV BN9 .... 68 C2
Second Av *PEAHV* BN10 ...... 66 C1
Sedbury Rd *LAN/SOMP* BN15 .. 39 E2
Sedgewick Rd *BRI* BN1 ...... 28 C1
Sefton Cl *SALV* BN13 .... 36 B4
Sefton Rd *PTSD* BN41 .... 43 F3
Segrave Cl *LEW* BN7 .... 16 D2
Selba Dr *ROTT* BN2 .... 29 E5
Selborne Pl *HOVE* BN3 ...... 45 E3
Selborne Rd *HOVE* BN3 ...... 45 E4
  WTHG BN11 .... 5 J2
Selden La *SALV* BN13 .... 34 B1
  WTHG BN11 .... 5 J4
Selden Rd *WTHG* BN11 .... 5 J5
Selden's Ms *SALV* BN13 ..... 36 D4
Selden's Wy *SALV* BN13 ..... 36 D4
Selham Cl *BRI* BN1 .... 29 E1
Selham Dr *BRI* BN1 .... 28 D1
Selhurst Rd *ROTT* BN2 ...... 48 C4
Selkirk Cl *SALV* BN13 ...... 54 C1
Selmestone Rd *ROTT* BN2 .... 47 F5
Selmeston Pl *ROTT* BN2 ..... 47 F4
Selsey Cl *BRI* BN1 .... 29 E1
  SALV BN13 .... 36 D5
Selsfield Dr *ROTT* BN2 ..... 28 D4
Semley Rd *BRI* BN1 .... 46 B1
Senlac Rd *NEWHV* BN9 .... 68 D1
Sevelands Cl *ROTT* BN2 ..... 47 F3
Seventh Av *LAN/SOMP* BN15 .. 39 G2
Seville St *ROTT* BN2 .... 46 C3
Seymour Sq *ROTT* BN2 .... 58 D1
Seymour St *ROTT* BN2 .... 58 D1
Shadwells Cl *LAN/SOMP* BN15 . 39 H3
Shadwells Rd *LAN/SOMP* BN15 . 39 H3
Shaftesbury Av *FERR* BN12 .. 54 C2
Shaftesbury Pl *BRI* BN1 .... 46 A2
Shaftesbury Rd *BRI* BN1 .... 46 A2
Shakespeare Rd *WTHG* BN11 .. 4 B3
Shakespeare St *HOVE* BN3 ... 44 C2
Shandon Gdns *FIN/BW* BN14 .. 37 H4
Shandon Rd *FIN/BW* BN14 .... 37 H4
Shandon Wy *FIN/BW* BN14 .... 37 H4
Shanklin Rd *ROTT* BN2 ...... 46 C2
Shannon Cl *PEAHV* BN10 ..... 62 C4
Sharpthorne Crs *PTSD* BN41 . 25 G5
Sheepbell Cl *PTSD* BN41 .... 25 F4
Sheepfair *LEW* BN7 .... 16 C2
Sheep Pen La *SEAF* BN25 .... 71 E5
  STEY/UB BN44 .... 7 F1
Sheep Wk *ROTT* BN2 .... 60 D4
Shelby Rd *SALV* BN13 .... 36 A4
Shelldale Av *PTSD* BN41 .... 43 F3
Shelldale Crs *PTSD* BN41 ... 43 E2
Shelldale Rd *PTSD* BN41 .... 43 E2
Shelley Cl *LEW* BN7 .... 16 D3
Shelley Rd *HOVE* BN3 .... 44 B3
  WTHG BN11 .... 4 C5
Shenfield Wy *BRI* BN1 ...... 28 B5
Shepham Av *ROTT* BN2 .... 61 G4
Shepherds Cl *NEWHV* BN9 .... 64 B3
Shepherds Cot *PEAHV* BN10 .. 63 F3
Shepherds Cft *BRI* BN1 ..... 27 E4
Shepherds Md *FIN/BW* BN14 .. 19 E4

Sheppard Wy *PTSD* BN41 ..... 25 E4
The Shepway *SEAF* BN25 ..... 71 F4
Sherbourne Cl *HOVE* BN3 .... 25 H4
Sherbourne Rd *HOVE* BN3 .... 25 H4
Sherbourne Wy *HOVE* BN3 .... 25 H4
Sherbrooke Cl *SALV* BN13 ... 36 B4
Sheridan Rd *FIN/BW* BN14 ... 37 H5
Sheridan Ter *HOVE* BN3 ..... 44 C2
Shermanbury Rd *FIN/BW* BN14 . 4 B1
Sherrington Rd *ROTT* BN2 ... 48 D2
Sherwood Ri *SEAF* BN25 ..... 70 D4
Sherwood Rd *SEAF* BN25 ..... 70 D4
Shetland Ct *SALV* BN13 ..... 35 H5
Shingle Rd *SHOR* BN43 ...... 41 C4
Shipley Rd *ROTT* BN2 .... 48 C3
Ship St *BRI* BN1 .... 3 F5
  NEWHV BN9 .... 64 C5
  SHOR BN43 .... 41 E3
Shirley Av *HOVE* BN3 .... 26 D5
Shirley Cl *FIN/BW* BN14 .... 37 F3
  SHOR BN43 .... 42 A2
Shirley Dr *FIN/BW* BN14 .... 37 F3
  HOVE BN3 .... 45 E1
Shirley Rd *HOVE* BN3 .... 45 E2
Shirley St *HOVE* BN3 .... 44 D3
Shopsdam Rd *LAN/SOMP* BN15 . 57 H1
Shoreham By-pass
  LAN/SOMP BN15 .... 40 C1
Shoreham Rd *STEY/UB* BN44 .. 8 B4
Short Brow *SEAF* BN25 ...... 71 E4
Shortgate Rd *PTSD* BN41 .... 29 F3
Sidehill Dr *PTSD* BN41 ..... 24 D5
Sillwood Pl *BRI* BN1 .... 2 C4
Sillwood Rd *BRI* BN1 .... 2 D4
Sillwood St *BRI* BN1 .... 2 C4
Silver Birch Dr *SALV* BN13 . 35 H5
Silverdale Av *HOVE* BN3 .... 45 F3
Silverdale La *LAN/SOMP* BN15 . 39 E5
Silverdale Rd *HOVE* BN3 .... 45 F3
Singleton Cl *FERR* BN12 .... 53 F2
Singleton Crs *FERR* BN12 ... 53 F2
Singleton Rd *BRI* BN1 ...... 28 A1
Sir George's Pl *STEY/UB* BN44 . 7 E1
Skyline Vw *PEAHV* BN10 ..... 63 F4
Slindon Av *PEAHV* BN10 ..... 67 F2
Slindon Rd *FIN/BW* BN14 .... 37 H4
Slinford Cl *ROTT* BN2 ...... 46 D5
Slonk Hill Rd *SHOR* BN43 ... 23 G5
Smugglers Wk *FERR* BN12 .... 54 C4
Snednore *LEW* BN7 .... 32 B2
Solway Av *BRI* BN1 .... 13 H5
Somerhall Av *HOVE* BN3 ..... 2 A1
Somerhill Rd *HOVE* BN3 ..... 2 B2
Somerset Cl *SALV* BN13 ..... 37 E5
  FERR BN12 .... 53 F5
Somerset St *ROTT* BN2 ...... 46 C5
Sompting Av *FIN/BW* BN14 ... 37 H5
Sompting By-pass *FIN/BW* BN14 . 38 A3
Sompting Cl *ROTT* BN2 ...... 47 F3
Sompting Rd *FIN/BW* BN14 ... 38 A3
  LAN/SOMP BN15 .... 39 F4
Sopers La *STEY/UB* BN44 .... 6 D5
Southall Av *ROTT* BN2 ...... 28 D5
Southampton St *ROTT* BN2 ... 3 K2
South Av *FERR* BN12 .... 54 C4
  ROTT BN2 .... 46 C5
South Coast Rd *PEAHV* BN10 . 62 A5
  PEAHV BN10 .... 67 E2
  ROTT BN2 .... 61 H5
Southcourt Rd *FIN/BW* BN14 . 4 D2
Southdown Av *BRI* BN1 ...... 46 A1
  LEW BN7 .... 16 C4
  PEAHV BN10 .... 67 G2
  PTSD BN41 .... 43 G2
Southdown Cl *NEWHV* BN9 .... 68 B2
Southdown Pl *BRI* BN1 ...... 46 A1
Southdown Rd *BRI* BN1 ...... 46 A1
  NEWHV BN9 .... 68 B2
  PTSD BN41 .... 25 E5
  SEAF BN25 .... 70 D4
  SHOR BN43 .... 41 F3
  STHW BN42 .... 42 C3
South Downs Rd *LEW* BN7 ... 17 F2
South Downs Wy *HFD* BN5 ... 10 D2
  LEW BN7 .... 30 D3
  SHOR BN43 .... 9 H2
  STEY/UB BN44 .... 6 C5
  STEY/UB BN44 .... 8 C4
Southdown Ter
  STEY/UB BN44 .... 7 G1
Southdown View Cl
  FIN/BW BN14 .... 38 B5
Southdown View Rd
  FIN/BW BN14 .... 38 A5
Southdown View Wy
  FIN/BW BN14 .... 38 A4
South Dr *FERR* BN12 .... 53 E5

Southey Rd *WTHG* BN11 .... 4 C6
South Farm Rd *FIN/BW* BN14 .... 37 G4
Southfield Rd *FIN/BW* BN14 ..... 37 H5
South La *NEWHV* BN9 .... 68 D1 🔢
Southmount *ROTT* BN2 .... 46 B1
Southon Cl *PTSD* BN41 .... 24 D4
Southover High St *LEW* BN7 .... 17 E4 🔢
Southover Pl *ROTT* BN2 .... 3 J1
Southover Rd *LEW* BN7 .... 17 E4
Southover St *ROTT* BN2 .... 3 J1
South Rd *BRI* BN1 .... 45 C1
  NEWHV BN9 .... 68 D1
Southsea Av *FERR* BN12 .... 54 C3
South Strd *ANG/EP* BN16 .... 52 A5
South St *BRI* BN1 .... 3 F5
  BRI BN1 .... 30 A1
  LAN/SOMP BN15 .... 39 C5
  LEW BN7 .... 17 G3
  PTSD BN41 .... 43 E1
  SALV BN13 .... 37 E5
  SEAF BN25 .... 72 C1
  WTHG BN11 .... 5 F5
South Vw *ANG/EP* BN16 .... 52 B5
Southview Cl *SHOR* BN43 .... 42 A3
  STHW BN42 .... 42 C1 🔢
Southview Dr *WTHG* BN11 ...... 55 E3
Southview Gdns *WTHG* BN11 ... 54 D3
Southview Rd *PEAHV* BN10 ...... 63 E5
  STHW BN42 .... 42 C2
Southwater Cl *FERR* BN12 ...... 53 H2 🔢
  ROTT BN2 .... 46 D4
South Wy *LEW* BN7 .... 16 C3
  NEWHV BN9 .... 68 D1 🔢
  SEAF BN25 .... 73 G2
Southways Av *FIN/BW* BN14 .... 38 A4
Southwick Sq *STHW* BN42 ...... 42 C3
Southwick St *STHW* BN42 ...... 42 C3
Southwold Cl *SALV* BN13 .... 36 C1
South Woodlands *BRI* BN1 ...... 27 G3
Sovereign Cl *SEAF* BN25 .... 71 E3 🔢
The Sparrows *PEAHV* BN10 ..... 63 F4 🔢
Speedwell Cl *SALV* BN13 .... 35 C5 🔢
Spencer Av *HOVE* BN3 .... 25 H4
Spencer Rd *LAN/SOMP* BN15 .... 39 F5
Spences Fld *LEW* BN7 .... 17 G2
Spences La *LEW* BN7 .... 17 G2
Spey Cl *SALV* BN13 .... 36 A2
Spinnals Gv *STHW* BN42 .... 42 B3
The Spinneys *LEW* BN7 .... 17 G2
The Spinney *ANG/EP* BN16 ..... 52 A5 🔢
  HOVE BN3 .... 27 E4
Spital Rd *LEW* BN7 .... 16 C3
Springate Rd *STHW* BN42 ...... 42 D2
Springfield Av *PEAHV* BN10 .... 62 B5
Springfield Rd *BRI* BN1 .... 45 H2
Spring Gdns *BRI* BN1 .... 3 G3
  LEW BN7 .... 17 F3 🔢
Spring St *BRI* BN1 .... 2 D4
Squadron Dr *SALV* BN13 .... 35 H4
Stable La *FIN/BW* BN14 .... 18 C1
Stafford Rd *BRI* BN1 .... 45 G2
  SEAF BN25 .... 70 D5
Standean Cl *BRI* BN1 .... 28 D1
Stanford Av *BRI* BN1 .... 45 H2
Stanford Cl *HOVE* BN3 .... 45 E1
Stanford Rd *BRI* BN1 .... 45 G2
Stanhope Rd *WTHG* BN11 ...... 4 E3
Stanley Av *PTSD* BN41 .... 24 D3
Stanley Rd *BRI* BN1 .... 46 A3
  PEAHV BN10 .... 62 D4
  PTSD BN41 .... 43 E2
  WTHG BN11 .... 5 F2
Stanley St *ROTT* BN2 .... 3 K4
Stanmer Av *ROTT* BN2 .... 61 H2
Stanmer Park Rd *BRI* BN1 ..... 28 A5
Stanmer St *BRI* BN1 .... 28 B5 🔢
Stanmer Vls *BRI* BN1 .... 28 B4
Stansfield Rd *LEW* BN7 .... 16 D2
Stanstead Crs *ROTT* BN2 ...... 48 D4
Staplefield Dr *ROTT* BN2 ...... 29 F4
Stapley Rd *HOVE* BN3 .... 43 H2
Station Ap *BRI* BN1 .... 29 H1
  SEAF BN25 .... 70 C5
Station Rd *BRI* BN1 .... 17 F4 🔢
  LEW BN7 .... 17 F4 🔢
  NEWHV BN9 .... 65 F4
  SEAF BN25 .... 69 H4
  STEY/UB BN44 .... 7 G1
  STHW BN42 .... 42 C3
  WTHG BN11 .... 5 F2
Station St *BRI* BN1 .... 3 G2
Steep Cl *FIN/BW* BN14 .... 18 C2
Steepdown Rd *LAN/SOMP* BN15.. 39 F2
Steep La *FIN/BW* BN14 .... 18 C2
Steeple Vw *SALV* BN13 .... 37 E5
Steine Gdns *ROTT* BN2 .... 3 H5
Steine La *BRI* BN1 .... 3 G5
Steine St *ROTT* BN2 .... 3 H6

Stephens Rd *BRI* BN1 .... 28 B5
Stevenson Rd *ROTT* BN2 .... 46 C5
Stewards Inn La *LEW* BN7 ..... 17 E4 🔢
Steyne Cl *SEAF* BN25 .... 72 D1 🔢
Steyne Gdns *WTHG* BN11 ...... 5 G5
Steyne Rd *SEAF* BN25 .... 72 C1
The Steyne *WTHG* BN11 .... 5 G5
Steyning Av *HOVE* BN3 .... 26 B4
  PEAHV BN10 .... 67 E1
Steyning By-pass *STEY/UB* BN44 .. 7 H3
Steyning Cl *SEAF* BN25 .... 53 H2 🔢
  LAN/SOMP BN15 .... 39 F2
  SEAF BN25 .... 73 G1 🔢
Steyning Rd *ROTT* BN2 .... 60 D4
  SEAF BN25 .... 73 G1
  SHOR BN43 .... 22 C2
Stirling Av *SEAF* BN25 .... 71 G4
Stirling Cl *SEAF* BN25 .... 71 C5 🔢
Stirling Pl *HOVE* BN3 .... 44 C4
Stoke Abbott Rd *WTHG* BN11 .. 4 E4
Stoke Cl *SEAF* BN25 .... 71 F5
Stoke Manor Cl *SEAF* BN25 ... 71 F5
Stone Cl *SALV* BN13 .... 36 D4
Stonecroft Cl *HOVE* BN3 ...... 26 A3
Stonecross Rd *ROTT* BN2 ...... 29 F3
Stoneham Cl *LEW* BN7 .... 17 E1
Stoneham Rd *HOVE* BN3 .... 44 B3
Stonehurst Ct *ROTT* BN2 ..... 46 C4 🔢
Stonehurst Rd *SALV* BN13 .... 36 D5
Stone La *SALV* BN13 .... 36 D4
Stoneleigh Av *BRI* BN1 .... 27 H1
Stoneleigh Cl *BRI* BN1 .... 27 H1
Stonery Cl *PTSD* BN41 .... 25 E5
Stonery Rd *PTSD* BN41 .... 25 E5
Stone St *BRI* BN1 .... 2 D4
Stonewood Cl *SEAF* BN25 ..... 71 G4 🔢
Stoney La *SHOR* BN43 .... 42 A2
Stopham Cl *FIN/BW* BN14 ..... 37 F5 🔢
Storrington Cl *HOVE* BN3 ..... 26 A5 🔢
Storrington Ri *FIN/BW* BN14 .. 18 D3
Stour Cl *SALV* BN13 .... 36 A2
Stour Rd *SALV* BN13 .... 36 A2
The Strand *FERR* BN12 .... 53 E5
  FERR BN12 .... 53 H2
  ROTT BN2 .... 59 C2
Strathmore Cl *SALV* BN13 .... 54 C1
Strathmore Rd *SALV* BN13 .... 54 C1
The Street *LAN/SOMP* BN15 ... 39 G2
  LEW BN7 .... 32 A2
  SALV BN13 .... 37 H1
  SHOR BN43 .... 40 D1
  STEY/UB BN44 .... 7 H2
Stringer Wy *BRI* BN1 .... 27 H4
Stuart Cl *WTHG* BN11 .... 5 K1
Sudeley Pl *ROTT* BN2 .... 58 D1
Sudeley Rd *ROTT* BN2 .... 58 D1
Sudeley St *ROTT* BN2 .... 58 D1
Sudeley Ter *ROTT* BN2 .... 58 D1 🔢
Suffolk St *HOVE* BN3 .... 44 B2
Sugden Rd *WTHG* BN11 .... 5 J2
Sullington Cl *ROTT* BN2 ...... 29 F3
Sullington Gdns *FIN/BW* BN14 . 18 D3
Sullington Wy *SHOR* BN43 .... 41 C2
Summer Cl *PTSD* BN41 .... 43 E3
Summerdale Rd *HOVE* BN3 .... 25 H5
Summerdown Cl *SALV* BN13 ... 35 H5 🔢
Summerfields *FIN/BW* BN14 ... 18 C1
Summersdeane *STHW* BN42 ... 42 C1
Sunningdale Cl *SEAF* BN25 ... 73 E1 🔢
Sunningdale Rd *SALV* BN13 ... 36 B4
Sunninghill Av *HOVE* BN3 .... 26 A5
Sunninghill Cl *HOVE* BN3 .... 26 A5 🔢
Sunny Cl *FERR* BN12 .... 54 C4
Sunnydale Av *BRI* BN1 .... 28 A1
Sunnydale Cl *BRI* BN1 .... 28 A1
Sunset Cl *PEAHV* BN10 .... 62 D4 🔢
Sun St *LEW* BN7 .... 17 E3
Sunview Av *PEAHV* BN10 ..... 67 F2
Surrenden Cl *BRI* BN1 .... 27 G4
Surrenden Crs *BRI* BN1 ...... 27 G4
Surrenden Holt *BRI* BN1 ..... 27 G5
Surrenden Pk *BRI* BN1 .... 28 A3
Surrenden Rd *BRI* BN1 .... 27 G4
Surrey Rd *SEAF* BN25 .... 70 A4
Surrey St *BRI* BN1 .... 3 F2
  WTHG BN11 .... 4 D6
Surry St *SHOR* BN43 .... 41 F3
Sussex Border Pth *BRI* BN1 .. 12 B2
  PTSD BN41 .... 24 C1
Sussex Pl *ROTT* BN2 .... 3 J3
Sussex Rd *HOVE* BN3 .... 44 D5 🔢
  LAN/SOMP BN15 .... 40 C4
  WTHG BN11 .... 5 F3
Sussex Sq *ROTT* BN2 .... 59 E1
Sussex St *ROTT* BN2 .... 3 J4
Sussex Wy *PEAHV* BN10 ..... 66 B1
Sutherland Rd *ROTT* BN2 .... 46 C5
Sutton Av *PEAHV* BN10 ...... 66 D1
  SEAF BN25 .... 73 E1

Sutton Av North *PEAHV* BN10 .. 62 D5
Sutton Cl *ROTT* BN2 .... 48 C1
Sutton Croft La *SEAF* BN25 ... 70 C5 🔢
Sutton Dro *SEAF* BN25 .... 70 D4
Sutton Park Rd *SEAF* BN25 ... 70 C5
Sutton Rd *SEAF* BN25 .... 70 C5
Swallows Cl *LAN/SOMP* BN15 .. 40 D2
Swallows Green Dr *SALV* BN13 .. 36 A5
The Swallows *PEAHV* BN10 ... 62 D4 🔟
Swanborough Dr *ROTT* BN2 ... 47 F3
Swanborough Dro *LEW* BN7 ... 32 B4
Swanborough Hollow *LEW* BN7 .. 32 C3
Swanborough Pl *ROTT* BN2 ... 47 F3 🔢
Swanbourne Cl *LAN/SOMP* BN15 .. 39 H2
Swannee Cl *PEAHV* BN10 ..... 63 F4 🔢
Swillage La *ANG/EP* BN16 .... 34 A1
Swiss Gdns *SHOR* BN43 ...... 41 E3
Sycamore Cl *PTSD* BN41 ..... 25 G4 🔢
  ROTT BN2 .... 48 C2
  SEAF BN25 .... 71 G5 🔢
The Sycamores *PEAHV* BN10 .. 63 F4 🔢
Sydney St *BRI* BN1 .... 3 G3
Sylvan Rd *LAN/SOMP* BN15 ... 38 D4
Sylvester Wy *HOVE* BN3 ..... 25 G4
Symbister Rd *PTSD* BN41 .... 43 G3 🔢

T

Talbot Crs *BRI* BN1 .... 28 D1
Talbot Ter *LEW* BN7 .... 17 E3
Tamar Av *SALV* BN13 .... 36 A2
Tamar Cl *SALV* BN13 .... 36 A3
Tamarisk Wy *FERR* BN12 .... 53 F5
Tamplin Ter *ROTT* BN2 ...... 3 J2
Tamworth Rd *HOVE* BN3 ..... 44 B3
Tandridge Rd *HOVE* BN3 .... 44 A4
Tangmere Rd *BRI* BN1 ...... 28 A1
Tanners Brook *LEW* BN7 .... 17 F4 🔢
Tanyard La *STEY/UB* BN44 .. 7 E1
Tarmount La *SHOR* BN43 .... 41 F3
Tarner Rd *ROTT* BN2 .... 3 K4
Tarragon Wy *SHOR* BN43 .... 42 A1
Tarring Cl *NEWHV* BN9 ..... 64 D3 🔢
Tarring Rd *WTHG* BN11 ..... 4 A2
Tasman Wy *SALV* BN13 ..... 36 A3
Taunton Rd *ROTT* BN2 ..... 47 F1
Taunton Wy *ROTT* BN2 ..... 47 G1 🔢
Tavistock Down *BRI* BN1 ... 28 A2
Tavy Cl *SALV* BN13 .... 36 A4 🔢
Tavy Rd *SALV* BN13 .... 36 A4
Taw Cl *SALV* BN13 .... 36 B3
Teg Cl *PTSD* BN41 .... 25 C5
Telegraph St *ROTT* BN2 .... 58 C1 🔢
Telgarth Rd *FERR* BN12 .... 53 E5
Telscombe Cliffs Wy *PEAHV* BN10 .. 66 B1
Telscombe Pk *PEAHV* BN10 . 63 E3 🔢
Telscombe Rd *PEAHV* BN10 . 63 E3
The Templars *BRI* BN1 ..... 38 A3
Temple Gdns *HOVE* BN3 .... 2 C2
Temple St *BRI* BN1 .... 2 C2
Ten Acres *WTHG* BN11 ..... 56 C2 🔢
Tenantry Down Rd *ROTT* BN2 .. 47 E3
Tenantry Rd *ROTT* BN2 .... 46 D2
Tennis Rd *HOVE* BN3 ...... 44 A4
Tennyson Rd *WTHG* BN11 .. 4 D4
Terminus Pl *BRI* BN1 ...... 3 F1 🔢
Terminus Rd *BRI* BN1 ..... 3 F1
Terminus St *BRI* BN1 ..... 3 F2
The Terrace *LAN/SOMP* BN15 .. 57 C1
Terringes Av *SALV* BN13 ... 36 C5
Test Rd *LAN/SOMP* BN15 ... 38 D4
Teville Pl *WTHG* BN11 .... 4 D1
Teville Rd *WTHG* BN11 .... 4 D1
Thackeray Rd *FIN/BW* BN14 .. 56 B1 🔢
Thakeham Cl *ANG/EP* BN16 .. 52 B2 🔢
  FERR BN12 .... 53 C3 🔢
Thakeham Dr *FERR* BN12 ... 53 C3 🔢
Thalassa Rd *WTHG* BN11 ... 56 D2 🔢
Thames Cl *ROTT* BN2 ...... 3 K4
Thames Wy *SALV* BN13 .... 36 B3
Thesiger Cl *WTHG* BN11 ... 56 C1
Thesiger Rd *WTHG* BN11 ... 56 C1
Third Av *FIN/BW* BN14 .... 37 H3
  HOVE BN3 .... 44 D5
  LAN/SOMP BN15 .... 39 G3
  NEWHV BN9 .... 65 H2
Third Rd *PEAHV* BN10 ..... 66 C1 🔢
Thirlmere Crs *FIN/BW* BN14 .. 38 D5
Thomas St *LEW* BN7 .... 17 G3 🔢
Thompson Rd *BRI* BN1 ..... 46 C1
  NEWHV BN9 .... 65 F3
Thomson Cl *SALV* BN13 .... 35 H4 🔢
Thornbush Crs *PTSD* BN41 .. 25 F4
Thorndean Rd *ROTT* BN2 ... 28 D4
Thornhill Av *BRI* BN1 ..... 14 A5

Thornhill Cl *HOVE* BN3 ...... 26 ..
Thornhill Ri *PTSD* BN41 ..... 2..
Thornhill Wy *PTSD* BN41 .... 2..
Thorn Rd *WTHG* BN11 ....
Thurlow Rd *WTHG* BN11 ....
Thyme Cl *SHOR* BN43 .... 42 ..
Ticehurst Rd *ROTT* BN2 ..... 4.
Tichborne St *BRI* BN1 ....
Tidy St *BRI* BN1 ....
Tilbury Pl *ROTT* BN2 ....
Tilbury Wy *ROTT* BN2 ....
Tilgate Cl *ROTT* BN2 .... 4.
Tillstone Cl *ROTT* BN2 ..... 28 ..
Tillstone St *ROTT* BN2 ....
Timber Cl *SALV* BN13 ...... 36 ..
Timber Yard Cottages *LEW* BN7 ... 1.
Tintern Cl *BRI* BN1 ....
Tisbury Rd *HOVE* BN3 ...... 4.
Titch Hl *LAN/SOMP* BN15 ... ..
Titian Rd *HOVE* BN3 .... 4.
Titnore La *FERR* BN12 ..... 3.
  SALV BN13 .... 3.
Titnore Wy *FERR* BN12 .... 3.
Tivoli Crs *BRI* BN1 .... 4.
Tivoli Crs North *BRI* BN1 ... 2.
Tivoli Pl *BRI* BN1 .... 2.
Tivoli Rd *BRI* BN1 .... 2.
Tollgate *PEAHV* BN10 ...... 6.
Tongdean Av *HOVE* BN3 ... 2.
Tongdean La *BRI* BN1 ..... 2.
Tongdean Ri *BRI* BN1 ..... 2.
Tongdean Rd *HOVE* BN3 ... 2.
Torcross Cl *ROTT* BN2 .... 2.
Toronto Cl *SALV* BN13 .... 36 .
Toronto Ter *LEW* BN7 ..... 1.
  ROTT BN2 ....
Torrance Cl *HOVE* BN3 .... 44 .
Torridge Cl *SALV* BN13 ...
Tor Rd *PEAHV* BN10 ...... 6.
Tor Rd West *PEAHV* BN10 . 6.
Totland Rd *ROTT* BN2 .... 4.
Tottington Wy *SHOR* BN43 . 41 .
Towergate *BRI* BN1 ......
Tower Rd *LAN/SOMP* BN15 . 3.
  ROTT BN2 .... 4.
  WTHG BN11 ....
Towers Rd *STEY/UB* BN44 ..
Trafalgar Cl *PEAHV* BN10 . 63 .
Trafalgar Ct *BRI* BN1 .... 3 .
Trafalgar Ga *ROTT* BN2 ... 5.
Trafalgar La *BRI* BN1 ....
Trafalgar Pl *BRI* BN1 .... 3 .
Trafalgar St *BRI* BN1 ....
Transit Rd *NEWHV* BN9 ... 6.
Tredcroft Rd *HOVE* BN3 .. 2.
Tree Tops Cl *ROTT* BN2 .. 4.
Treharne Cl *SALV* BN13 .. 36 .
Tremola Av *ROTT* BN2 ... 6.
Trent Cl *LAN/SOMP* BN15 . 3.
Trent Rd *WTHG* BN11 ....
Treveor Cl *WTHG* BN11 ...
Treyford Cl *SALV* BN13 .. 4.
Trinity St *ROTT* BN2 ....
Tristram Cl *LAN/SOMP* BN15 . 3.
Troon Cl *SEAF* BN25 ..... 69 .
Truleigh Cl *ROTT* BN2 ...
Truleigh Dr *PTSD* BN41 .. 2.
Truleigh Rd *STEY/UB* BN44 .
Truleigh Wy *SHOR* BN43 .. 4.
Tudor Cl *FIN/BW* BN14 ...
  HOVE BN3 .... 2.
  SEAF BN25 .... 7.
Tudor Dr *STEY/UB* BN44 ..
Tumulus Rd *ROTT* BN2 ... 6.
Tunsgate *STEY/UB* BN44 . 7 .
Turner Rd *FIN/BW* BN14 .
Turnpike Cl *PEAHV* BN10 . 6.
Turton Cl *ROTT* BN2 ....
Twineham Cl *ROTT* BN2 .. 4.
Twitten Cl *STHW* BN42 .. 42 .
The Twitten *STHW* BN42.. 4.
Twitten Wy *SALV* BN13 .. 5.
Twyford Cl *SALV* BN13... 3.
Twyford Gdns *SALV* BN13.. 3.
Twyford Rd *BRI* BN1 .... 2.
  SALV BN13 .... 3.
Tye Cl *ROTT* BN2 .... 3.
Tyedean Rd *PEAHV* BN10 . 6.
Tye Vw *PEAHV* BN10 ..... 62 .
Tyne Cl *SALV* BN13 ..... 3.
The Tynings *LAN/SOMP* BN15 . 39 .

U

Uckfield Cl *ROTT* BN2 .... 4.
Ullswater Rd *LAN/SOMP* BN15 ..

...erdown Rd *STHW* BN42........... 42 C2
...ermill Rd *STEY/UB* BN44 ...... 8 B2
...n Pl *WTHG* BN11............... 5 F4
...n Rd *ROTT* BN2................ 3 J1
...n St *BRI* BN1................. 3 F5
...nds Av *SALV* BN13............ 36 D1
...nds Rd *BRI* BN1.............. 28 C5
...er Abbey Rd *ROTT* BN2........ 58 D1
...er Bannings Rd *ROTT* BN2..... 62 A2
...er Bedford St *ROTT* BN2...... 58 C1
...er Belgrave Rd *SEAF* BN25.... 70 D3
...er Bevendean Rd *ROTT* BN2.... 47 E1
...er Boundstone La
N/BW BN15.................... 39 F3
...er Brighton Rd
N/BW BN14.................... 37 G4
N/SOMP BN15.................. 38 C3
...er Chalvington Pl *ROTT* BN2.. 47 E5
...er Chyngton Gdns
AF BN25...................... 71 F3 ⊡
...er Dr *ANG/EP* BN16........... 52 B5
...Upper Dr *HOVE* BN3........... 45 E2
...er Gardner St *BRI* BN1....... 3 F3 ⊡
...er Gloucester Rd *BRI* BN1 ... 3 F3 ⊡
...er Hamilton Rd *BRI* BN1...... 45 G2
...er High St *WTHG* BN11........ 5 G2
...er Hollingdean Rd *BRI* BN1... 46 B1
...er Kingston La *STHW* BN42.... 42 B1
...er Lewes Rd *ROTT* BN2........ 46 B3
...er Market St *HOVE* BN3....... 2 B4
...er North St *BRI* BN1......... 2 D3
...er Park Pl *ROTT* BN2......... 3 K4
...er Rock Gdns *ROTT* BN2....... 3 K6
...er St James's St *ROTT* BN2... 3 K6
...er Sherwood Rd *SEAF* BN25.... 70 D4
...er Shoreham Rd *SHOR* BN43 ... 41 E2
HW BN2....................... 42 B1
...er Sudeley St *ROTT* BN2 .. 58 D1 ⊡
...er Valley Rd *NEWHV* BN9...... 68 B2
...er Wellington Rd *ROTT* BN2... 46 C3
...er West Dr *FERR* BN12........ 53 E4
...er West La *LAN/SOMP* BN15.... 39 G3
...er Winfield Av *BRI* BN1...... 27 H1
...on Av *STHW* BN42............. 42 C1
...on Gdns *SALV* BN13........... 54 D1
...on Rd *SALV* BN13............. 54 D1

V

...e Av *BRI* BN1................. 13 G5
N/BW BN14.................... 18 D5
...e Cl *SEAF* BN25............. 71 E4
...e Dr *FIN/BW* BN14........... 18 D5
...e Gdns *PTSD* BN41........... 43 F3
...ance Rd *LEW* BN7............ 16 D3
...encia Rd *WTHG* BN11......... 55 E2
...entine Cl *FIN/BW* BN14 ... 37 F5 ⊡
...erie Cl *PTSD* BN41.......... 25 F5
...e Rd *PTSD* BN41............. 43 G3
...OTT* BN2..................... 61 H2
...SAF* BN25.................... 70 D4
...Vale *ROTT* BN2.............. 48 C5
...e Wk *FIN/BW* BN14........... 18 D5
...ance Gdns *HOVE* BN3......... 44 C4
...ance Rd *HOVE* BN3........... 44 C4
...ey Cl *BRI* BN1.............. 27 E3
...EWHV* BN9.................... 64 B5
...ey Dene *NEWHV* BN9.......... 68 B1
...ey Dr *BRI* BN1.............. 27 E3
...SAF* BN25.................... 71 E3
...ey Ri *SEAF* BN25............ 70 D4
...ey Rd *LAN/SOMP* BN15........ 39 E2
...EW* BN7...................... 16 C4
...ey Rd *FIN/BW* BN14.......... 68 B1
...EAHV* BN10................... 63 E3
...TSD* BN41.................... 43 G3
...ancouver Cl *SALV* BN13 ... 36 B4 ⊡
...ancouver Rd *SALV* BN13...... 36 A4
...aguard Wy *SEAF* BN25........ 73 E2
...ey Rd *SALV* BN13............ 35 H4
...ndean Cl *BRI* BN1........... 27 G4
...ndean Dr *BRI* BN1........... 27 G4
...ndean Gdns *BRI* BN1......... 27 G4
...ndean Holt *BRI* BN1......... 27 H4
...ndean Rd *BRI* BN1........... 27 G4
...atnor Vls *HOVE* BN3......... 44 D4
...mont Av *BRI* BN1............ 46 A2
...mont Dr *ANG/EP* BN16........ 52 A4
...mont Wy *ANG/EP* BN16........ 52 A4
...mon Av *PEAHV* BN10.......... 67 F2
...mon Rd *BRI* BN1............. 48 A1
...mon Ter *BRI* BN1............ 2 D2
...onica Cl *ANG/EP* BN16 ... 52 A5 ⊡
...onica Wy *ROTT* BN2.......... 3 K6
...duct Rd *BRI* BN1............ 46 A3
...BN2.......................... 46 B3

Vicarage Cl *NEWHV* BN9 ...... 65 E3 ⊡
SEAF BN25.................... 70 D5
Vicarage Flds *SALV* BN13..... 36 B3
Vicarage La *ROTT* BN2 ... 60 D4 ⊡
STEY/UB BN44................. 7 F1
Vicarage Ter *ROTT* BN2 ... 60 D4 ⊡
Victor Cl *SEAF* BN25......... 70 B3
Victoria Av *PEAHV* BN10...... 67 E2
Victoria Gv *HOVE* BN3 ... 45 E4 ⊡
Victoria Park Gdns *WTHG* BN11 ... 4 C3
Victoria Pl *BRI* BN1......... 2 D3 ⊡
Victoria Rd *BRI* BN1......... 2 D3
PTSD BN41.................... 43 F2
SHOR BN43.................... 41 E3
STHW BN42.................... 42 B3
WTHG BN11.................... 4 D3
Victoria St *BRI* BN1......... 2 D3
Victory Ms *ROTT* BN2......... 59 G2
View Rd *PEAHV* BN10.......... 63 E5
Viking Cl *SEAF* BN25......... 69 G2
The Village Barn *BRI* BN1.... 13 G5
Village Wy *BRI* BN1.......... 30 A1
Villiers Cl *ROTT* BN2........ 48 C2
Vincent Cl *LAN/SOMP* BN15.... 39 F4 ⊡
Vineries Cl *SALV* BN13 ... 37 E4 ⊡
Vines Cross Rd *ROTT* BN2..... 47 F3
Vine St *BRI* BN1............. 3 H3

W

Wadhurst Dr *FERR* BN12....... 53 H3
Wadhurst Ri *ROTT* BN2........ 47 F5
Waite Cl *LEW* BN7............ 17 F2
Wakefield Rd *ROTT* BN2....... 46 B2
Waldegrave Rd *BRI* BN1....... 27 H5
Waldron Av *BRI* BN1.......... 27 E3
Waldshut Rd *LEW* BN7......... 16 C1
Walesbeech Rd *ROTT* BN2...... 61 H5
Wallace Av *WTHG* BN11........ 54 D3
Wallands Crs *LEW* BN7........ 17 E2
Walmer Crs *ROTT* BN2......... 47 G1
Walmer Rd *SEAF* BN25......... 71 G4
Walnut Cl *BRI* BN1........... 27 G4
Walnut Tree Wy *SALV* BN13 ... 35 H5 ⊡
Walpole Av *FERR* BN12........ 54 B3
Walpole Rd *ROTT* BN2......... 58 C1
Walpole Ter *ROTT* BN2........ 46 D5
Walsingham Rd *HOVE* BN3...... 44 B4
Walton Bank *BRI* BN1......... 29 E2
Walton Cl *SALV* BN13......... 36 D4
Walton Ldg *SALV* BN13 ... 36 D4 ⊡
Wanderdown Cl *ROTT* BN2...... 60 C1
Wanderdown Rd *ROTT* BN2...... 60 C1
Wanderdown Wy *ROTT* BN2...... 60 B1
Wantley Rd *FIN/BW* BN14...... 37 E1
Warbleton Cl *ROTT* BN2....... 47 G1
Warenne Rd *HOVE* BN3......... 25 G4
Warleigh Rd *BRI* BN1......... 46 A2
Warmdene Av *BRI* BN1......... 27 H1 ⊡
Warmdene Cl *BRI* BN1......... 27 H2 ⊡
Warmdene Rd *BRI* BN1......... 27 H1
Warmdene Wy *BRI* BN1......... 27 H1
Warner Rd *FIN/BW* BN14....... 56 B1
Warnham Cl *SALV* BN13 ... 54 B4 ⊡
Warnham Ri *BRI* BN1.......... 28 A2
Warnham Rd *FERR* BN12........ 54 B3
Warren Av *ROTT* BN2.......... 48 A1
Warren Cl *LEW* BN7........... 16 D4
ROTT BN2..................... 47 H2 ⊡
Warren Dr *LEW* BN7........... 16 C4
Warren Gdns *FIN/BW* BN14 .... 37 F3 ⊡
Warren Rd *FIN/BW* BN14....... 47 H2
Warren Rd *ROTT* BN2.......... 47 F3
ROTT BN2..................... 47 F3
The Warren *FERR* BN12........ 54 D4
Warren Wy *PEAHV* BN10........ 62 C4
ROTT BN2..................... 48 B2
Warr Gn *LEW* BN7............. 16 D1
Warrior Cl *PTSD* BN41........ 25 F5
Warwick Gdns *WTHG* BN11...... 5 G5
Warwick Pl *WTHG* BN11........ 5 H4
Warwick Rd *SEAF* BN25 ... 70 C5 ⊡
WTHG BN11.................... 5 H5
Warwick St *WTHG* BN11........ 5 F5
Washington St *ROTT* BN2...... 3 K2
Waterdyke Av *STHW* BN42 ... 42 C3 ⊡
Waterford Cl *PEAHV* BN10..... 63 E3
Watergate La *LEW* BN7 ... 17 F4 ⊡
Waterhall Rd *BRI* BN1........ 27 E1
Water La *ANG/EP* BN16........ 34 A4
Waterloo Pl *LEW* BN7 ... 17 F3 ⊡
Watersfield Rd *FIN/BW* BN14.. 37 F5
Watling Cl *STHW* BN42 ... 42 C3 ⊡
Waverley Crs *BRI* BN1........ 46 B1

Wavertree Rd *FERR* BN12...... 54 B2
Wayfield Av *HOVE* BN3........ 44 A1
Wayfield Cl *HOVE* BN3 ... 44 B1 ⊡
Wayland Av *BRI* BN1.......... 27 E3
Wayland Hts *BRI* BN1......... 27 E3
Wayside *BRI* BN1............. 27 F1
Wayside Av *SALV* BN13........ 36 B3
The Way *ANG/EP* BN16......... 52 A5
Weald Av *HOVE* BN3........... 44 B1
Weald Cl *LEW* BN7 .... 17 E2 ⊡
Weald Dyke *SHOR* BN43........ 41 F4
Wear Cl *SALV* BN13........... 36 A3
Wear Rd *SALV* BN13........... 36 A3
Weavers Hl *ANG/EP* BN16...... 34 A4
Weavers Ring *ANG/EP* BN16.... 34 A5
Welbeck Av *HOVE* BN3......... 44 A4
Welesmere Rd *ROTT* BN2....... 61 E2
Welland Cl *SALV* BN13........ 36 B2
Welland Rd *SALV* BN13........ 36 B2
Wellesley Av *FERR* BN12...... 54 B3
Wellgreen La *LEW* BN7........ 32 B2
Well House Pl *LEW* BN7 ... 17 E4 ⊡
LEW BN7...................... 17 E3 ⊡
Wellingham La *SALV* BN13..... 36 C1
Wellington Pk *SEAF* BN25..... 71 E5
Wellington Rd *NEWHV* BN9..... 65 E3
PEAHV BN10................... 67 G2 ⊡
PTSD BN41.................... 43 F4
ROTT BN2..................... 46 B3
Wellington St *LEW* BN7 ... 17 F3 ⊡⊡
ROTT BN2..................... 46 C3
Wembley Av *LAN/SOMP* BN15.... 39 F4
Wembley Gdns
LAN/SOMP BN15................ 39 F4 ⊡
Wenban Rd *WTHG* BN11......... 4 E3
Wenceling Cottages
LAN/SOMP BN15................ 40 C5 ⊡
Wendale Dr *PEAHV* BN10....... 63 F3
Went Hill Pk *SEAF* BN25 ... 71 E5 ⊡
Wentworth Cl *SALV* BN13...... 36 D2
Wentworth St *ROTT* BN2....... 3 J6
West Av *LAN/SOMP* BN15....... 40 A5
WTHG BN11.................... 55 E3 ⊡
West Beach La *LAN/SOMP* BN15 ... 40 C5
Westbourne Av *FIN/BW* BN14... 4 E1
Westbourne Gdns *HOVE* BN3.... 44 C4
Westbourne Pl *HOVE* BN3...... 44 C4
Westbourne St *HOVE* BN3...... 44 C3
Westbourne Vls *HOVE* BN3..... 44 B4
Westbrooke *WTHG* BN11........ 4 E4
Westbrook Wy *STHW* BN42...... 42 D3
West Buildings *WTHG* BN11.... 4 D6
Westcourt Pl *FIN/BW* BN14.... 4 D1
Westcourt Rd *FIN/BW* BN14.... 4 D2
Westdean Av *NEWHV* BN9....... 68 A3
West Dean Ri *SEAF* BN25...... 71 E4
Westdean Rd *FIN/BW* BN14..... 37 F5
Westdene Dr *BRI* BN1......... 27 E2
Westdown Rd *SEAF* BN25....... 70 B4
West Dr *FERR* BN12........... 53 E5
ROTT BN2..................... 3 K4
West End Wy *LAN/SOMP* BN15... 57 F1
Westergate Cl *FERR* BN12..... 53 F3
Westergate Rd *ROTT* BN2...... 29 E3
Western Cl *LAN/SOMP* BN15.... 57 E1
Western Pl *WTHG* BN11........ 4 D6
Western Rd *HOVE* BN3......... 2 A3
LAN/SOMP BN15................ 57 E1
LEW BN7...................... 16 D3
NEWHV BN9.................... 68 C2
SHOR BN43.................... 41 E3
Western Rd North
LAN/SOMP BN15................ 39 E3 ⊡
Western Rw *WTHG* BN11........ 4 D6
Western St *BRI* BN1.......... 2 B5
Western Ter *BRI* BN1......... 2 C4
Westfield Av *ANG/EP* BN16.... 52 A5
ROTT BN2..................... 61 H2
Westfield Av North *ROTT* BN2.. 61 H2
Westfield Av South *ROTT* BN2.. 61 H2
Westfield Cl *BRI* BN1........ 28 A3
Westfield Crs *BRI* BN1....... 28 A2
Westfield Ri *ROTT* BN2....... 61 H2
Westgate St *LEW* BN7 .... 17 E4 ⊡
West Hl *SALV* BN13........... 18 C5
West Hill Av *SALV* BN13 .... 18 C5 ⊡
West Hill Pl *BRI* BN1........ 2 E1
West Hill Rd *BRI* BN1........ 2 E1
West Hill St *BRI* BN1........ 2 E2
Westlake Cl *SALV* BN13....... 36 D5
Westland Av *FIN/BW* BN14..... 55 E1
Westlands *FERR* BN12......... 53 E4
West La *LAN/SOMP* BN15....... 39 G4
Westmeston Av *ROTT* BN2...... 61 G3
Westmount Cl *STHW* BN42 ... 42 B2 ⊡
West Onslow Cl *FERR* BN12.... 53 E2 ⊡
West Pde *WTHG* BN11.......... 4 D5
Westpark La *FERR* BN12....... 54 C3

West Rd *PTSD* BN41........... 43 E3
West St *BRI* BN1............. 3 F5
LAN/SOMP BN15................ 38 D3
PTSD BN41.................... 43 G3
ROTT BN2..................... 60 D4
SEAF BN25.................... 72 C1 ⊡
SHOR BN43.................... 41 E3
WTHG BN11.................... 4 D6
West Tyne *SALV* BN13......... 36 B5
West Vw *SEAF* BN25........... 72 C1 ⊡
Westview Ter *FIN/BW* BN14.... 18 C1
West Wy *HOVE* BN3............ 25 H5
LAN/SOMP BN15................ 40 A5
SALV BN13.................... 36 B1
Westway Cl *PTSD* BN41 ... 24 C3 ⊡
Westway Gdns *PTSD* BN41...... 24 C3
Wheatfield Wy *ROTT* BN2...... 29 F4
Wheatland Cl *ROTT* BN2 ... 62 D3 ⊡
Wheatsheaf Gdns *LEW* BN7..... 17 G2
Whichelo Pl *ROTT* BN2........ 46 C4
Whippingham Rd *ROTT* BN2..... 46 C2
Whippingham St *ROTT* BN2 ... 46 C2 ⊡
Whipping Post La *ROTT* BN2 ... 60 D4 ⊡
Whitebeam Rd *SALV* BN13...... 36 A5
Whitecross St *BRI* BN1....... 3 H2
Whitehawk Cl *ROTT* BN2....... 47 E4
Whitehawk Crs *ROTT* BN2...... 47 E5
Whitehawk Hill Rd *ROTT* BN2.. 46 D5
Whitehawk Rd *ROTT* BN2....... 47 E4
Whitehawk Wy *ROTT* BN2....... 47 F4
Whitelot Cl *STHW* BN42....... 42 C1
Whitelot Wy *STHW* BN42....... 24 C5
Whiterock Pl *STHW* BN42...... 42 C1
White St *ROTT* BN2........... 3 J5
White Styles Rd *LAN/SOMP* BN15.. 38 D3
Whitethorn Dr *BRI* BN1....... 26 D3
White Wy *LEW* BN7............ 50 D1
Whiteway Cl *SEAF* BN25....... 70 C2
Whiteway La *ROTT* BN2........ 61 E3
Whittingehame Gdns *BRI* BN1.. 27 H4
Whylands Av *SALV* BN13....... 36 B2
Whylands Cl *SALV* BN13....... 36 B2
Whylands Crs *SALV* BN13...... 36 B2
Wickhurst Cl *PTSD* BN41...... 24 D4
Wickhurst Ri *PTSD* BN41...... 24 D4
Wickhurst Rd *PTSD* BN41...... 24 D4
Wicklands Av *ROTT* BN2....... 61 H4
Widdicombe Wy *ROTT* BN2...... 29 E5
Widewater Cl
LAN/SOMP BN15................ 40 C5 ⊡
Wigmore Cl *BRI* BN1.......... 46 B1
Wigmore Rd *FIN/BW* BN14...... 37 H4
Wilbury Av *HOVE* BN3......... 45 F3
Wilbury Crs *HOVE* BN3........ 45 F3
Wilbury Gdns *HOVE* BN3....... 45 E3
Wilbury Gv *HOVE* BN3......... 45 E4
Wilbury Rd *HOVE* BN3......... 45 E3
Wilbury Vls *HOVE* BN3........ 45 E3
Wilby Av *STHW* BN42.......... 42 C1
Wild Park Cl *ROTT* BN2....... 29 E4
Wilfrid Rd *HOVE* BN3......... 43 H2
Wilkinson Cl *ROTT* BN2....... 60 D2
Wilkinson Wy *SEAF* BN25...... 70 C4
Williams Rd *SHOR* BN43....... 41 H2
William St *PTSD* BN41........ 43 F3
ROTT BN2..................... 3 H4
Willingdon Rd *ROTT* BN2...... 47 E1
Willowbrook Rd *FIN/BW* BN14.. 56 B1
Willow Cl *LAN/SOMP* BN15 ... 40 C5 ⊡
ROTT BN2..................... 48 C2
Willow Ct *WTHG* BN11 .... 55 E2 ⊡
Willow Crs *SALV* BN13........ 36 A5
Willow Dr *SEAF* BN25......... 71 G5
Willowhayne Av *ANG/EP* BN16 .. 52 A5 ⊡
Willowhayne Cl *ANG/EP* BN16 .. 52 A5 ⊡
Willowhayne Crs *ANG/EP* BN16 .. 52 A5
Willow Wk *NEWHV* BN9......... 64 C5
Wilmington Cl *BRI* BN1....... 28 A2
Wilmington Pde *BRI* BN1...... 27 H2 ⊡
Wilmington Rd *NEWHV* BN9..... 68 B2
SEAF BN25.................... 70 B4
Wilmington Wy *BRI* BN1....... 27 H2
Wilmot Rd *SHOR* BN43......... 42 A2
Wilson Av *ROTT* BN2.......... 59 F1
Winchelsea Cl *SEAF* BN25.... 71 G3 ⊡
Winchelsea Gdns *WTHG* BN11... 54 D4
Winchester Rd *WTHG* BN11..... 4 B5
Winchester St *BRI* BN1....... 46 A2
Wincombe Rd *BRI* BN1 .... 45 F1 ⊡
Windermere Crs *FERR* BN12.... 36 B5
Windlesham Av *HOVE* BN3...... 2 C2
Windlesham Cl *PTSD* BN41..... 43 E1
Windlesham Gdns
ANG/EP BN16.................. 52 A3 ⊡
BRI BN1...................... 2 D2
SHOR BN43.................... 41 F2
Windlesham Rd *BRI* BN1....... 2 C2
SHOR BN43.................... 41 F2

Windmill Cl *HOVE* BN3 .... 26 B5
STEY/UB BN44 .... 8 B2
Windmill Dr *BRI* BN1 .... 27 E1
Windmill Rd *STHW* BN42 ...... 42 C1
Windmill St *ROTT* BN2 .... 3 K4
Windmill Ter *ROTT* BN2 .... 3 K3
Windmill Vw *BRI* BN1 .... 28 A1
Windover Crs *LEW* BN7 .... 16 C2
Windrush Cl *SALV* BN13 .... 36 A2
Windsor Cl *HOVE* BN3 .... 26 C4
SEAF BN25 .... 69 H2
Windsor Rd *HOVE* BN11 .... 5 K3
Windsor St *BRI* BN1 .... 3 F4
Windsor Wy *LAN/SOMP* BN15 ... 40 B4
Winfield Av *BRI* BN1 .... 27 H1
Winfield Cl *BRI* BN1 .... 27 H2
PTSD BN41 .... 25 E3
Winston Rd *LAN/SOMP* BN15 .. 57 E2
Winterbourne Cl *LEW* BN7 .. 16 D4
SALV BN13 .... 35 H5
Winterbourne Hollow *LEW* BN7 .. 16 D4
Winterbourne La *LEW* BN7 .... 16 C4
Winterbourne Ms *LEW* BN7 .... 16 D4
Winterbourne Wy *SALV* BN13 .. 35 H5
Winterton Wy *SHOR* BN43 .... 41 H4

Winton Av *ROTT* BN2 .... 61 G3
Winton Pl *WTHG* BN11 .... 4 E4
Wish Rd *HOVE* BN3 .... 44 A4
Wiston Av *FIN/BW* BN14....... 37 F5
Wiston Cl *FIN/BW* BN14 ...... 37 F5
Wiston Rd *ROTT* BN2............ 47 F3
Wiston Wy *ROTT* BN2 .... 47 F3
Withdean Av *BRI* BN1 .... 27 F5
FERR BN12 .... 53 H5
Withdean Cl *BRI* BN1 .... 27 F4
Withdean Court Av *BRI* BN1 ... 27 F4
Withdean Crs *BRI* BN1 .... 27 G4
Withdean Ri *BRI* BN1 .... 27 F4
Withdean Rd *BRI* BN1 .... 27 F5
Withyham Av *ROTT* BN2......... 61 G5
Wivelsfield Rd *ROTT* BN2 .... 61 G2
Woburn Pl *BRI* BN1 .... 29 F2
Wolseley Rd *BRI* BN1 .... 28 D1
PTSD BN41 .... 43 E2
Wolstonbury Rd *HOVE* BN3 ... 45 G3
Wolverstone Dr *BRI* BN1 ...... 28 C5
Woodard Rd *LAN/SOMP* BN15... 39 H3
Woodards Vw *SHOR* BN43....... 40 D5
Woodbourne Av *BRI* BN1....... 27 H3
Woodbridge Pk *ANG/EP* BN16 ... 52 A4

Woodhouse Rd *HOVE* BN3........... 44 A3
Woodland Av *HOVE* BN3 .... 26 D3
SALV BN13 .... 36 C1
Woodland Cl *HOVE* BN3 .... 26 D5
Woodland Dr *HOVE* BN3........... 26 D4
Woodlands *HOVE* BN3 .... 27 E5
Woodlands Cl *ANG/EP* BN16 .... 34 A3
PEAHV BN10 .... 62 D4
SALV BN13 .... 35 F1
The Woodlands *BRI* BN1 .... 27 G2
Woodland Wk *ROTT* BN2 .... 60 B1
Woodland Wy *BRI* BN1.......... 27 H3
Woodlea Rd *SALV* BN13 .... 55 E1
Woodmancote Rd *FIN/BW* BN14 .. 55 F1
Woodpecker Wy *SALV* BN13 ... 36 A5
Woodruff Av *HOVE* BN3 .... 27 E5
Woodside Av *BRI* BN1........... 27 F5
Woodside Rd *FIN/BW* BN14...... 4 B1
Woods Wy *FERR* BN12 .... 54 A2
Woodview *SHOR* BN43 .... 41 F1
Woodview Cl *BRI* BN1........... 28 D1
Worcester Vls *HOVE* BN3 .... 43 G3
Wordsworth Rd *WTHG* BN11......... 4 B5
Wordsworth St *HOVE* BN3....... 44 C3
Wychwood Gdns *WTHG* BN11 ... 56 D2

Wyke Av *WTHG* BN11
Wykeham Cl *STEY/UB* BN44
Wykeham Rd *WTHG* BN11
Wyndham St *ROTT* BN2
Wynnes Ms *HOVE* BN3 44

Y

Yardley St *BRI* BN1
Yeoman Rd *SALV* BN13
Yeoman Wy *SALV* BN13
York Av *HOVE* BN3
York Gv *BRI* BN1
York Hl *BRI* BN1
York Pl *BRI* BN1
York Rd *HOVE* BN3
PEAHV BN10
WTHG BN11
York Vls *BRI* BN1
Youngsmere Cl *BRI* BN1 28

Index - featured places

Adur District Council
LAN/SOMP BN15 .... 39 G4
Adur District Council
STHW BN42 .... 42 C3
Albion Doctors Surgery
ROTT BN2 .... 3 J2
Aldrington House Hospital
HOVE BN3 .... 44 B4
A M F Bowling
WTHG BN11 .... 4 E6
Aquarena Swimming Pool
WTHG BN11 .... 5 J5
The Arden Foot & Health Clinic
ROTT BN2 .... 3 H5
Ardmore School
WTHG BN11 .... 4 E4
Art Gallery
BRI BN1 .... 3 G3
Assembly Hall
WTHG BN11 .... 4 E4
Balfour Junior School
BRI BN1 .... 28 A4
Bartholomews Tutorial College
BRI BN1 .... 3 G5
Beach House Surgery
FERR BN12 .... 54 A4
Bellerbys College
HOVE BN3 .... 45 E3
Bell Tower Industrial Estate
ROTT BN2 .... 59 F1
Benfield County Junior School
PTSD BN41 .... 43 G2
Benfield Valley Golf Course
PTSD BN41 .... 25 G4
Bevendean County
Primary School
ROTT BN2 .... 47 F1
Blatchington Mill School
HOVE BN3 .... 44 C1
Booth Museum of
Natural History
BRI BN1 .... 45 G2
Bowden House School
SEAF BN25 .... 70 C4
Bramber Castle
STEY/UB BN44 .... 7 H2
Bramber First School
FIN/BW BN14 .... 38 A4
Brighton Business Centre
BRI BN1 .... 45 H2
Brighton Business Centre
BRI BN1 .... 46 A2
The Brighton Centre
BRI BN1 .... 2 E5
Brighton College
ROTT BN2 .... 46 C5
Brighton College of Technology
BRI BN1 .... 3 H2
Brighton College of Technology
HOVE BN3 .... 44 A2
Brighton College of Technology
HOVE BN3 .... 44 D4
Brighton College of Technology
ROTT BN2 .... 3 J1
Brighton County Court
ROTT BN2 .... 3 H4

Brighton Fishing Museum
BRI BN1 .... 3 F6
Brighton General Hospital
ROTT BN2 .... 46 D3
Brighton & Hove Council
BRI BN1 .... 3 H1
Brighton & Hove Council
BRI BN1 .... 28 B1
Brighton & Hove Council
HOVE BN3 .... 44 B1
Brighton & Hove Council
HOVE BN3 .... 44 D3
Brighton & Hove Council
HOVE BN3 .... 45 E4
Brighton & Hove Council
PTSD BN41 .... 43 E1
Brighton & Hove Council
PTSD BN41 .... 43 G2
Brighton & Hove Council
ROTT BN2 .... 29 E4
Brighton & Hove Council
ROTT BN2 .... 46 C3
Brighton & Hove Girls
Day School
BRI BN1 .... 2 C3
Brighton & Hove Golf Course
HOVE BN3 .... 26 A1
Brighton & Hove High Schools
BRI BN1 .... 2 C2
Brighton & Hove Progressive
Synagogue
HOVE BN3 .... 2 A3
Brighton Hove & Sussex
Sixth Form College
HOVE BN3 .... 45 G2
Brighton Islamic Centre &
Mosque
HOVE BN3 .... 45 G3
Brighton Library & Museum
BRI BN1 .... 3 G4
Brighton Media Centre
BRI BN1 .... 3 F5
Brighton Municipal Market
ROTT BN2 .... 3 H3
Brighton Racecourse
ROTT BN2 .... 47 G2
Brighton Rugby Club
BRI BN1 .... 26 D1
Brighton Technical College
BRI BN1 .... 45 H2
Brighton Youth Centre
ROTT BN2 .... 3 K5
Broadwater C of E School
FIN/BW BN14 .... 37 G5
Broadwater Manor School
FIN/BW BN14 .... 37 H5
Broadway Surgery
ROTT BN2 .... 59 F1
Brooklands Trading Estate
FIN/BW BN14 .... 4 B2
Bross Estate
NEWHV BN9 .... 65 E5
Buckingham Middle School
SHOR BN43 .... 41 G2
Cardinal Newman School
HOVE BN3 .... 45 F2

Carlton Hill Cp School
ROTT BN2 .... 3 J4
Castledean School
BRI BN1 .... 28 B5
Centenary Industrial Estate
BRI BN1 .... 46 B1
The Central Hove Surgery
HOVE BN3 .... 44 D4
Charter Medical Centre
HOVE BN3 .... 2 A1
Chelsea College
SHOR BN43 .... 40 D3
Chesswood Middle School
WTHG BN11 .... 5 H1
Child Clinic
ROTT BN2 .... 3 H4
Churchill Square
Shopping Centre
BRI BN1 .... 2 E5
Church Surgery
ROTT BN2 .... 46 C1
Civic Centre
SHOR BN43 .... 41 F3
Clairmonte Galleries
BRI BN1 .... 3 G4
Clapham & Patching
C of E Primary School
SALV BN13 .... 35 E1
Clermont C P U School
BRI BN1 .... 27 G5
Cliffe Business Centre
LEW BN7 .... 17 G3
Cliffe Industrial Estate
LEW BN7 .... 17 H4
Club House
FIN/BW BN14 .... 37 F1
Coldean Junior & Infant School
BRI BN1 .... 28 D1
Connaught Theatre
WTHG BN11 .... 5 F4
The Constable Gallery Artshop
WTHG BN11 .... 4 C6
Conway Court Clinic
HOVE BN3 .... 44 D2
Coombe Road County
Primary School
ROTT BN2 .... 46 D1
Corn Exchange Theatre
BRI BN1 .... 3 G4
Cottage Surgery
PEAHV BN10 .... 67 E2
Cottesmore St Marys RC Primary
School
HOVE BN3 .... 45 F2
County First School
SALV BN13 .... 35 H4
County Hall
LEW BN7 .... 17 F3
County Middle School
STHW BN42 .... 42 D2
County Primary School
BRI BN1 .... 28 B5
Cradle Hill Cp School
SEAF BN25 .... 71 E3
Crown Court
HOVE BN3 .... 2 A2

The Cyril Richings
Business Centre
SHOR BN43 4
Davigdor County Infant School
HOVE BN3
Davison C of E Secondary
School for Girls
WTHG BN11 .... 4 B5
Denton County Primary School
NEWHV BN9 6
Dolphin House Clinic for Adults
BRI BN1
Downsbrook CP School
FIN/BW BN14 3
Downsbrook Middle School
FIN/BW BN14 3
Downsbrook Trading Estate
FIN/BW BN14 3
Downs County First School
BRI BN1 4
Downs Junior School
BRI BN1 4
Downs Leisure Centre
SEAF BN25 7
Downs Park School
PTSD BN41 2
Downs View School
ROTT BN2 4
The Dr Jan De Winter Clinic
for Cancer Prevention Advice
BRI BN1 3
DSS
ROTT BN2 3
Durrington First & Middle School
SALV BN13 3
Durrington Health Centre
SALV BN13 3
Durrington High School
SALV BN13 3
East Preston Cp School
ANG/EP BN16 52
East Sussex Brighton &
Hove Health Authority
LEW BN7 17
East Sussex County Council
BRI BN1 3
East Sussex County Council
HOVE BN3 26
East Sussex County Council
LEW BN7 16
East Sussex County Council
LEW BN7 17
East Sussex County Council
LEW BN7 17
East Sussex County Council
NEWHV BN9 65
East Sussex County Council
NEWHV BN9 68
East Sussex County Council
PEAHV BN10 67
East Sussex County Council
PEAHV BN10 67
East Sussex County Council
ROTT BN2 47
East Sussex County Council
SEAF BN25 70

Sussex County Music School
 EW BN7 .... 17 E4
Sussex Health Authority
 EWHV BN9 .... 64 D5
Grove County First School
 THG BN11 .... 54 D2
Grove CP School
 OTT BN2 .... 46 C3
ish Martyrs RC School
 ERR BN12 .... 36 B5
 Business Park
 ERR BN12 .... 64 D5
ution Health Centre
 RI BN1 .... 2 D3
ight County Primary School
 OTT BN2 .... 46 C2
 Gallery
 EW BN7 .... 17 F3
ing C of E Primary School
 ERR BN12 .... 53 F3
ing Football Club
 ERR BN12 .... 53 E3
yfield Industrial Estate
 EWHV BN9 .... 69 E1
ersgate First School
 TSD BN41 .... 43 E3
Fold School
 OVE BN3 .... 43 H3
hill Surgery
 EWHV BN9 .... 68 D3
 Gallery
 PEAHV BN10 .... 62 D4
Framing Studio & Gallery
 AN/SOMP BN15 .... 39 G5
shbrook County First School
 AN/SOMP BN15 .... 39 G4
shbrook School
 AN/SOMP BN15 .... 39 G4
ery
 OTT BN2 .... 58 C1
 Gallery
 RI BN1 .... 2 E4
 Gallery
 OVE BN3 .... 44 C3
 Gallery
 THG BN11 .... 4 A7
ini Business Centre
 OVE BN3 .... 44 C2
rge Pringle School
 ERR BN12 .... 36 B5
rge Street Gallery
 OTT BN2 .... 3 H5
rgian House Business Centre
 OTT BN2 .... 3 H5
e CP School
 THW BN42 .... 42 B3
dstone Junior School
 OVE BN3 .... 44 A1
ing C of E School
 ERR BN12 .... 54 A3
ing Cricket Club
 ERR BN12 .... 53 G3
ys County Infants School
 EWHV BN9 .... 68 D2
dbourne Shopping Centre
 THG BN11 .... 5 F5
n Bridge Trading Estate
 FIN/BW BN14 .... 56 C1
n Business Centre
 SHOR BN43 .... 41 G3
nilton Lodge School
 OTT BN2 .... 46 D5
gleton County
 Junior & Infant School
 OVE BN3 .... 26 A5
 Hawthorns School
 SALV BN13 .... 36 A5
el Cottage Clinic
 OTT BN2 .... 48 A2
elwood Trading Estate
 FIN/BW BN14 .... 56 B1
alth Clinic
 EW BN7 .... 17 F3
ene C of E First School
 THG BN11 .... 4 C3
bert Hone Clinic
 OTT BN2 .... 46 B3
ons Dale School
 SHOR BN43 .... 42 A1
hdown School
 SALV BN13 .... 36 C5
hdown Surgery
 PTSD BN41 .... 37 E5
side School
 PTSD BN41 .... 25 H4
podrome Bingo
 BRI BN1 .... 3 F5

Hoddern County Junior School
 PEAHV BN10 .... 62 D5
Holmbush County Infants School
 SHOR BN43 .... 42 A1
Homecare Business Centre
 LEW BN7 .... 17 G3
Home Farm Business Centre
 BRI BN1 .... 28 D4
Hove Business Centre
 HOVE BN3 .... 44 D2
Hove General Hospital
 HOVE BN3 .... 44 C3
Hove Medical Centre
 HOVE BN3 .... 25 H5
Hove Metal Galleries
 BRI BN1 .... 2 E1
Hove Park Upper School
 HOVE BN3 .... 44 C1
Hove Polyclinic
 HOVE BN3 .... 44 B1
Hove Rugby Football Club
 HOVE BN3 .... 44 D1
Ice Rink
 BRI BN1 .... 3 F4
Iford & Kingston C of E School
 LEW BN7 .... 32 B1
The John Horniman School
 WTHG BN11 .... 5 H4
John Selden County First School
 FERR BN12 .... 54 B1
Kings Manor School
 SHOR BN43 .... 42 B2
Kingston Buci School
 SHOR BN43 .... 41 G2
Knoll Business Centre
 HOVE BN3 .... 43 H2
Lancing College Chapel
 LAN/SOMP BN15 .... 22 A5
Lancing Health Centre
 LAN/SOMP BN15 .... 39 G5
Lancing Parish Council
 LAN/SOMP BN15 .... 39 G5
Law Courts
 ROTT BN2 .... 3 J4
Lewes Business Centre
 LEW BN7 .... 17 F2
Lewes Castle & Museums
 LEW BN7 .... 17 E3
Lewes District Council
 NEWHV BN9 .... 64 C5
Lewes District Council
 SEAF BN25 .... 70 C5
Lewes Gallery
 LEW BN7 .... 17 E4
Lewes Grammar School
 LEW BN7 .... 17 E4
Lewes Leisure Centre
 LEW BN7 .... 17 G4
Lewes Little Theatre
 LEW BN7 .... 17 E3
Lewes Magistrates Court
 LEW BN7 .... 17 F3
Lewes Sports Club
 LEW BN7 .... 16 D5
Lewes Tertiary College
 LEW BN7 .... 17 F4
Lewes Victoria Hospital
 LEW BN7 .... 16 C3
Lewes Wallands Cp School
 LEW BN7 .... 16 C2
Limetree Surgery
 FIN/BW BN14 .... 19 E5
Little Theatre
 SEAF BN25 .... 72 C1
Longhill School
 ROTT BN2 .... 60 C1
Longley Industrial Estate
 BRI BN1 .... 45 H3
Lyndhurst CP School
 WTHG BN11 .... 5 K2
Manor House Hospital
 HOVE BN3 .... 44 C3
Manor Sports Ground Pavilion
 FIN/BW BN14 .... 37 H5
Marine Clinic
 ROTT BN2 .... 61 E4
Marlborough Business Centre
 LAN/SOMP BN15 .... 57 E1
Marlipins Museum
 SHOR BN43 .... 41 E4
Meeching Valley CP School
 NEWHV BN9 .... 68 B1
Meridian CP School
 PEAHV BN10 .... 63 E4
Meridian Leisure Centre
 PEAHV BN10 .... 67 E1
Meridian Surgery
 PEAHV BN10 .... 62 D5

Middle Street Primary School
 BRI BN1 .... 3 F5
Mile Oak Clinic
 PTSD BN41 .... 24 D4
Mile Oak Junior School
 PTSD BN41 .... 24 D4
Mill View Hospital
 HOVE BN3 .... 44 A1
Modern Moulds Business Centre
 WTHG BN11 .... 57 E1
Montague Shopping Centre
 WTHG BN11 .... 5 F5
Morley Street Health Centre
 ROTT BN2 .... 3 J3
Moulscoomb Clinic
 ROTT BN2 .... 29 E4
Moulsecoomb County
 Junior School
 ROTT BN2 .... 29 E4
Mowden School
 HOVE BN3 .... 45 F1
Museum
 SHOR BN43 .... 40 D3
The Museum
 STEY/UB BN44 .... 7 F1
Newhaven Flea Market
 NEWHV BN9 .... 68 C2
Newhaven Health Centre
 NEWHV BN9 .... 68 D1
Newhaven Town Council
 NEWHV BN9 .... 68 C1
Newlands Preparatory School
 SEAF BN25 .... 71 F4
Newlands Senior School
 SEAF BN25 .... 71 E4
Newmans Loner School
 HOVE BN3 .... 45 F2
New Pond Row Surgery
 LAN/SOMP BN15 .... 39 G5
New Venture Theatre
 BRI BN1 .... 2 B4
Northbourne Medical Centre
 SHOR BN43 .... 41 G2
Northbrook College
 FIN/BW BN14 .... 37 G5
Northbrook College
 SALV BN13 .... 53 H1
Northbrook College
 WTHG BN11 .... 5 F4
Northbrook Trading Estate
 FIN/BW BN14 .... 38 A4
Northease Manor School
 LEW BN7 .... 51 E1
Odeon Cinema
 BRI BN1 .... 2 E5
Old Darlington Mushroom
 Farm Ind Est
 ANG/EP BN16 .... 34 A5
Old Grammar School
 LEW BN7 .... 16 D3
Old Grammar School
 LEW BN7 .... 17 E3
Old School Surgery
 SEAF BN25 .... 72 C1
Orchards Middle School
 FERR BN12 .... 54 B1
Our Lady of Lourdes School
 ROTT BN2 .... 60 D3
Our Lady of Sion Junior School
 ROTT BN2 .... 4 E4
Our Lady of Sion School
 ROTT BN2 .... 4 D5
Ovingdean Hall School
 ROTT BN2 .... 60 B1
Palace Pier
 ROTT BN2 .... 3 H7
Parkland Business Centre
 LAN/SOMP BN15 .... 57 F1
Park View Leisure Centre
 HOVE BN3 .... 44 A3
Patcham CP School
 BRI BN1 .... 27 H1
Patcham First School
 BRI BN1 .... 27 G1
Patcham High School
 BRI BN1 .... 27 H1
Patcham House School
 BRI BN1 .... 27 G1
The Pavilion Clinic
 BRI BN1 .... 2 D4
Pavilion Theatre
 BRI BN1 .... 3 G4
Pavilion Theatre
 WTHG BN11 .... 5 F6
Paxton Business Centre
 HOVE BN3 .... 43 H2
Peacehaven Infant School
 PEAHV BN10 .... 66 D1

Peacehaven Sports Centre
 PEAHV BN10 .... 67 F1
Peacehaven Town Council
 PEAHV BN10 .... 63 E5
Peacock Industrial Estate
 HOVE BN3 .... 45 F3
Pells C of E Infant School
 LEW BN7 .... 16 D2
Pells Primary School
 LEW BN7 .... 17 E2
Peregrine Gallery
 FERR BN12 .... 53 E5
Peter Gladwin School
 PTSD BN41 .... 25 E5
Phoenix Industrial Estate
 LEW BN7 .... 17 F2
Portfolio Studio Gallery
 BRI BN1 .... 3 G5
Portland Business Park
 HOVE BN3 .... 43 H3
Portland Industrial Estate
 HOVE BN3 .... 44 A2
Portland Road Ind Est
 HOVE BN3 .... 43 H2
Portland Surgery
 HOVE BN3 .... 44 B3
Portslade Community College
 PTSD BN41 .... 25 E4
Portslade Community College
 PTSD BN41 .... 43 E1
Portslade Community College
 STHW BN42 .... 24 D5
Portslade Health Centre
 PTSD BN41 .... 43 F3
Preston Furniture Gallery
 BRI BN1 .... 27 H5
Preston Park Clinic
 BRI BN1 .... 46 A1
Preston Park Surgery
 BRI BN1 .... 46 A2
Primary School
 STEY/UB BN44 .... 8 A2
Prince Regent Swimming
 Complex
 BRI BN1 .... 3 H4
Prinnys Antique Gallery
 BRI BN1 .... 3 F5
Priory School
 LEW BN7 .... 17 F4
Queen Alexandra Hospital Home
 WTHG BN11 .... 4 B5
Queensdown School
 BRI BN1 .... 28 C4
Queens Park County Primary
 School
 ROTT BN2 .... 46 C5
Ranalah Estate
 NEWHV BN9 .... 65 E5
Register Office
 WTHG BN11 .... 4 A4
Rich Industrial Estate
 NEWHV BN9 .... 65 E4
Riverbank Business Centre
 SHOR BN43 .... 40 D3
River Lodge Surgery
 LEW BN7 .... 17 F3
Riverside Business Centre
 SHOR BN43 .... 41 F4
Riverside Industrial Estate
 LEW BN7 .... 17 F2
Rodmell Primary School
 LEW BN7 .... 51 G1
Roedean School
 ROTT BN2 .... 60 A2
Rottingdean Football Club
 ROTT BN2 .... 60 D2
Rottingdean Primary School
 ROTT BN2 .... 61 E3
Rottingdean Surgery
 ROTT BN2 .... 60 C2
Royal Alexandra Hospital
 BRI BN1 .... 2 E2
Royal Pavilion
 BRI BN1 .... 3 H4
Royal Sussex County Hospital
 NHS Trust
 ROTT BN2 .... 58 D1
Rudyard Kipling Primary School
 ROTT BN2 .... 48 C3
Sackville Road First School
 FIN/BW BN14 .... 56 A1
St Andrews C of E High
 School for Boys
 FIN/BW BN14 .... 56 A1
St Andrews C of E School
 HOVE BN3 .... 44 D4
St Andrews Surgery
 LEW BN7 .... 17 F4

St Annes Special School
LEW BN7 ...... 16 D4
St Aubyns School
ROTT BN2 ...... 61 E4
St Bartholomews C of E Primary
School
BRI BN1 ...... 3 G1
St Bernadettes First Middle
Va School
BRI BN1 ...... 27 G5
St Christophers School
HOVE BN3 ...... 44 C3
St Faith Clinic
ROTT BN2 ...... 59 E1
St John Baptist Primary School
FIN/BW BN14 ...... 18 B1
St Johns Residential School
ROTT BN2 ...... 46 D5
St John the Baptist RC
Primary School
ROTT BN2 ...... 46 D5
St Lawrence Surgery
FIN/BW BN14 ...... 55 E1
St Lukes Junior & Infant School
ROTT BN2 ...... 46 C4
St Lukes Swimming Pool
ROTT BN2 ...... 46 C4
St Marks C of E Primary School
ROTT BN2 ...... 47 E5
St Martins C of E Primary School
ROTT BN2 ...... 46 C2
St Mary Magdalene School
BRI BN1 ...... 2 D4
St Marys Hall School for Girls
ROTT BN2 ...... 58 D1
St Marys RC Primary School
WTHG BN11 ...... 4 C4
St Marys RC School
PTSD BN41 ...... 43 F3
St Nicholas & St. Mary School
SHOR BN43 ...... 41 G2
St Pancras RC Primary School
LEW BN7 ...... 16 D3
St Pauls C of E School
BRI BN1 ...... 3 F5
St Peters County Infant School
PTSD BN41 ...... 43 F4
St Peters Medical Centre
BRI BN1 ...... 3 H1
St Peters R C School
SHOR BN43 ...... 41 G2
Saltdean County Primary School
ROTT BN2 ...... 61 G3
Sandhurst School
WTHG BN11 ...... 5 J4
The Seaford Business Centre
SEAF BN25 ...... 70 C5
Seaford CP School
SEAF BN25 ...... 70 C4
Seaford Day Hospital
SEAF BN25 ...... 70 D5
Seaford Golf Club
SEAF BN25 ...... 70 D2
Seaford Head Community College
SEAF BN25 ...... 73 E1
Seaford Head Lower School
SEAF BN25 ...... 72 D1
Seaford Health Centre
SEAF BN25 ...... 70 C5
Seaford Sports & Leisure Centre
SEAF BN25 ...... 70 C5

Sea Life Centre
ROTT BN2 ...... 3 H6
Secondary School
ROTT BN2 ...... 47 E4
The Seven Dials Medical Centre
BRI BN1 ...... 2 E2
Sheila Cashin Gallery
BRI BN1 ...... 2 E3
Shelley Surgery
WTHG BN11 ...... 4 D5
Shoreham Beach County
First School
SHOR BN43 ...... 41 G4
Shoreham College
SHOR BN43 ...... 42 B3
Shoreham County First School
SHOR BN43 ...... 41 E2
Shoreham Football Club
PTSD BN41 ...... 43 F3
Shoreham Health Centre
SHOR BN43 ...... 41 E3
Somerhill County Junior School
HOVE BN3 ...... 2 A2
Somerstones Independent School
HOVE BN3 ...... 2 B3
Southdown Business Park
LEW BN7 ...... 17 F2
Southdown CP School
NEWHV BN9 ...... 68 C1
South Downs Health Clinic
BRI BN1 ...... 3 F2
South Malling Primary School
LEW BN7 ...... 17 F1
Southover C of E Primary School
LEW BN7 ...... 17 E4
Southwick Business Centre
PTSD BN41 ...... 42 C4
Southwick Manor Hall County
First School
STHW BN42 ...... 42 D3
Stanford Junior School
BRI BN1 ...... 45 H2
Stanley Deason Leisure Centre
ROTT BN2 ...... 47 F5
Steyning Athletic Club
STEY/UB BN44 ...... 7 E1
Steyning Grammar School
STEY/UB BN44 ...... 7 F1
Steyning Health Centre
STEY/UB BN44 ...... 7 F1
Stonelands School of
Ballet & Theatre
HOVE BN3 ...... 44 D4
The Strand Surgery
FERR BN12 ...... 54 B1
Sussex Clinic Ltd
WTHG BN11 ...... 4 C5
Sussex County Cricket Club
HOVE BN3 ...... 45 E3
Sussex Eye Hospital
ROTT BN2 ...... 58 D1
Sussex House Industrial Estate
HOVE BN3 ...... 44 B2
Sussex Nuffield Hospital
HOVE BN3 ...... 44 B4
Sussex Nuffield Hospital
ROTT BN2 ...... 48 A2
The Sussex Toy & Model Museum
BRI BN1 ...... 3 F2
Sussex University
LEW BN7 ...... 17 G2

Swandean Hospital
SALV BN13 ...... 36 B2
Synagogue
BRI BN1 ...... 3 F5
Telscombe Cliffs Primary School
PEAHV BN10 ...... 62 C5
Templars County Infants School
LAN/SOMP BN15 ...... 38 D4
Theatre Royal
BRI BN1 ...... 3 G4
Thomas A Becket First School
SALV BN13 ...... 37 E5
Thomas A Becket Middle School
FIN/BW BN14 ...... 37 F5
Thornberry Middle School
LAN/SOMP BN15 ...... 39 H5
Ticehurst Clinic
HOVE BN3 ...... 44 C4
Tideway School
NEWHV BN9 ...... 68 B2
University of Brighton
BRI BN1 ...... 29 E1
University of Brighton
BRI BN1 ...... 29 H2
University of Brighton
ROTT BN2 ...... 3 H4
University of Brighton
ROTT BN2 ...... 28 C5
University of Sussex
BRI BN1 ...... 15 H5
Uplands School
BRI BN1 ...... 28 C5
Upper Beeding Surgery
STEY/UB BN44 ...... 8 A2
Vale CP School
SALV BN13 ...... 18 D5
Varndean College
BRI BN1 ...... 27 H4
Varndean High School
BRI BN1 ...... 28 A4
Victoria Recreation Ground
WTHG BN11 ...... 4 C3
Victoria Road Surgery
WTHG BN11 ...... 4 D3
Virgin Cinemas
ROTT BN2 ...... 59 E2
Waterhall Golf Course
BRI BN1 ...... 12 D5
Waytefield Clinic
BRI BN1 ...... 27 G5
Welfare Clinic
HOVE BN3 ...... 26 A5
Westdene Primary School
BRI BN1 ...... 27 E2
Westholme Clinic Ltd
FERR BN12 ...... 54 B3
Westholme Clinic Ltd
WTHG BN11 ...... 4 C5
West Hove Middle School
HOVE BN3 ...... 44 A3
West Park C of E Controlled
First & Middle School
FERR BN12 ...... 54 B3
West Pier (Under Repair)
BRI BN1 ...... 2 D6
West Sussex Area Health
Authority
WTHG BN11 ...... 5 K4
West Sussex County Council
FERR BN12 ...... 54 A3
West Sussex County Council
SHOR BN43 ...... 41 H3

West Sussex County Council
WTHG BN11 ......
West Sussex Health Authority
FERR BN12 5
The White Gallery
HOVE BN3 ......
The White Gallery
HOVE BN3 4
Whitehawk Clinic
ROTT BN2 4
Whitehawk Infant School
ROTT BN2 4
Whitehawk Junior School
ROTT BN2 4
White Styles County
Junior School
LAN/SOMP BN15 3
Whytemead Cp School
FIN/BW BN14 3
Wigmore Athletic Football Club
FIN/BW BN14 3
The Willow Surgery
ROTT BN2 4
Windlesham School
HOVE BN3 4
Window Gallery
BRI BN1 ......
Window Gallery
BRI BN1 ......
Winston Business Centre
LAN/SOMP BN15 3
Woodingdean Primary School
ROTT BN2 4
Worthing Auction Galleries
WTHG BN11 ......
Worthing Borough Council
WTHG BN11 ......
Worthing Borough Council
WTHG BN11 ......
Worthing District Health
Authority
SHOR BN43 4
Worthing & District
Magistrates Court
WTHG BN11 ......
Worthing Football Club
FIN/BW BN14 ......
Worthing Golf Course
FIN/BW BN14 3
Worthing Health Authority
WTHG BN11 ......
Worthing High School
FIN/BW BN14 55
Worthing Leisure Centre
WTHG BN11 56
Worthing Museum
WTHG BN11 5
Worthing Rugby Club
ANG/EP BN16 52
Worthing Sixth Form College
SALV BN13 56
Worthing & Southlands
Hospitals NHS Trust
SHOR BN43 41
Worthing & Southlands
Hospitals NHS Trust
WTHG BN11 5
YMCA
BRI BN1 3
Zoo
WTHG BN11 4